istruzioni

directions

per l'uso e la manutenzione delle vetture

for use and upkeed of the

Ferrari
cars

250 Granturismo

NOTICE

The original Ferrari factory publications for the 250 GT - the *'Use and Upkeep'* and the *'Spare Parts'* manuals - were printed in landscape format and measured approximately 9" x 6.75" with a text width of 7" on each page.

For the purpose of this publication the front and back of each page has been merged into a single page. This is best illustrated by this title page – the top and bottom outlines are approximately the size of two pages of text in the original publication.

The 250 GTE *'Operating, Maintenance and Service Handbook'* is also included and is formatted at a slightly larger size than the original.

CONTENTS

250 GT Use and Upkeep Manual	Page 1
250 GT Spare Parts Manual	Page 25
250 GT/E Service Handbook	Page 59

PREFACE

TRADEMARKS & COPYRIGHT

Ferrari ® is the registered trademark of Ferrari S.p.A. This publication is not sponsored by or endorsed by the trademark owner. We recognize that some words, model names and designations, for example, mentioned herein are the property of the trademark holder. We use them for identification purposes only. This is not an official publication however; it may include non-copyright works of the trademark holder.

INTRODUCTION

Welcome to the world of digital publishing ~ the book you now hold in your hand was printed using the latest state of the art digital technology. The advent of print-on-demand has forever changed the publishing process, never has information been so accessible and it is our hope that this book serves your informational needs for years to come. If this is your first exposure to digital publishing, we hope that you are pleased with the results. Many more titles of interest to the classic automobile and motorcycle enthusiast, collector and restorer are available via our website at www.VelocePress.com. We hope that you find this title as interesting as we do.

NOTE FROM THE PUBLISHER

The information presented is true and complete to the best of our knowledge. All recommendations are made without any guarantees on the part of the author or the publisher, who also disclaim all liability incurred with the use of this information.

INFORMATION ON THE USE OF THIS PUBLICATION

This manual is an invaluable resource for those interested in performing their own maintenance. However, in today's information age we are constantly subject to changes in common practice, new technology, availability of improved materials and increased awareness of chemical toxicity. As such, it is advised that the user consult with an experienced professional prior to undertaking any procedure described herein. While every care has been taken to ensure correctness of information, it is obviously not possible to guarantee complete freedom from errors or omissions or to accept liability arising from such errors or omissions. Therefore, any individual that uses the information contained within, or elects to perform or participate in do-it-yourself repairs or modifications acknowledges that there is a risk factor involved and that the publisher or its associates cannot be held responsible for personal injury or property damage resulting from the use of the information or the outcome of such procedures.

WARNING!

One final word of advice, this publication is intended to be used as a reference guide, and when in doubt the reader should consult with a qualified technician.

GENERALITÀ

MOTORE

	250 GT.
N° dei cilindri disposti a V con apert. di 60°	12
Alesaggio e corsa m/m	73 x 58,8
Cilindrata totale cm³	2953,211
Rapporto di compressione 1:	9
Potenza C. V.	240
Regime di potenza massima giri minuto	7000

CAMBIO

Numero delle velocità in avanti	4
Retromarce	1
Velocità silenziose	Tutte
Velocità sincronizzate	1ª-2ª-3ª-4ª
Rinvio del cambio	30 23
Rapporto in 1ª velocità	2,536
Rapporto in 2ª velocità	1,701
Rapporto in 3ª velocità	1,256
Rapporto in 4ª velocità	1
Rapporto in 5ª velocità	—
Rapporto della retromarcia	2,6

AUTOTELAIO

Passo m.	2,60
Carreggiata anteriore m/m	1.354
Carreggiata posteriore m/m	1.349
Altezza minima da terra m/m	170
Raggio sterzata m.	7
RUOTE Cerchi R. W. Anteriore	5,50 x 16
Posteriore	5,50 x 16
Gomme Anteriore	6,00 16
Posteriore	6,00 16
Peso a vuoto dell'autovettura carrozzata Kg.	1.050
Posizione della guida	Sinistra
Carburante consigliabile	Super SHELL
Consumo carburante ogni 100 Km. lt.	18
Capacità del serbatoio lt.	120

GENERAL SPECIFICATIONS

ENGINE

	250 GT.
Number and arrangement of cylinders	V-12 "60"
Bore and stroke	73 x 58,8
Total piston displacement	2953,211
Compression ratio	1:9
Bhp	240
Maximum power at	7000 rpm

TRANSMISSION CASE (GEAR-BOX)

Number of speeds, forward	4
reverse	1
Silent speeds	all
Synchronized speeds	1st-2nd-3rd-4th
Countershaft drive gear	30 23
Gear ratios 1st	2,536
2nd	1,701
3rd	1,256
4th	1
5th	—
reverse	2,6

CHASSIS

Wheelbase	2,60
Tread (Track) Front	1354 mm
Rear	1349 mm
Minimum clearance from ground	170 mm
Turning radius	7 m
WHEELS Rims Front	5,50 x 16
Rear	5,50 x 16
Tires Front	6,00 x 16
Rear	6,00 x 16
Weight car dry, bodied	1050 kgs
Drive	left-hand
Fuel, advisable	Super SHELL
Fuel consumption per 100 kms	18 lts
Fuel tank capacity	120 lts

PRESTAZIONI

N. giri motore = 7000/1' - Gomme 6,00 x 16 ($\varnothing$ = 700)

Rapporti al ponte	Velocità in Km/h			
	1°	2°	3°	4°
7/34 = 4,858	75	112	151	190
7/32 = 4,57	80	119	161	202
8/34 = 4,25	86	128	173	217
8/32 = 4	91	136	184	231
9/34 = 3,778	97	144	195	245
9/32 = 3,666	100	148	200	252

PERFORMANCE

at 7000 r.p.m. - Tires: 6,00x16 ($\varnothing$ = 700)

Rear axle ratio	Speeds attainable: mph & kmph			
	1st	2nd	3st	4th
7/34 = 4,858	Ms 46,6 / Kms 75	69,6 / 112	93,8 / 151	118 / 190
7/32 = 4,57	Ms 49,7 / Kms 80	74 / 119	100 / 161	125,5 / 202
8/34 = 4,25	Ms 53,5 / Kms 86	79,5 / 128	107,5 / 173	134,8 / 217
8/32 = 4	Ms 56,5 / Kms 91	84,5 / 137	114,3 / 184	143,6 / 231
9/34 = 3,778	Ms 60,3 / Kms 97	89,5 / 144	121,2 / 195	152,2 / 245
9/32 = 3,666	Ms 62,1 / Kms 100	92 / 148	124,3 / 200	156,6 / 252

CARATTERISTICHE GENERALI	GENERAL FEATURES
Basamento — In lega leggera ad alta resistenza con canne cilindri in ghisa speciale riportate.	**Crankcase** — Of high resistance light alloy, with forced-in special cast-iron cylinder liners.
Testa cilindri — In lega leggera con camere di scoppio di forma speciale.	**Cylinder Head** — Of light alloy, with specially shaped combustion chambers.
Albero motore — In acciaio di alta resistenza perfettamente contrappesato e montato su 7 supporti dei quali 1 speciale per la tenuta assiale.	**Crankshaft** — Of high resistance steel, perfectly counterbalanced and mounted on 7 bearings, one of which specially designed for axial holding.
Distribuzione — A valvole in testa disposte a « V » e comandate, a mezzo di bilancieri, da due alberi con eccentrici azionati da catena silenziosa munita di tenditore semiautomatico.	**Timing** — By V-overhead valves, actuated, through rockers, by two shafts with eccentrics driven by silent chain with semi-automatic tightener.
Lubrificazione — A pressione per mezzo di pompa ad ingranaggi, filtro e valvolina limitatrice di pressione. Un manometro, sul quadro di bordo, indica la pressione.	**Lubrication** — Forced, by geared pump, filter, and pressure limiting valve. A manometer, on dashboard, shows the pressure.
Raffreddamento — Con pompa centrifuga, radiatore a tubetti e lamelle. La circolazione è regolata dal termostato.	**Cooling** — By centrifugal pump; laminated multi-tubular radiator. Circulation regulated by thermostat.
Accensione — Mediante 2 spinterogeni a 6 scintille con anticipo automatico e 2 bobine alta tensione.	**Ignition** — By two 6-spark distributors, with automatic advance and 2 high tension coils.
Alimentazione — Mediante 2 pompe meccaniche a membrana AC tipo FISPA AF ed una pompa elettrica FISPA.	**Feeding** — By 2 mechanical leaf (membrane) pumps AC, FISPA AF type, and an electric FISPA pump.
Carburatori — N. 3 Carburatori WEBER a doppio corpo invertito tipo 36 DCL 3.	**Carburetors (Carburetters)** — 3 WEBER carburetors with double down-draft (down draught) body, 36 DCL 3 type.
Avviamento — Elettrico mediante chiave nel quadro di bordo.	**Starting** — Electric by key on dash-board.
Sospensione motore — Elastica mediante 4 silentblocks antivibranti.	**Engine suspension** — Elastic, by 4 antivibrating silentblocks.
Frizione — A 2 dischi FRENDO e mozzo elastico.	**Clutch** — Double FRENDO plate and elastic hub.
Cambio — In blocco col motore. Nella scatola del cambio è incorporata una pompa olio e filtro per la lubrificazione degli ingranaggi e delle bronzine.	**Transmission Case (Gear-Box)** — In block with engine. An oil pump and filter, for lubricating the gears and bearings, is incorporated in the transmission casing (gear-box).
Albero di trasmissione — Oscillante su snodo cardanico e giunto SAGA.	**Transmission Shaft** — Oscillating, on cardan joint and SAGA joint.
Ponte posteriore — Del tipo rigido, con scatola centrale in lega leggera e bracci laterali in acciaio ad alta resistenza.	**Rear Axle** — Of the rigid type, with light alloy central casing and lateral high resistance steel arms.
Telaio — Monoblocco con struttura tubolare ellittica in acciaio ad alta resistenza saldato elettricamente.	**Chassis (Frame)** — Monoblock, with elliptical tubular structure of electrically welded high resistance steel.
Sospensione anteriore — A ruote indipendenti con parallelogramma trasversale integrata da tamponi in gomma ed ammortizzatori Houdaille.	**Front suspension** — With independent wheels with transverse parallelogram, integrated by rubber buffers and Houdaille shock absorbers.
Sospensione posteriore — A 4 puntoni con balestre longitudinali a grande flessibilità integrate da tamponi in gomma ed ammortizzatori Houdaille.	**Rear suspension** — With 4 radius rods and superflexible, longitudinal leaf springs, integrated by rubber buffers and Houdaille shock absorbers.
Sterzo — Con parallelogramma articolato ed indipendente dalle oscillazioni delle ruote. Guida con vite senza fine ed ingranaggio elicoidale.	**Steering** — With parallel motion, independent of the oscillations of the wheels. Worm screw drive and helical gear.
Freni — A pedale: idraulico sulle 4 ruote - A mano: meccanico sulle ruote posteriori.	**Brakes** — Pedal operated: hydraulic on the four wheels; hand operated: mechanical on the rear wheels.

USO DELLA VETTURA

Avviamento a freddo del motore — Prima dell'avviamento del motore a freddo si inserisce mediante l'apposito interruttore la pompa elettrica ausiliaria di alimentazione del carburante.
Tirare completamente il pomello dello starter (con motore caldo questa operazione non si deve compiere) Si introduca a fondo nel quadretto di distribuzione dell'impianto elettrico la chiave relativa e la si ruoti in senso orario abbandonandola non appena il motore è avviato. E' buona norma spingere a fondo il pedale della frizione mentre si fa l'avviamento del motore.

Avviamento a caldo — Se il motore è molto caldo non si deve usare lo starter, si eviterà così eccessiva introduzione di carburante nei cilindri. Potrà invece essere opportuno agire molto lentamente sul pedale dell'acceleratore fino a metà corsa per aprire le farfalle e procurare un impoverimento della miscela che faciliterà la partenza a motore caldo. Se l'avviamento risultasse difficoltoso o non avvenisse occorrerà verificare gli organi di accensione — candele, spinterogeni — e gli apparecchi di alimentazione del carburante — getti del minimo del carburatore, pompa benzina e filtri.

Prima di porre in moto la vettura — Dopo qualche minuto dall'avviamento del motore a freddo si rimetta lo starter nella posizione primitiva.
Si eviti in modo assoluto di accelerare il motore a fondo finchè esso non sia caldo.
Si osservi che il manometro dell'olio indichi una pressione di 40-50 m. con motore a media velocità.

Durante la marcia della vettura — Si eviti di fare funzionare il motore oltre il numero dei giri prescritto (vedi generalità). Si arresti il motore se funzionando ad alti regimi la pressione dell'olio scendesse sotto i 30 m.
Si osservi saltuariamente se l'indicatore luminoso di carica batteria rimane spento allorchè la vettura, in presa diretta supera i 30 Km. ora, il che indica che la dinamo carica regolarmente la batteria.
Si eviti di tenere il piede sul pedale della frizione quando non è necessario.
Il pedale del freno deve compiere metà della sua corsa perchè le ruote risultino bloccate e non deve mai superare i due terzi di quella totale.

USE OF THE CAR

To start up the engine cold — Before starting up the engine cold, insert, by means of the apposite switch, the electric auxiliary fuel pump.
Pull all the way the carburetor (carburetter) choke control button (this operation should not be performed when the engine is warm). Introduce the proper key, as far as it will go, into the distributing board of the electric plant, turn it clockwise, and leave hold of it as soon as engine starts up. It is a good rule to push the clutch pedal all the way while starting up the engine.

To start up the engine warm — If the engine is very hot, do not use the starter, thus avoiding excessive introduction of fuel into the cylinders. It may be advisable, on the contrary, to act very slowly on the accelerator pedal, to half its way, in order to open the throttles and, by thus impoverishing the mixture, facilitate the start with engine warm. Should starting be difficult or not take place at all, check the ignition system (plugs, ignition distributors) and the fuel apparatuses (slow running jets, petrol pump, and filters).

Before starting the car — A few minutes after starting the engine cold, replace the starter in its primitive position.
Absolutely avoid accelerating the engine all the way until it is not warm.
Do not forget that the oil pressure gauge should indicate a pressure of 43,6-54,5 yds (40-50 meters) with engine at average speed.

When running — Avoid making the engine work beyond the number of revolutions prescribed (see General Specifications). If, working at high ranges, the oil pressure should fall below 32,7 yds (30 meters), stop the engine.
Observe, from time to time, whether the luminous gauge of the battery charge remains unlighted when the car, in direct drive, exceeds 18,64 mph (30 kmph), which indicates that the dynamo is regularly charging the battery. Avoid keeping your foot on the clutch pedal when unnecessary.
To block the wheels, the brake pedal must run to middle of stroke, but this should never exceed 2/3 of its total length.

IRREGOLARITA'	CONSTATAZIONI	CAUSE E RIMEDI
Il motore non parte.	Gira troppo piano:	Controllare carica batteria.
	Motore troppo duro:	Allacciamento di qualche cuscinetto od aggiustaggio troppo preciso dei cuscinetti (se già revisionati).
	Olio troppo denso:	Sostituire l'olio con altro più fluido, del tipo prescritto dalla Casa.
	Non c'è scintilla alle candele o c'è ad una sola fila di cilindri:	Verificare fusibili - Umidità nei distributori. Contatti interruttori ossidati o sregistrati. Interruttore di massa guasto o relativo filo in corto circuito.
	Il carburante non arriva al carburatore:	Vaschetta vuota - Serbatoio vuoto. Pompa avariata. Raccordi tubazioni allentati. Filtro pompa o filtro serbatoi intasati.
	Il carburante arriva al carburatore ma il motore non parte:	Verificare lo starter, controllare i minimi se sono tappati. Acqua nel carburante. Entrata aria dalle flange tubazione aspirazione (mettere olio sulle flange per individuare la perdita). Compressione scarsa per eccessivo lavaggio dei pistoni, per prolungato uso dello starter (mettere un po' d'olio nei cilindri). Scarsa compressione per deficente tenuta valvole o cattiva registrazione. Candele umide o con puntine eccessivamente distanti.

IRREGOLARITA'	CONSTATAZIONI	CAUSE E RIMEDI
Il motore non dà tutta la sua potenza:	Il funzionamento non è regolare.	Candele troppo fredde o con puntine troppo staccate. Candele troppo calde (sostituirle con altre di tipo prescritto). Candele troppo usate. Candela sporca o qualche filo staccato su qualche cilindro. Acceleratore che non apre interamente. Gioco valvole non regolato. Carburante non adatto. Getti massimi non adatti. Pressione carburante scarsa.
	Perdita carburante da un carburatore	Galleggiante forato. Tappo spillo sporco.
	Il motore è stato revisionato e non provato al banco.	Controllare: fasatura valvole e registrazione punterie. Anticipo accensione.
Il motore non è regolare ad alto regime:	Le candele sono del tipo prescritto.	Candele troppo usate. Candele con puntine troppo staccate (5/10). Sfarfallamento valvole per eccesso di giri o per qualche molla rotta.
Il motore ad alto regime dà delle detonazioni:		Candele troppo calde. Qualche candela con isolante spaccato. Anticipo accensione eccessivo. Carburante non adatto.

FAULT	ASCERTAINMENT	CAUSES AND REMEDIES
The engine will not start:	It turns too slowly:	Check battery charge.
	It is too hard:	Bearing jamming or bearings too tight adjusted (if already overhauled).
	The oil is too thick:	Replace it by a fluider oil, of the type prescribeb by the Firm.
	No sparking at the plugs or only at one row of cylinders:	Control fuses. - Moisture in the distributors. - Switch contacts oxydized or out of order. - Earth switch defective or wire short-circuited.
	The fuel does not arrive at carburetor (carburetter):	Float chamber empty. - Fuel tank empty. - Pump defective - Tube coupling got loose. - Pump filter or tank filter choked.
	The fuel arrives at carburetor (carburetter), but engine does not start:	Control starter; see whether slow running (idling) jets are choked. - Water in the fuel. - Inlet manifold flanges are not air tight (to locate loss, put oil on the flanges). Compression insufficient, due to excessive washing of the pistons, to protracted use of starter (apply a little oil to the cylinders). - Compression insufficient due to defective tightness of the valves or to faulty adjustment. - Spark plugs moist or with too distant points.

FAULT	ASCERTAINMENT	CAUSES AND REMEDIES
The engine does not yield all its power efficiency:	Working is unsatisfactory:	Plugs too cold or points too distant. Plugs too hot (replace them by others, of the type prescribed). Plugs too worn-out. Plug dirty or some wire detached on some cylinder. Accelerator does not open entirely. - Valve play not adjusted. - Fuel unfit. - Main jets unfit. - Fuel pressure insufficient.
	Loss of fuel from a carburetor (carburetter):	Float with a hole. Needle plug dirty.
	The engine has been overhauled, but not tested on the bench:	Control: valve timing and valve lifter (tappet) adjustment. - Ignition advance.
The engine works unsatisfactorily at high range:	The spark plugs are of the prescribed type:	Plugs too worn-out. Plug points too distant (5/10). Valve fluttering due to excess of revolutions or to breakage of some spring.
The engine gives detonations at high range:		Plugs too hot. - Some plug split. - Ignition overadvance. - Fuel unfit.

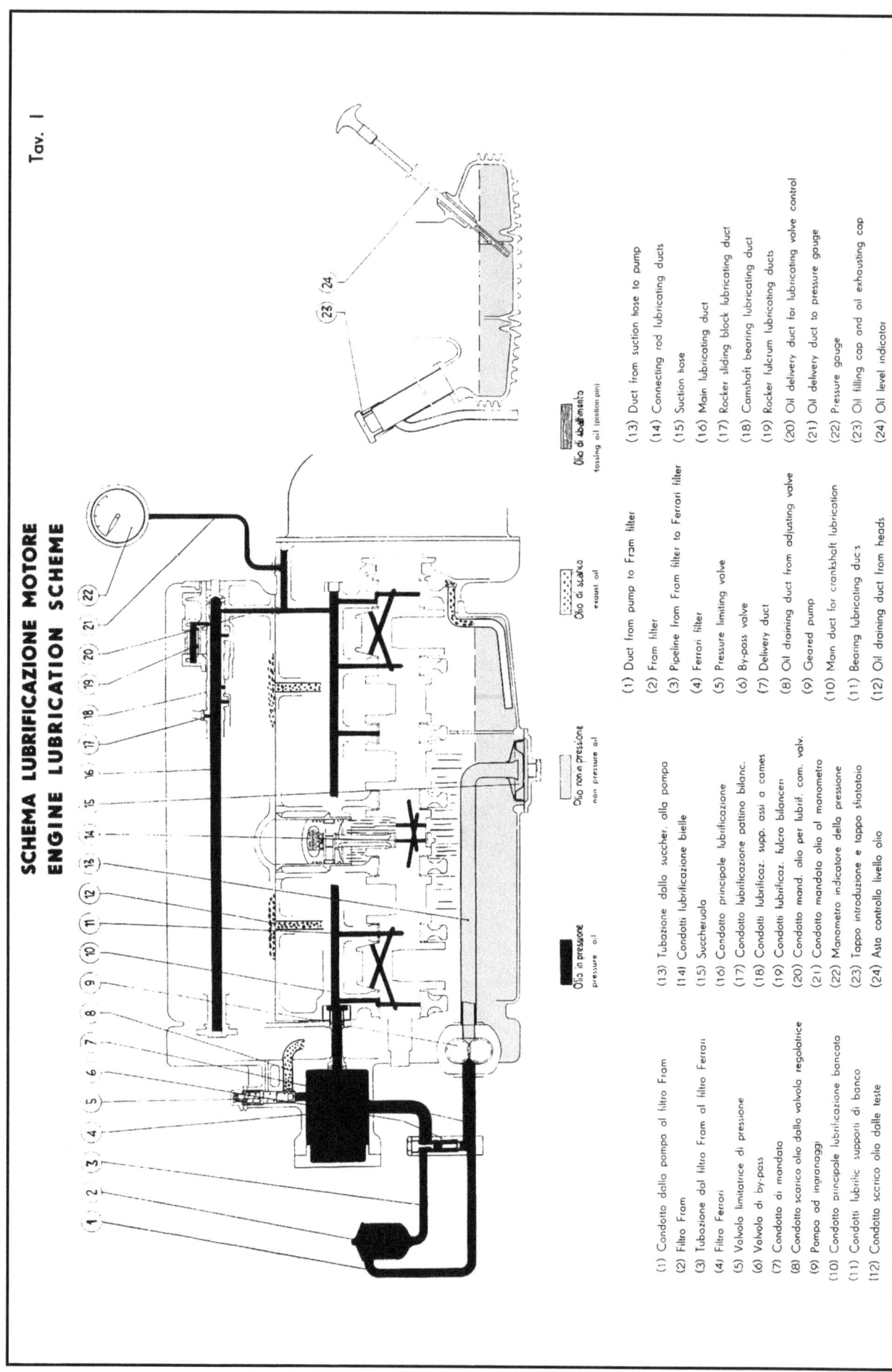

Tav. I

SCHEMA LUBRIFICAZIONE MOTORE
ENGINE LUBRICATION SCHEME

Olio in pressione / pressure oil
Olio non in pressione / non pressure oil
Olio di scarico / exaust oil
Olio di sbattimento / tossing oil (piston pin)

(1) Condotto dalla pompa al filtro Fram
(2) Filtro Fram
(3) Tubazione dal filtro Fram al filtro Ferrari
(4) Filtro Ferrari
(5) Valvola limitatrice di pressione
(6) Valvola di by-pass
(7) Condotto di mandata
(8) Condotto scarico olio dalla valvola regolatrice
(9) Pompa ad ingranaggi
(10) Condotto principale lubrificazione bancata
(11) Condotti lubrific. supporti di banco
(12) Condotto scarico olio dalle teste
(13) Tubazione dallo succher. alla pompa
(14) Condotti lubrificazione bielle
(15) Succheruola
(16) Condotto principale lubrificazione
(17) Condotto lubrificazione pattino bilanc.
(18) Condotti lubrificaz. supp. assi a cames
(19) Condotti lubrificaz. fulcro bilancieri
(20) Condotto mand. olio per lubrif. com. valv.
(21) Condotto mandata olio al manometro
(22) Manometro indicatore della pressione
(23) Tappo introduzione e tappo sfiatatoio
(24) Asta controllo livello olio

(1) Duct from pump to Fram filter
(2) Fram filter
(3) Pipeline from Fram filter to Ferrari filter
(4) Ferrari filter
(5) Pressure limiting valve
(6) By-pass valve
(7) Delivery duct
(8) Oil draining duct from adjusting valve
(9) Geared pump
(10) Main duct for crankshaft lubrication
(11) Bearing lubricating ducts
(12) Oil draining duct from heads
(13) Duct from suction hose to pump
(14) Connecting rod lubricating ducts
(15) Suction hose
(16) Main lubricating duct
(17) Rocker sliding block lubricating duct
(18) Camshaft bearing lubricating duct
(19) Rocker fulcrum lubricating ducts
(20) Oil delivery duct for lubricating valve control
(21) Oil delivery duct to pressure gauge
(22) Pressure gauge
(23) Oil filling cap and oil exhausting cap
(24) Oil level indicator

ISTRUZIONI PER LA LUBRIFICAZIONE

Motore — La lubrificazione del motore avviene secondo lo schema della Tav. I. Nelle coppe l'olio non deve mai scendere sotto il livello minimo e neppure deve superare quello massimo. A livello massimo il contenuto d'olio nelle coppe è di litri 7. Circa la qualità d'olio da usare per il motore e per i diversi gruppi attenersi alle indicazioni dello schema generale della lubrificazione (Tav. II). Con olio caldo e con motore funzionante a pieno regime la pressione non deve mai essere inferiore a 30 m. - Normalmente è di 50 m.

Cambio — Come risulta dalle caratteristiche generali della vettura la lubrificazione avviene a mezzo di una pompa ad ingranaggi e filtro.
Per l'olio da usare e per la periodica sostituzione attenersi alle indicazioni dello schema generale della lubrificazione (Tav. II).

Balestre — Per mantenere le balestre nelle migliori condizioni di funzionamento ed eliminare i rumori è necessario, ogni 3000 Km., lavare con petrolio ed iniettare con siringa un po' d'olio grafitato tra foglia e foglia sollevando la vettura con un cricchetto fino a che le ruote non si sollevino da terra e togliendo i bulloncini delle staffette di chiusura delle foglie. Operazione da eseguire nelle balestre senza inserto di polietilene.

DIRECTIONS FOR LUBRICATION

Engine — To lubricate the engine proceed according to the diagram on Table I. In the pans (sumps) oil shall never go below minimum level, nor exceed maximum level. At maximum level the pans (sumps) contain 7 liters (12,317 pints) of oil. As to the quality of oil to be used for engine and the various sets, keep to the indications of the General Diagram of Lubrication (Table II). When oil is hot and engine working at full speed, pressure should never go below 30 m (32,7 yds). Normal pressure: 50 m (54,5 yds).

Transmission Case (Gear-Box) — As already specified under « General Features », proper lubrication is assured by a geared pump and filter. As to the oil to be used, and its periodical replacement, keep to the indications of the General Diagram of Lubrication (Table II).

Leaf Springs — To maintain the leaf springs in the best working conditions, and eliminate noises, it is necessary, every 1864 miles (3000 kms), to wash with petroleum and to inject, by means of a grease gun (syringe), a little graphitized oil between the leaves after lifting the car by means of a jack until the wheels leave the ground, and taking off the small bolts of the spring clips.
Operation to be carried out only on the leaf-springs without polyethylene inserts.

Tav. II

SCHEMA GENERALE DELLA LUBRIFICAZIONE
GENERAL LUBRICATION AND GREASING OF CHASSIS
SHELL

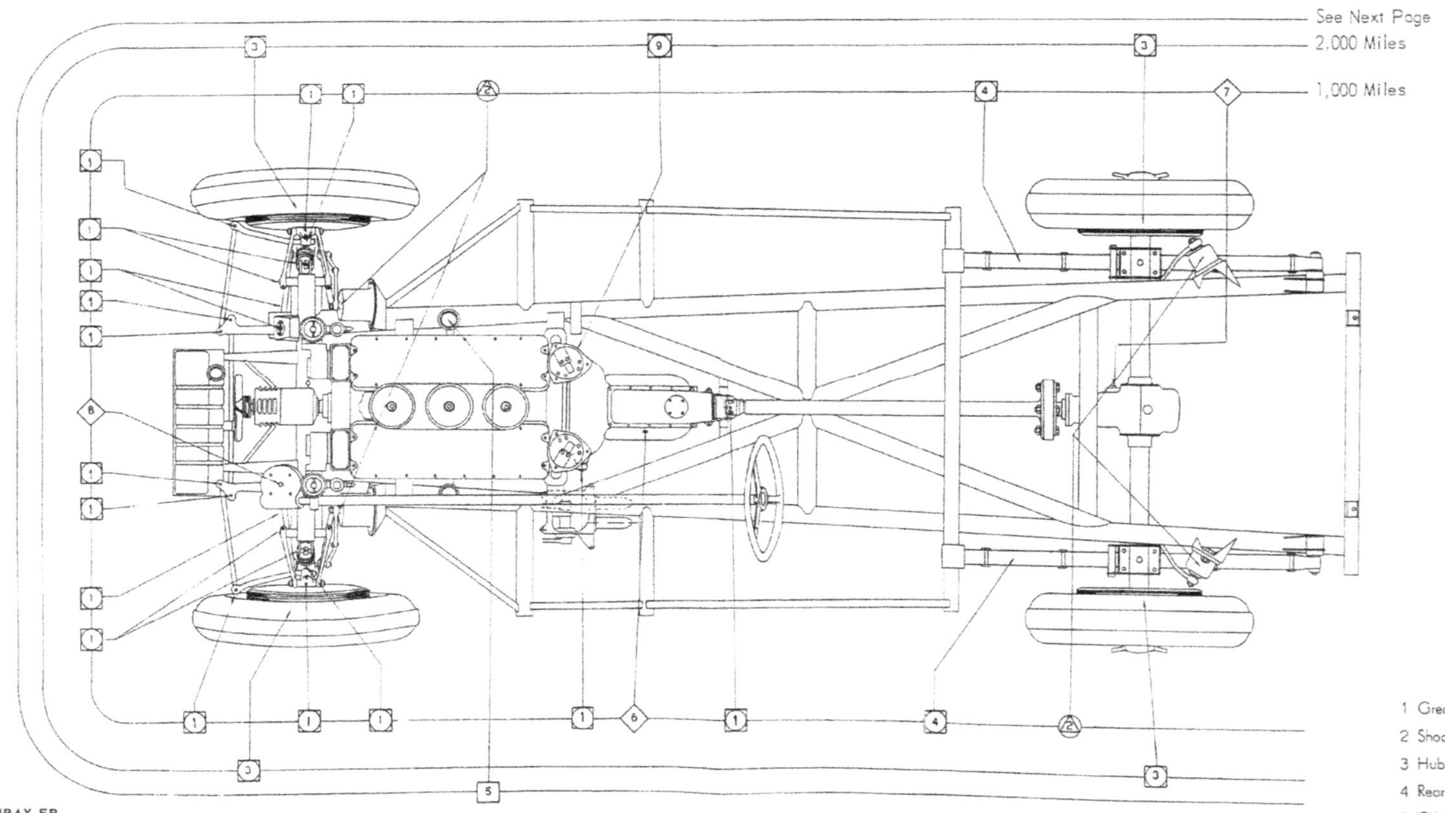

See Next Page
2,000 Miles
1,000 Miles

- ☐ Shell X-100 Motor Oil (See Next Page)
- ◇ Shell Spirax E P (See Box at Left)
- ▲ Shell Retinax A
- △ Shell Donax A4

1 Tegemot — 6 Ingresso olio cambio
2 Ammortizzatori — 7 Ingresso olio ponte
3 Cuscinetti ruote ant. e post. — 8 Scatola guida
4 Balestre posteriori — 9 Spinterogeno
5 Ingresso olio motore

1 Grease nipples
2 Shock absorbers
3 Hub bearings
4 Rear springs
5 Oil inlet to engine
6 Oil inlet to gear box
7 Oil inlet to rear axle
8 Steering box
9 Distributor

SHELL SPIRAX EP

Transmission	Above 10°F.	90
	Below 10°F.	80
Rear Axle	Above 90°F.	140
	Below 90°F.	90
Steering Gearbox		90

Change transmission and rear axle lubricant every 10,000 miles or at least twice each year.

FERRARI ENGINE OIL RECOMMENDATIONS

Shell X-100 Motor Oil
250 Granturismo
Above 50°F............40
10 to 50°F........ 10/30 or 30
Below 10°F.......... 10W/30
Berlinetta & 4.9
Above 50°F.......... 40
Below 50°F.......... 30

The following outline is a general guide to good practice for various operating conditions.

OPERATING CONDITIONS	OIL DRAIN - MILES	OIL FILTER RENEWAL - MILES	AIR CLEANER AND BREATHER SERVICE - MILES
A	1,000	4,000/6,000	2,000
B	500	4,000/6,000 2,000/3,000 *	2,000 500*
C	2,000	4,000/6,000	2,000

Under dusty conditions, also see remarks under B.

SUPPLEMENT - TAV. II

A. **City and Suburban Driving:** This represents the ordinary use of a typical car on short-run, start-and-go service on paved roads under moderate temperatures. It also includes some longer-distance travel at normal speeds.

B. **Very Cold Weather or Dusty Conditions:** Vehicle operation in zero or subzero weather, especially in start-and-go driving, with much engine idling, is a form of adverse service. The hours of engine running, rather than the miles driven, should govern the oil drain interval. Generally, the oil change should be made at not over 500 miles or 60 days, whichever comes first, and more often in extreme cases. Consistent driving over dusty roads is another adverse condition in which it is advisable to change the oil at not more than 500 miles; in the event a vehicle is driven through a dust storm, the oil should be changed as soon as possible, the filter renewed, and air cleaner serviced.

C. **Open Highway Driving:** The most favorable driving condition is essentially that done on the open highway, such as intercity travel on paved, dust-free roads, with little engine idling. The engine operates at a desirable temperature for efficient combustion. Using high-quality oil, there is relatively little or no oxidation, and objectionable condensation and fuel by-products are usually held to a minimum in the oil circulating system.

| ALTRE ISTRUZIONI | ADDITIONAL DIRECTIONS |

Distribuzione — Il gioco tra bilancere e valvola di aspirazione deve essere di 15/100 e quello tra bilancere e valvola di scarico di 20/100. Il controllo di tale gioco deve essere fatto ogni 5000 Km.

Accensione — La registrazione e la sostituzione dei contatti dei due ruttori dei distributori di accensione va effettuata solo presso la Casa o presso le officine autorizzate dal costruttore degli apparecchi. - Le candele che consigliamo sono: MARCHAL 34 HF che vanno sostituite ogni 8-10.000 Km. La distanza fra le puntine della candela deve essere normalmente da mm. 0,5 a 0,6.

Carburatore — La registrazione della carburazione non deve essere alterata. Sconsigliamo anche di procedere a smontaggio delle parti interne. - La variazione della ricchezza della miscela al minimo si ottiene agendo sulle apposite viti inclinate del carburatore (Tav. IV pos. 5), svitandole si arricchisce la miscela, avvitandole si impoverisce. Il règime minimo del motore è di 800 giri al minuto. Esso si regola agendo sulle farfalle a mezzo delle apposite viti orizzontali (pos. 4).

Ponte Posteriore — Per la ripresa dei giochi è necessario smontare il ponte. Detta operazione non presenta speciali difficoltà.

Guida — La guida non richiede speciali cure; eventuali giochi tra vite e settore sono facilmente eliminabili togliendo la scatola dal telaio e rotando, nel senso richiesto, la boccola eccentrica che porta il settore avendo cura di togliere prima la piastrina di sicurezza. La scatola deve essere mantenuta piena di olio denso, operazione che si esegue facilmente togliendo il coperchio superiore (vedi schema generale della lubrificazione - Tav. II).

Ammortizzatori — Ad ogni 3000 km. togliere il tappo che chiude il pozzetto di riserva (Tav. III) di ogni singolo ammortizzatore e riempire completamente con olio (vedi schema generale della lubrificazione Tav. II). Se necessitasse il loro smontaggio consigliamo rivolgersi alla Casa od a qualche officina autorizzata.

Frizione — Il pedale di comando, in buone condizioni di funzionamento, prima di agire sul manicotto disinnesto frizione, deve fare una corsa a vuoto di cm. 3 circa. Quando la frizione tende a slittare è necessario controllare:
1) che la corsa a vuoto del pedale sia quella prescritta, in caso contrario agire sull'apposito registro collocato nel tirantino di collegamento delle due leve di comando (vedi Tav. V);
2) che sulle superfici delle guarnizioni non vi sia olio od altra sostanza untuosa;
3) che non sia avvenuta la rottura di qualche guarnizione;
4) che le guarnizioni non siano eccessivamente logore o di qualità non adatta.

Ad ogni montaggio necessita rimettere i dadi delle colonnette nella loro posizione primitiva.

Freni — Il grande diametro dei tamburi, in lega leggera molto resistente, con anello in ghisa speciale,

Timing — The clearance between rocker and inlet valve should be of 15/100, and the clearance between rocker and exhaust valve of 20/100. Clearance should be checked every 3107 miles (5000 kms).

Ignition — Adjustment and eventual replacement of the contacts of the two contact breakers of the distributors must be exclusively excuted either by the manufacturing Firm or by workshops authorized by the constructor of the apparatuses. We recommend MARCHAL 34 HF spark plugs, to be replaced every 5000-6200 miles (8000-10.000 kms). The distance between the plug points should be, as a rule, from 0,5 to 0,6 mm.

Carburetor (Carburetter) — Never alter the carburetion adjustment! Disassembling of the internal parts is likewise unadvisable. To vary the richness of the mixture for slow running, act upon the proper inclined screws on the carburetor (Table IV/5) to enrich the mixture: unscrew! — to impoverish it: screw up! — The minimum engine running rate is 800 r.p.m.; it may be adjusted by acting on the throttles through the apposite horizontal screws (4).

Rear Axle — To correct clearance it is necessary to dismount the rear axle. This operation does not present any particular difficulty.

Drive — The drive system does not require special care; eventual clearances between screw and sector may be easily compensated by taking casing off chassis, and turning in the proper direction, after removing the locking plate, the sector carrying eccentric bush. Casing shall be kept full with thick oil, operation which can be easily done by taking the upper cover off (see General Lubrication scheme, Table II).

Shock Absorbers — Every 1864 miles (3000 kms) remove the plug closing the reserve bowl (Table III) of each separate shock absorber and fill up with oil (see General Diagram of Lubrication, Table II). If dismounting should appear, however, absolutely necessary, it is advisable to apply either to the Firm or to some authorized workshop.

Clutch — The idle stroke of the pedal, in good working conditions, should be about 1,18 in. (3 cm) before acting on the throw-out (withdrawal) sleeve. Whenever the clutch tends to slip, it is necessary to control:
1) whether the idle stroke of the pedal corresponds to the length prescribed; in the contrary case, act on the adjusting screw located in the link connecting the two gear shift (control) levers (see Table V);
2) whether there is some oil, or other greasy substance, on the lining surfaces;
3) whether breakage of some lining occurred;
4) whether the linings are either excessively worn down or of unsuitable quality.

When mounting, be careful to replace the nuts of the small columns exactly where they stood before.

Brakes — The large diameter of the drums, of high resistance light alloy, with rings of special cast-iron,

permette di avere una frenatura efficace e costante anche alle alte velocità.

Le ganasce ad espansione sono comandate da doppia pompa sul pedale e da due cilindri sul portaceppi.

Il gioco viene ripreso: per i freni anteriori mediante due eccentrici sui portaceppi; per i freni posteriori mediante quattro eccentrici sui portaceppi (vedi Tavola VI).

E' necessario, ogni 1000 Km., provvedere al controllo del livello del liquido, e ogni 3000 Km. effettuare la sostituzione.

I freni posteriori sono muniti di comando meccanico delle ganasce che fa capo alla leva del comando a mano.

Quando lo spessore delle guarnizioni è ridotto a metà necessita la loro sostituzione.

Difficilmente i tamburi richiedono la ripassatura della superficie frenante se sono impiegate le guarnizioni del tipo prescritto dalla Casa.

Anche le deformazioni sono escluse se i freni vengono usati in modo normale.

NORME PARTICOLARI - Con temperatura invernale scaricare sempre l'acqua di raffreddamento aprendo l'apposito rubinetto del radiatore. E' però consigliabile l'uso di miscele anticongelanti. Ogni 3000 Km. controllare il livello dell'olio nel cambio, nel ponte posteriore, nella scatola guida, negli ammortizzatori, e pulire il filtro olio della pompa del cambio.

assures efficacious and constant braking even at the highest speeds.

The expanding shoes are controlled by a double master cylinder on the pedal and two cylinders on the brake shoe holders.

The clearance is compensated: for the front brakes by means of two eccentrics on the brake shoe holders; for the rear brakes by means of four eccentrics on the brake shoe holders (see Table VII).

The level of the fluid must be checked every 620 miles (1000 kms); after 1864 miles (3000 ks) the fluid must be replaced.

The rear brakes are provided with mechanical brake shoe control actuated by the hand brake lever.

Replace the shoe linings whenever their thickness is reduced to half.

Provided the type of lining prescribeb by the Firm is employed, drums seldom require overhauling of the braking surfaces.

No deformation is liable to occur as long as the brakes are used in the normal way.

Particular Rules — In cold weather always discharge the cooling water by turning the drain tap of the radiator. The use of non-freezing mixtures is to be recommended. Every 1864 miles (3000 kms) check the oil level in the transmission casing (gear-box), rear axle, steering box, shock absorbers, and clean the oil filter of the transmission (gear-box) pump.

REGISTRAZIONE CARBURATORI

Registrazione minimo e progressione — Premesso che è indispensabile che tutti i cilindri al minimo abbiano la stessa potenza, si deve operare come segue:

1) Togliere i minimi di una fila, mettere in moto il motore lasciandolo girare al minimo (800 giri) poscia operando sulle viti registro minimo, della fila opposta, ottenere la migliore regolarità con tendenza ad avere una miscelazione leggermente ricca.

2) Ripetere l'operazione di cui al punto 1) invertendo le file, previo montaggio dei minimi precedentemente tolti (naturalmente s'intende che vanno smontati quelli della fila opposta).

3) Togliere i getti del minimo di ambo le file dei carburatori 2° e 3°, rimettere in moto registrando le viti regolazione farfalle, del 1° carburatore, in maniera che il motore giri al numero minimo di giri.

4) Identica operazione si deve eseguire, escludendo i minimi dei carburatori 1° e 3°, quindi registrare il 2° carburatore.

5) C. S. escludendo il 1° e 2° carburatore, quindi regolazione del 3° carburatore.

Tenere presente che tutte le 5 operazioni di cui sopra debbono essere effettuate con esclusione delle aste comando farfalle che vanno dall'alberino, sul coperchio testa destra, ai carburatori.

6) Rimontare le aste e senza rimettere in moto il motore registrare le aste in maniera tale che le aperture delle farfalle siano tutte della stessa ampiezza.

CARBURETOR ADJUSTMENT

Adjustment of slow running and progression — Since it is indispensable that, when running slow, the same power may be developed by all the cylinders, proceed as follows:

1) Remove the slow running jets of one row, start up the engine letting it run at minimum range (800 rpm), then acting on the screws for slow running of the opposite row, try to obtain the best possible regularity with a tendency to a rather rich mixture.

2) Repeat the same operation (1) by inverting the rows and having previously mounted the slow running jets removed according to 1); now, dismount the jets of the opposite row.

3) Remove the slow running jets from both rows of carburetors 2 and 3; start up while adjusting the throttle adjusting screws of carburetor 1 so that the engine may run at minimum range.

4) Perform the same operation excluding the slow running jets of carburetors 1 and 3; then adjust carburetor 2.

5) As above excluding carburetors 1 and 2; then adjust carburetor 3.

Bear in mind that all the above described operations are to be performed excluding the throttle control rods going from the spindle, on right head cover, to the carburetors.

6) Remount the rods and, without starting the engine up, adjust the rods in such a manner that the opening of all the throttles may present the same width.

AMMORTIZZATORE DELLE SOSPENSIONI
SHOCK ABSORBERS

Tav. III

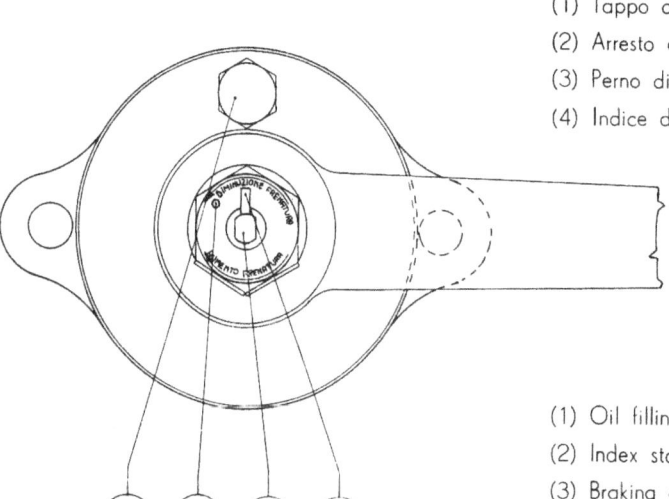

(1) Tappo del foro introduzione olio
(2) Arresto dell'indice
(3) Perno di regolazione dell'azione frenante
(4) Indice del perno di regolazione

(1) Oil filling hole cap
(2) Index stop
(3) Braking action adjusting pin
(4) Adjusting pin index

CARBURATORE
CARBURETTOR

Tav. IV

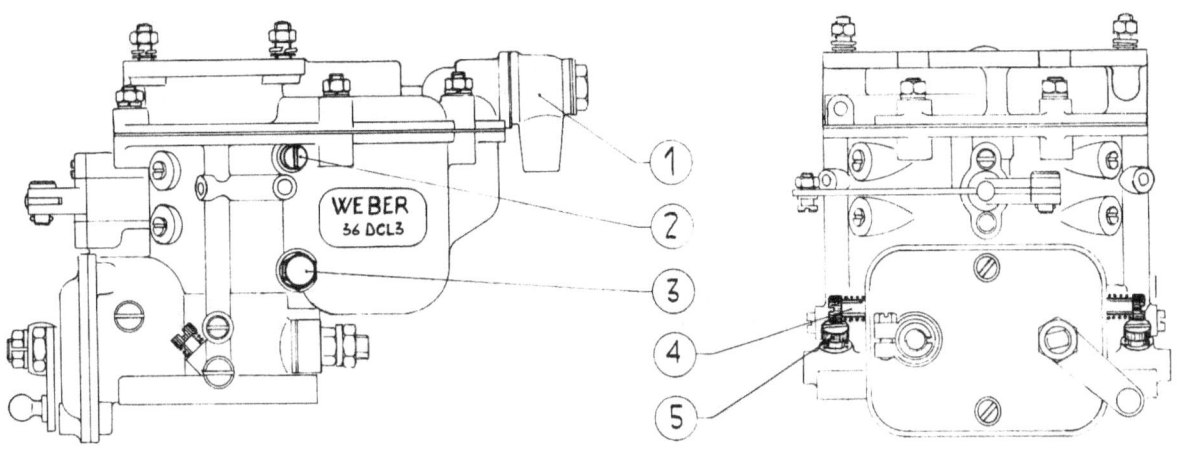

(1) Filtro benzina
(2) Porta getto minimo
(3) Porta getto principale
(4) Registro apertura farfalla
(5) Registro miscela al minimo

(1) Fuel filter
(2) Idling jet screw
(3) Main jet screw
(4) Throttle opening screw
(5) Idling mixture screw

Tav. V

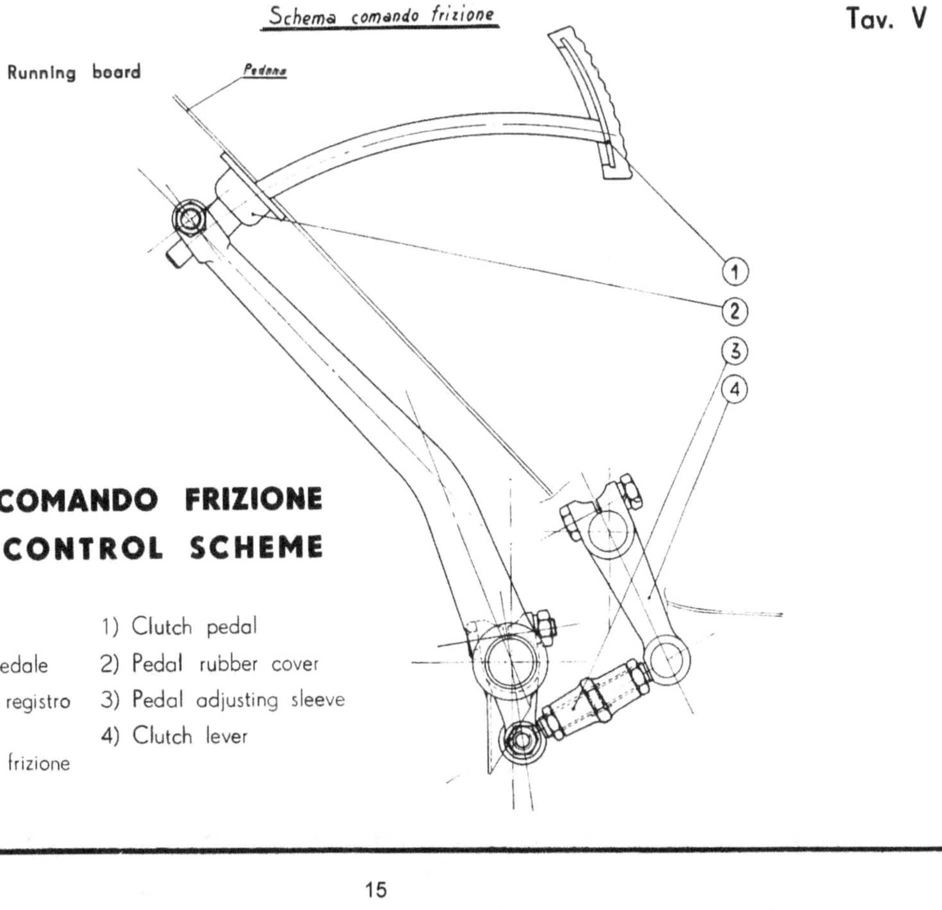

Schema comando frizione

Running board — Pedana

SCHEMA COMANDO FRIZIONE
CLUTCH CONTROL SCHEME

1) Pedale frizione
2) Soffietto per pedale
3) Manicotto per registro pedale
4) Leva comando frizione

1) Clutch pedal
2) Pedal rubber cover
3) Pedal adjusting sleeve
4) Clutch lever

SCHEMA DELL'INSTALLAZIONE DEI FRENI
BRAKE ASSEMBLY SCHEME

Tav. VI

1) Cilindri comando freni
2) Perni eccentrici registrazione freni
3) Dado regolazione fissa del gioco pedale
4) Leva comando freni a mano sulle ruote posteriori
5) Pedale comando freni idraulici sulle 4 ruote
6) Pompe alimentazione cilindri freni
7) Serbatoi del liquido (olio SHELL DONAX B Controllare livello olio ogni 1000 Km.)

1) Wheel brake cylinders
2) Adjusting cams
3) Brake adjuster
4) Hand brake lever on rear wheels
5) Brake pedal on four wheels
6) Brake master cylinders
7) Oil tanks (SHELL DONAX B oil - check oil level every 1000 kms)

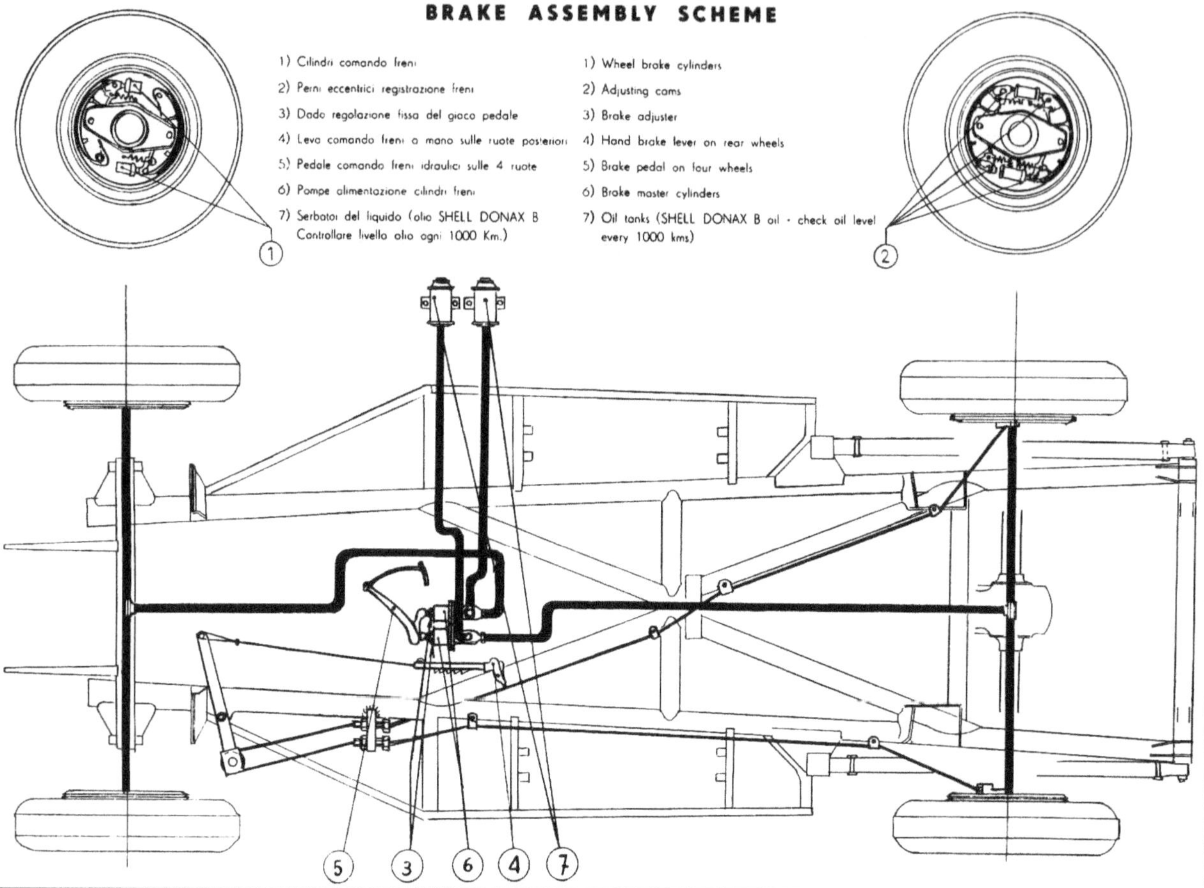

SCHEMA DELL' ORDINE DI ACCENSIONE DEI CILINDRI
CYLINDER IGNITION ORDER's SCHEME

Tav. VII

(1) Bobine (N. 2)
(2) Spinterogeni a 6 scintille (N. 2)
(3) Candele (N. 12)

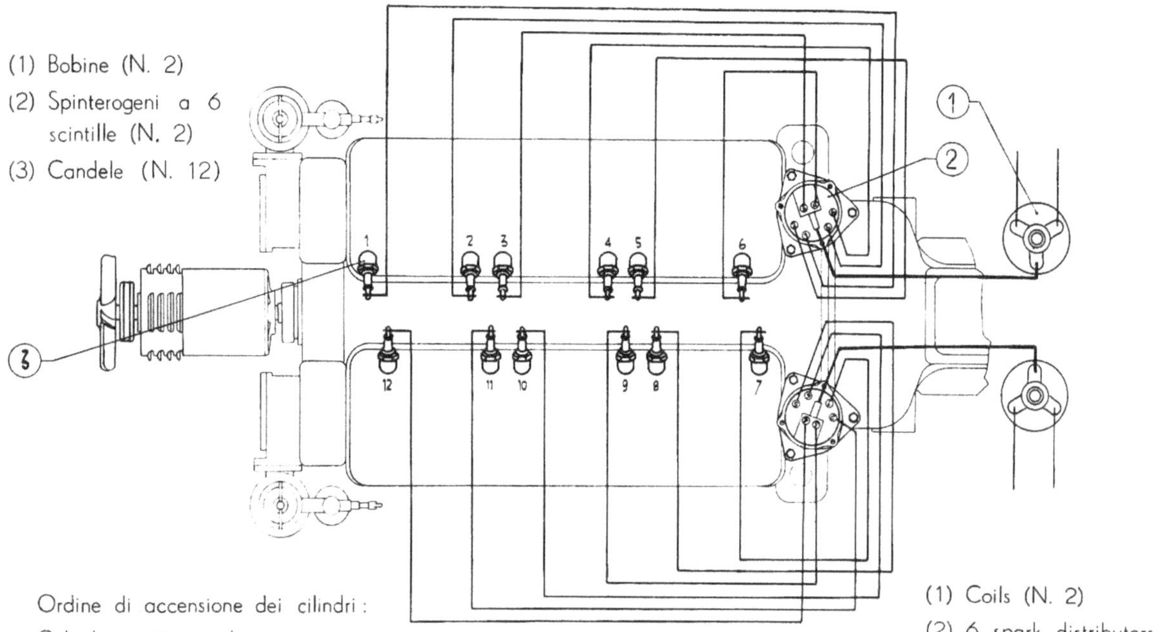

Ordine di accensione dei cilindri:
Cylinder ignition order:

1-7-5-11-3-9-6-12-2-8-4-10

(1) Coils (N. 2)
(2) 6 spark distributors (N. 2)
(3) Spark plugs (N. 12)

16

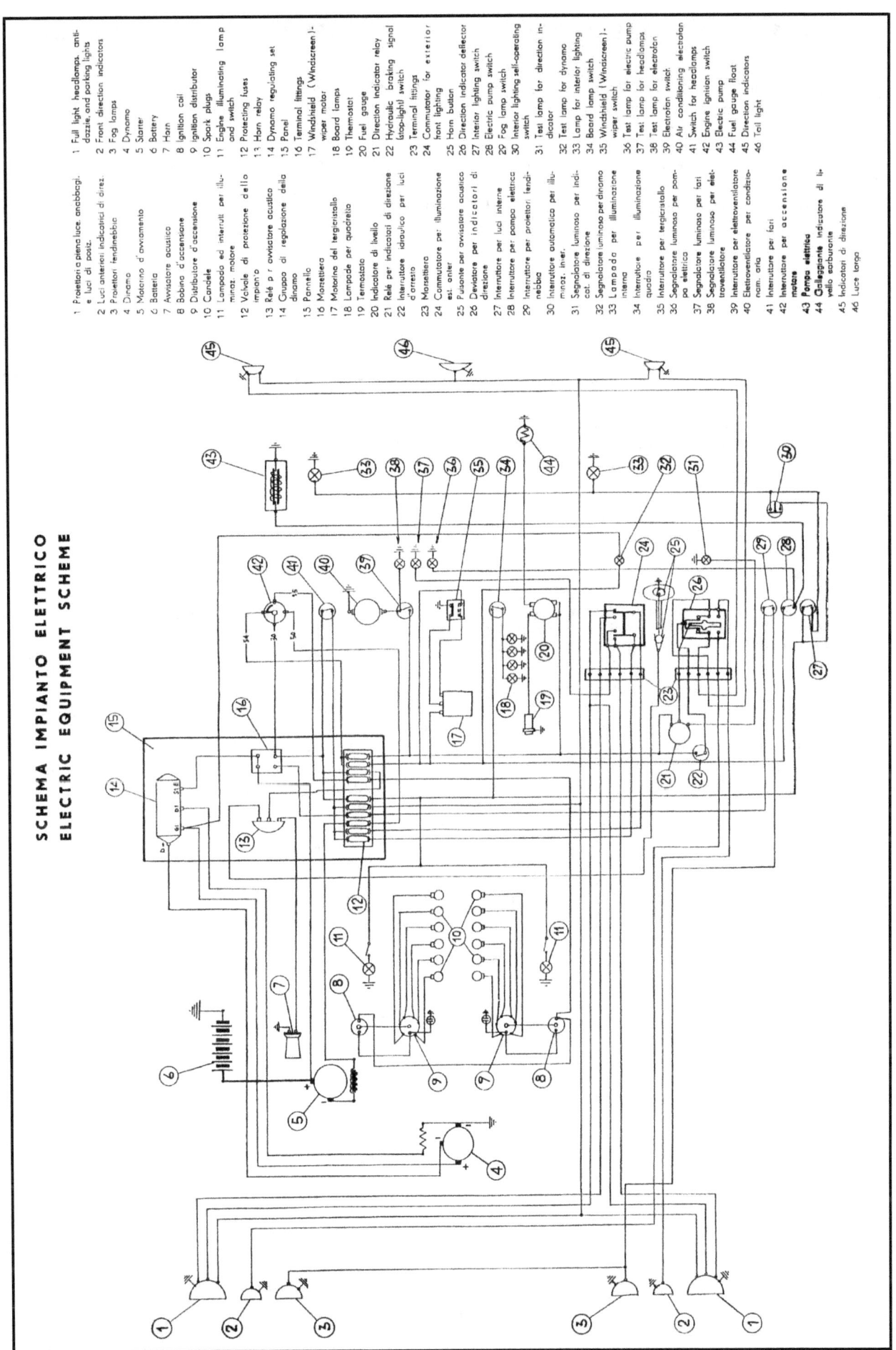

SMONTAGGIO DEL MOTORE

E' necessario disporre di un cavalletto che permetta il fissaggio del motore sulle quattro zampe.

Fissato il motore su di esso, si scarica completamente l'olio dalla coppa, svitando l'apposito tappo quindi l'acqua degli scomparti laterali, levando i due tappi sui fianchi del basamento.

Dopo di ciò si smonta la coppa stessa.

Rimesso il motore coi cilindri in alto, si procede allo smontaggio dei carburatori.

Si smontano altresì la dinamo e i due spinterogeni, unitamente a questi i loro supporti e relativi pignoni di comando. Si procede quindi allo smontaggio dei coperchi della scatola di distribuzione prima e quelli delle valvole poi. Si tolgano in seguito tutti i supporti degli alberi di distribuzione, completi di bilancieri e di bulloni, che fissano le ruote della distribuzione ai rispettivi alberi.

Sulla scatola distribuzione, al posto dei supporti spinterogeno, si fissano due perni a flangia di diametro corrispondente al foro di centraggio delle ruote distribuzione. E' facile allora staccare con due cacciaviti le ruote stesse dagli alberi distribuzione facendole scorrere sui perni a flangia senza per nulla togliere la catena, perchè questa è senza giunto e quindi non apribile.

E' possibile così togliere i due alberi distribuzione dalla loro sede ed anche le due testate, dopo naturalmente aver tolto i dadi che le fissano al basamento, con l'apposita chiave. In queste condizioni lo smontaggio dell'intera scatola distribuzione è semplice: basta togliere il tendicatena affinchè questa, distendendosi, possa disimpegnarsi dal pignone di comando dell'albero, e togliere i dadi dei prigionieri e i bulloni che la fissano al basamento compresi anche il bullone centrale a colonnetta situato nell'interno del corpo filtro olio ed il dado che fissa il tubo di aspirazione olio della pompa al supporto dell'albero motore.

Lo smontaggio dei singoli gruppi che compongono l'assieme della scatola distribuzione non offre speciali difficoltà ad eccezione del corpo pompa acqua il quale richiede qualche cura.

Per togliere bielle e pistoni è meglio ruotare di 90° il cavalletto in modo che il motore venga a trovarsi in posizione verticale col volano in basso, dopo di che, svitati i due bulloni di ciascuna biella, la coppia biella-pistone esce con facilità lungo la canna.

Le canne cilindri non devono mai essere tolte se non per sostituzione.

Eventuali operazioni di ripassatura e levigatura debbono essere eseguite con canne montate.

TO DISMOUNT THE ENGINE

A trestle, on which the engine may be fixed on its four brackets, cannot be dispensed with. After fixing the engine on it, drain off sump oil completely by unscrewing the proper plug, then draw the water off the lateral compartments by removing the two plugs on the crankcase sides.

Then dismount the sump.

Replace the engine cylinders upwards, and dismount the carburetors (carburetters).

Then dismount the dynamo and the two distributors together with their supports and control pinions. Dismount the timing gear casing, then the valve tappet covers.

Take off all the camshaft bearings along with their rockers and the bolts fixing the timing wheels to their respective shafts.

On the timing gear case, in the place of the distributor supports, fix two flange pins of a diameter corresponding to the centering hole of the timing wheels. It is then easy to detach, by means of two screw-drivers, the wheels themselves from the camshafts by making them slide along the flange pins without taking off the chain which, being jointless, is unopenable.

It is thus possible to remove the two camshafts from their seats, as well as the two heads, after taking off — needless to say —, by means of the proper key, the nuts fixing them to the crankcase. Under these conditions it is easy to dismount the complete timing case: merely take off the chain tightener, that the chain, by loosening, may be disengaged from the shaft control pinion; then remove the stud nuts and the bolts fixing it to the crankcase, inclusive of the column-shaped bolt inside the oil filter body and of the nut fixing the pump oil suction pipe to the crankshaft bearing.

The disassembling of the various groups making up the timing casing assembly does not present any particular difficulty, with the exception of the water pump casing which requires a little care.

To take off the connecting rods and the pistons, it is advisable to rotate the trestle through an angle of 90 degrees, so as to set the engine in upright position, flywheel downwards; unscrew the two bolts of each connecting rod, after which the couple connecting rod-piston easily slides along the liner.

Never remove the cylinder liners, except to replace them.

Eventual overhauling and polishing operations should be performed with the liners mounted.

| REVISIONE DEL MOTORE | OVERHAULING OF THE ENGINE |

Cuscinetti di banco — Essi sono del tipo a guscio sottile. L'albero motore essendo di acciaio nitrurato e ben contrappesato, non è soggetto ad usura apprezzabile ed anche i cuscinetti, se lubrificati con olio pulito e della qualità prescritta dalla Casa, ben raramente esigono la sostituzione.

Cuscinetti bielle — Anche questi del tipo a guscio sottile, devono avere da 3 a 5/100 di gioco sui propri perni di manovella. Quando tale gioco raggiunge il valore di 10/100 i cuscinetti sono da sostituire.

Se esiste usura di albero motore in maniera tale da richiedere la ripassatura dei perni, necessita disporre di cuscinetti tali che messi in opera diano il gioco prescritto, senza ritoccare assolutamente il cuscinetto per non danneggiare il trattamento specialissimo che esso presenta alla superfice.

Tra le due bielle affiancate sullo stesso perno, il gioco laterale deve risultare di 10÷15/100 di mm. Per la disposizione delle bielle necessita osservare attentamente i numeri di riferimento.

Le minorazioni previste per i perni di biella e di banco sono quattro e sono elencate nella tabella a ultima pag.

Pistoni — Ad ogni smontaggio di motore è buona norma togliere i segmenti, i raschiaolio e lo spinotto ed osservare se esiste qualche screpolatura sul pistone. Per individuare anche quelle più recondite basta sollevare fra due dita il pistone nella parte superiore e con lo spinotto colpirlo leggermente in basso. Se il suono che ne risulta non è metallico esso è sicuramente difettoso.

Il gioco minimo fra pistone e canna deve essere di 10÷12/100 di mm. misurando il pistone in corrispondenza del fianco superiore della cava del raschiaolio inferiore.

Segmenti e raschiaolio — Sono da sostituire ogni qualvolta, misurando l'apertura del taglio nell'apposita canna con feritoia entro la quale viene introdotto il pistone con segmenti e raschiaolio montati, essa risulti superiore ai 6÷7/10.

Quelli nuovi debbono avere aperture di taglio non inferiore a 3/10 e non superiore a 5/10.

Raschiaolio e segmenti di tenuta debbono essere liberissimi nelle loro sedi.

Valvole — Ripassatura delle sedi, se necessario, e controllo concentricità dei funghi coi gambi.

Bilancieri — Controllare che il rullo non abbia eccessivo gioco nel perno.

Teste — Bisogna procedere alla pulizia delle camere di scoppio, dei condotti di scarico, dei condotti acqua, liberando questi ultimi il più possibile dai sedimenti calcarei.

Controllo dei fori delle guide valvole sostituendo quelle eccessivamente usurate (oltre mm. 0,1) e ripassatura con la fresa delle sedi valvole se è necessario. Per questa operazione è necessario che il gambo del mandrino porta fresa sia forzato nella guida valvola. Dopo la smerigliatura ed il montaggio accurato delle valvole controllarne la tenuta procedendo nel seguente modo:

Crankshaft Main Bearings — They are of the « thin wall » type. Since the crankshaft is of nitrogenized steel and well balanced, no appreciable wear is likely to occur; the bearings also, if lubricated with clean oil of the quality prescribed by the Firm, very seldom require replacement.

Connecting Rod Bearings — These are, likewise, of the « thin wall » type; they should have a clearance of 3-5/100 on their crank pins. Whenever this clearance attains 10/100, they should be replaced. If the crankshaft is so far worn down as to require grinding of the pins, it is necessary to employ such bearings as may assure the clearance prescribed, without having to retouch, in any way, the bearings, lest the very special treatment their surfaces have undergone, should be impaired.

Between the two connecting rods side-by-side on the same pin, the lateral clearance must be 10÷15/100 of millimeter. As to the arrangement of the connecting rods, attention should be given to the bench numbers.

The undersizes foreseen for connecting rod and main pins are four; they are tabulated on last page.

Pistons — At every dismounting of engine it is advisable to take off the compression rings, the oil scraper rings, and the pin, and to note whether there is some crack in the piston. In order to detect even the most hidden ones, merely grip the piston at its upper end, and, keeping it suspended between forefinger and thumb, strike, with the pin, its lower end. If the resulting sound is non-metallic, the piston is certainly faulty.

The minimum clearance between piston and liner should be 10÷12/100 of millimeter, the piston being measured in correspondence to the upper flank of the lower scraper ring cavity.

Compression rings and oil scraper rings — These should be replaced whenever the width of the cut on the apposite liner with window into which the piston, with compression rings and oil scraper rings mounted, is inserted, exceeds 6÷7/10 of millimeter. The new ones should have a cut no less than 3/10 and no more than 5/10 wide.

Oil scraper rings, as well as compression rings, must be quite free on their seats.

Valves — Grind their seats, if necessary, and check concentricity of the valve heads with the stems.

Rockers — Make sure the play of the roller in the pin is not excessive.

Heads — It is necessary to clean the combustion chambers, the exhaust and water ducts, which latter must be freed, as far as possible, from any calcareous sediment.

Check the holes of the valve guides, and replace those which are excessively worn down (over 0,1 mm); mill, if necessary, the valve seats. To perform this operation it is necessary to force the milling cutter shank into the valve guide. After grinding with emery and careful mounting of the valve, check seal as follows:

1) avvitare in ogni camera di scoppio una candela possibilmente di scarto;

2) riempire la camera di scoppio di benzina, petrolio o nafta;

3) con un getto di aria compressa soffiare in ognuno dei canali di aspirazione e di scarico osservando se nel liquido si manifestano bolle d'aria. In caso affermativo è necessario procedere ad una più accurata smerigliatura.

Canne cilindri — Per eseguire l'operazione di controllo dell'usura delle canne è necessario disporre di un ottimo comparatore.

Se l'usura rilevata raggiunge i 10/100 è indispensabile eseguire la ripassatura portando il diametro a +20/100 oppure, procedere alla sostituzione.

In tal caso è consigliabile scaldare a 60° il basamento e controllare che l'interferenza a freddo fra la nuova canna e la sede del basamento risulti di 4÷5/100.

Dopo la sostituzione, avendo cura che siano ben pressate sulla propria sede nel basamento, ritoccare il piano superiore delle canne sostituite, in modo che risulti uguale a quello del basamento. Non è assolutamente tollerabile che sia più alto o più basso. Eliminare il più possibile i residui calcarei intorno alle canne.

Pompa olio — Raramente necessita revisionarla perchè non soggetta a logorio.

Pompa acqua — Sostituzione dell'anello tenuta acqua se logorato eccessivamente.

Catena — Controllare se i rullini delle maglie sono intatti e se il gioco fra di essi ed il loro asse non è eccessivo.

Controllare che anche i cuscinetti a sfere fissi alle scatole e che supportano il pignone della catena siano in buone condizioni e che non abbiano eccessivo gioco.

Tendicatena — Raramente necessita di revisione.
Per tendere la catena è sufficiente togliere il dado cieco che blocca il morsetto del perno tenditore, quindi spingere nella posizione esatta il tenditore. Bloccare nuovamente il morsetto e rimettere il dado cieco.

1) screw, in each combustion chamber, a sparking plug, preferably a discarded one;

2) fill up with gasoline (petrol), petroleum, or Diesel oil, the combustion chamber;

3) direct a jet of compressed air into each inlet or exhaust duct, and note whether air bubbles originate in the liquid. In the affirmative, a more careful grinding is indispensable.

Liners — To check the wear of liners an excellent comparison gauge cannot be dispensed with.

If the wear ascertained attains 10/100 of millimeter, it is necessary either to overhaul and bring the diameter up to +20/100 or to replace. In this latter case it is advisable to warm the crankcase up to 60° C (=140° F) and make sure that the interference, in a cold state, between the new liner and the crankcase seat, is 4÷5/100 of millimeter.

After replacement, and having ascertained that the liners are well forced into position in the crankcase, retouch the upper plane to render them flush with the crankcase plane. Differences of level, either way, are absolutely inadmissible. Remove, as far as possible, eventual calcareous residues around the liners.

Oil Pump — Not being subject to any appreciable wear, overhauling of this is only exceptionally required.

Water Pump — Replace the sealing ring if excessively worn down.

Chain — Check whether the link rollers are unimpaired and whether the play between them and their axes is excessive.

Make sure that the ball bearings fixed on the boxes and supporting the chain sprocket are in good working conditions and do not present an excessive play.

Chain Tightener — It seldom requires overhauling.
To tighten the chain merely take off the box nut locking the clamp of the tightening pin, then push the tightener into position. Relock the clamp and replace the box nut.

MONTAGGIO DOPO REVISIONE

La prima operazione consiste nel montaggio dell'albero motore, con speciale riguardo alla pulizia accurata del basamento e dell'albero. E' indispensabile che dopo la chiusura dei supporti di banco l'albero giri liberissimo. Si proceda poscia al montaggio delle bielle già preventivamente accoppiate ai rispettivi pistoni.

Se questi sono stati sostituiti è necessario assicurarsi che i controlli richiesti nelle norme di revisione siano stati eseguiti. Il montaggio bielle-pistoni sull'albero a gomiti avviene rimettendo il basamento in posizione verticale col volano in basso e facendo molta attenzione alla corrispondenza dei numeri segnati su ciascuna biella e sull'albero motore, assicurandosi infine che ogni biella, dopo la chiusura definitiva dei bulloni, sia ben libera sul proprio perno.

Eseguito ciò e rimessa in opera la scatola distribuzione con tutti i suoi organi, assicurarsi prima che i 2 distanziali interni siano al loro posto e togliere solo il tendicatena, per poter avvolgere la catena sul pignone dell'albero motore, rimettendolo poi a posto. Prima del montaggio delle teste, accuratamente preparate come descritto nelle norme di revisione, è indispensabile controllare le guarnizioni tra basamento e testa.

Tutti i dadi dei prigionieri di fissaggio teste debbono essere chiusi energicamente ed uniformemente (meglio con chiave tarata). E' buona regola a questo punto del montaggio procedere alla pressatura delle camere acqua a 3-4 atm. togliendo naturalmente le candele alle camere di scoppio, girando il motore con le teste in basso. Se l'operazione di montaggio è stata accuratamente eseguita nessuna goccia d'acqua dovrà uscire dai fori delle candele nè dal basamento e neanche attorno alla guarnizione delle testate. Constatata la perfetta tenuta si può procedere al montaggio degli alberi distribuzione agendo secondo le norme qui sotto elencate.

E' importante far presente che l'operazione di messa in fase della distribuzione richiede la massima attenzione poichè uno sbaglio, anche di un sol dente, è già sufficiente per danneggiare le valvole specie nei motori con rapporto di compressione molto elevato.

Sul volano sono segnate freccie ben visibili a 60° che rappresentano i punti morti superiori dei cilindri 1 e 2, il numero 1 della linea destra vicina alla scatola distribuzione ed il numero 2 della linea sinistra vicina al volano, sempre, naturalmene, guardando il motore dal volano stesso.

Si porti allora il punto morto n. 1 in corrispondenza del riferimento segnato sul basamento nell'apposita finestra di ispezione e si metta in opera l'albero distribuzione in modo che il segno esistente su di esso, in prossimità del centraggio della ruota catena, risulti in corrispondenza ad un analogo segno sul cappello del supporto.

Si montino i due gruppi bilancieri corrispondenti ai cilindri 1-6 senza mettere i dadi di bloccaggio.

Si faccia allora scorrere la ruota dal mozzo provvisorio, fissato alla scatola distribuzione (vedi norme di smontaggio), al centraggio proprio sull'albero di distribuzione e si osservi se i riferimenti segnati sulla ruota corrispondono a quelli segnati sull'albero.

TO MOUNT THE ENGINE AFTER OVERHAULING

Mount, first of all, the crankshaft, after ascertaining that both crankcase and shaft have been carefully cleaned. It is indispensable that, after closing of the main journals, the crankshaft can turn quite freely. Then mount the connecting rods, previously coupled to the respective pistons.

If these have been replaced, make sure the controls required by the rules given in the preceding chapter (concerning the overhauling of the engine) have been effected. To mount the couple «connecting rods-pistons» on the crankshaft, reset the crankcase upright, flywheel downwards, and carefully note the correspondence between the numbers marked on each connecting rod and on the crankshaft; make finally sure each connecting rod, after definitive closing of the bolts, is perfectly free on its pin.

After which, and the timing gear casing being restored, with all its parts, to its former place, make sure, first of all, that the spacer sleeves are in their proper places, then merely take off the chain tightener, to make it possible to wind the chain on the crankshaft pinion, and then put it back in its place. Before mounting the heads, carefully prepared as described in the overhauling rules, it is necessary to check the gaskets between crankcase and head.

All the nuts of the head fixing stud bolts should be firmly and uniformly tightened (preferably by means of a rated wrench / spanner /). It is advisable, at this point, to subject the water chambers to a test pressure of 3-4 atmospheres, after removing — needless to say — the spark plugs and turning the engine upside down. If mounting was carefully effected, no drop of water should drip either from the plug holes or the crankcase or around the head gaskets. Having thus ascertained the water-tightness, the camshafts may be mounted according to the rules given here below.

Kindly bear in mind that the timing operation requires the utmost care inasmuch as the slightest mistake, were it limited to ony one tooth, suffices to impair the valves especially in engines with very high compression ratio.

Well visible arrows at 60° are marked on the flywheel; they represent the upper dead points of the cylinders 1 and 2: number 1 of the right-hand row, near the timing gear casing, and number 2 of the left-hand row near the flywheel, looking at the engine, of course, from this latter.

Bring then dead point N° 1 into correspondence with the fixed datum marked, on the crankcase, in the peep-window provided for this purpose, and mount the camshaft in such a way that the fixed bench mark on it, near the centering of the chain wheel, exactly correspond to an analogous mark on the support cap.

Mount the two rocker sets corresponding to cylinders 1-6 without applying the lock nuts. Then make the wheel slide from the provisional hub, fixed on the timing gear casing (see Instructions for Dismounting the Engine), to its own centering on the camshaft, and note whether the bench marks on the wheel do correspond to the ones on the shaft.

Should they not coincide, merely count by how many teeth it is necessary to diplace the wheel with respect

Se non coincidono basta contare di quanti denti bisogna spostare la ruota rispetto alla catena, allentare i quattro dadi che fissano il tendicatena della scatola distribuzione in modo da allontanarlo di circa un centimetro dalla propria base e, facendo uscire la ruota dal centraggio dell'albero di distribuzione, si può spostarla in un senso o nell'altro della quantità richiesta. Quando i riferimenti corrispondono esattamente si blocca con cura la ruota sull'albero.

Constatato che i riferimenti dell'albero rispetto al supporto, e della ruota rispetto all'albero, si corrispondono, si faccia girare di 60° il volano nel senso di rotazione del motore in modo che il punto morto superiore n. 2 venga a trovarsi davanti alla finestra di ispezione, mentre il punto morto superiore n. 1 si troverà esattamente in corrispondenza del punto morto superiore del cilindro n. 2 della linea di sinistra.

Si ripeta l'operazione eseguita per la linea destra dei cilindri, e cioè montaggio dell'albero di distribuzione sinistro e gruppi bilancieri dei cilindri estremi senza tuttavia chiuderli, ma solo per avere un riferimento per l'albero di distribuzione.

Se anche in questo caso i riferimenti fra albero e ruota non si corrispondono, si allontana ancora il tendicatena, si fa saltare la ruota sulle maglie della catena finchè, rimesso a posto il tendicatena, si constata che i riferimenti si corrispondono.

Nell'eseguire l'operazione di spostamento della catena sui denti delle ruote, è necessario fare attenzione che la catena non salti fuori dai denti del pignone dell'albero a gomito. Per questo è bene non staccare il tendicatena oltre quanto detto.

Eseguite tutte queste operazioni, si possono bloccare i due gruppi bilancieri di ogni albero, controllare se il gioco tra bilanciere e valvola è di 15/100 per l'aspirazione e 20/100 per lo scarico e fare il rilievo delle aperture e chiusure delle valvole.

Se le fasature risultano come indicate nella tabella a ultima pag., con una tolleranza di 2°, si possono ritenere esatte.

Per eseguire questa operazione è necessario, s'intende, disporre di un disco graduato da fissare sulla flangia d'attacco cambio del motore.

Quando, per effetto dell'allungamento della catena distribuzione dovuto all'uso, si riscontrano dei dati di fasatura diversi da quelli esposti, necessita rifare le messe a punto, agendo nel modo sotto indicato ed iniziando naturalmente dalla linea di cilindri destra. Allentare per prima cosa i bulloni di chiusura dei gruppi bilancieri in modo che l'albero possa girare senza comandare le valvole. Vedere dai rilievi eseguiti, di quanti gradi è lo spostamento che si deve fare e se è in anticipo od in ritardo, tenendo conto che lo spostamento minimo che si può operare è di 4° (sul volano) e che, per ottenerlo, è necessario spostare in un senso la ruota con l'albero a cammes di ben 7 denti rispetto alla catena ed in senso opposto il solo albero a cammes rispetto alla ruota di 1/5 di giro.

Ora, se è necessario anticipare di quattro gradi la fasatura, si farà lo spostamento della ruota e dell'albero di sette denti rispetto alla catena in anticipo (cioè nel senso di rotazione del motore), perchè, corrispondendo ogni spostamento di un dente della ruota a 21°10' (letti naturalmente sul volano e quindi 7 × 21°10' = 148°10'), si ha uno spostamento in anticipo maggiore di 4°10' rispetto a quello ottenuto spostando poi nel senso opposto di 1/5 di giro (720° : 5 = 144°) il solo albero distribuzione. Se lo spostamento da operare fosse di 8° circa, si fa due volte l'operazione suaccennata.

to the chain, loosen the four nuts which hold the chain tightener of the timing gear casing in place, so as to remove it by about 0,39" (10 mm) from its base and, by taking out the wheel from the centering of the camshaft, render it possible to displace it in either direction by the quantity required. After ascertaining that the bench marks exactly correspond to each other, carefully block the wheel on the shaft.

Make it sure the bench marks on the shaft with respect to the support, and the ones on the wheel with respect to the shaft, correspond to each other, turn the flywheel by 60° in the direction of rotation of the engine so as to bring upper dead point N° 2 to face the peep-window, while upper dead point N° 1 will exactly correspond to the upper dead point of cylinder N° 2 of the left-hand row.

Repeat the same operation for the right-hand cylinder row, viz, mount the left camshaft and the rocker sets of the outermost cylinders, yet without closing them, but merely to obtain a fixed datum for the camshaft.

If the marks between shaft and wheel do not yet correspond, remove the chain tightener again, and make the wheel spring over the chain links until, having replaced the chain tightener, the marks exactly correspond to each other.

In displacing the chain over the teeth of the wheels be careful that the chain does not spring off the crankshaft pinion teeth. It is therefore advisable not to remove the chain tightener more than prescribed above.

This done, the rocker sets of each shaft may be blocked; check whether the play between rocker and valve is 15/100 of millimeter for the inlet and 20/100 for the exhaust valves, and control the opening and closing of the valves.

If timings result as shown in the Table on last page, with a tolerance of 2°, they may be considered exact.

To effect this operation, a graduated disc, to be fixed on the flange connecting the transmission case (gearbox) to the engine, is, of course, indispensable.

When, owing to elongation of the timing chain due to wear, the timing data prove different from the tabulated ones, it is necessary to tune up again proceeding as indicated here below, and beginning, of course, at the right cylinder row. Loosen, first of all, the blocking bolts of the rocker sets that the shaft may turn without controlling the valves. See by how many degrees it is necessary to displace, and whether there is lead or lag, bearing in mind that the least possible displacement is of 4° (on the flywheel), and that, to obtain it, ment is necessary to displace in one direction, by no less than 7 teeth with respect to the chain, the wheel with the camshaft, and in opposite direction only the camshaft, by 1/5 revolution, with respect to the wheel.

Now, if it is necessary to advance the timing by four degrees, both the wheel and the shaft must be displaced by seven teeth with respect to the chain in advance (i.e. in the direction of rotation of the engine), for, since each displacement of one tooth of the wheel correspond to 20°10' (read, of course, on the flywheel and, therefore, 7 × 21°10' = 148°10'), the displacement in advance is greater by 4°10' with respect to the one obtained by then displacing in opposite direction, by 1/5 of a revolution (720° : 5 = 144°), the camshaft only. Should the displacement required be of about 8°, the above operation should be performed twice.

Controllata così l'esatta fasatura (toll. ±2°), si ripete l'operazione sull'altra linea di cilindri.

S'intende che i segni di riferimento tra ruota ed albero a boccioli non si corrispondono più; è pertanto necessario rifarne altri sulla ruota e cancellare i primi. Ciò fatto, si montano i gruppi bilanceri assicurandosi che, dopo la chiusura dei dadi, i bilanceri risultino liberissimi sul proprio perno. Particolare molto importante in quanto il grippaggio di un bilancere può provocare gravi danni al motore.

Per la messa in fase dei magneti è necessario rimettere il punto morto numero 1, segnato sul volano, in corrispondenza col riferimento della finestra di spia e controllare che il riferimento delle camme corrisponda a quello del supporto bilancere vicino alla ruota.

Ciò significa che il cilindro numero 1 è in fase di scoppio.

Ciò fatto, si gira il volano di 8° in senso opposto a quello di rotazione e si caletta lo spinterogeno con la spazzola distributrice in posizione 1 e le puntine dell'interruttore che appena accennino a staccarsi (usare apposita lametta o carta sottile). Spostato di 60° il volano nel senso della marcia, si ripete la stessa operazione per la fasatura del secondo spinterogeno.

CAMBIO DI VELOCITÀ

Smontaggio — La prima operazione da eseguire è quella di togliere il coperchietto superiore, lo snodo cardanico e relativa forcella fissa sul primario. Togliere quindi il coperchietto posteriore e quello anteriore che porta la leva del disinnesto frizione. Si svita poscia la ghiera anteriore del secondario e si spinge l'albero fuori dal cuscinetto a sfere anteriore, finchè l'ingranaggio fisso del rinvio cada sul fondo della scatola. Solo allora è possibile svitare la ghiera avvitata sul primario e quindi togliere gli ingranaggi sfilando il primario stesso.

Having thus checked the exact timing (tolerance ±2°), repeat the same operation on the other cylinder row.

Now, needless to say, the fixed data between wheel and camshaft do no longer correspond to each other; it is therefore necessary to fix and mark other data, and to cancel the former. This done, mount the rocker sets, and make sure that, after tightening the nuts, the rockers are quite free on their pins. This is a detail of the utmost importance inasmuch as the jamming of a rocker may seriously damage the engine.

To time the magnetos it is necessary to replace dead point N° 1, marked on the flywheel, in correspondence with the fixed datum in the peep-window, and check whether the fixed datum on the cams corresponds to the one on the rocker support near the wheel. This indicates that cylinder N° 1 is in the explosion phase.

This done, turn the flywheel by 8° in the direction opposite that of rotation and drive in the ignition distributor, with the distributing brush in position 1 and the switch points hardly diverging from each other (use a suitable blade or thin paper). Having displaced the flywheel by 60° in the direction of rotation, time, in the same way, the second ignition distributor.

GEAR CONTROL

Dismounting — First of all, remove the upper cover, the universal joint and respective gear shift fork (gear control fork) fixed on the third motion shaft (main shaft). Then take off the rear cover and the front cover bearing the clutch lever. Then unscrew the front sleeve of the countershaft and push the shaft out of the front ball bearing until the fixed gear of the countershaft falls on the bottom of the box. Only then is it possible to unscrew the sleeve screwed on the third motion shaft (main shaft) and then take off the gears and draw out said shaft itself.

TABELLA DELLE FASATURE DEL MOTORE

MOTORE	ASPIRAZIONE		SCARICO	
	ANT. APERTURA	POS. CHIUSURA	ANT. APERTURA	POS. CHIUSURA
250 GT	22°	66°	67°	17°

TIMINGS OF THE ENGINE

ENGINE	INLET		EXHAUST	
	OPENING ADVANCE	CLOSING RETARD	OPENING ADVANCE	CLOSING RETARD
250 GT	22°	66°	67	17°

TABELLA DELLE MINORAZIONI PREVISTE PER I PERNI DI BIELLA E DI BANCO

	Biella	Banco
⌀ nominale	41,275	55
1ª minorazione	41,021	54,746
2ª minorazione	40,767	51,492
3ª minorazione	40.513	54,238
4ª minorazione	40,259	53,984

Oltre queste minorazioni necessita la sostituzione dell'albero motore.

UNDERSIZES FORESEEN FOR THE CONNECTING ROD AND MAIN BEARINGS

	Connecting rod bearings	Main bearings
Nominal ⌀	41,275	55 ·
1st undersize	41,021	54,746
2nd undersize	40,767	54.492
3rd undersize	40,513	54,238
4th undersize	40,259	53,984

Beyond these undersizes, the crankshaft must be replaced.

Non dimenticate di interpellarci per qualsiasi quesito relativo al funzionamento delle nostre macchine.

E' consuetudine della Ditta assistere la CLIENTELA, dietro semplice richiesta, con personale specializzato.

TELEGRAFARE A **Ferrari** : MODENA o TELEFONARE AL 24081 - MODENA

Do not forget to consult us about any problem concerning the working of our cars.

Our firm makes a point of assisting its customers, on application, by placing its skilled staff at their disposal.

WIRE TO: **Ferrari** - MODENA or PHONE 24-081 MODENA

catalogo
parti di ricambio

spare parts
catalogue

Ferrari
cars
250 Granturismo

**norme da osservare per
l'ordinazione delle parti di ricambio:**

per le ordinazioni di parti di ricambio, indicare sempre chiaramente, oltre alla denominazione del pezzo, anche i numeri di matricola e disegno desunti dall'allegato catalogo e citare i numeri di matricola del motore e del telaio da riparare.

**rules to be observed
when ordering spare parts:**

when ordering spare parts, clearly indicate the denomination of each piece, its classification numbers, as mentioned in the enclosed catalogue, and also state the number of engine and chassis of the car to be repaired.

Elenco delle tavole

Tavola 1 -	Basamento motore	
Tavola 2 -	Coppa olio	
Tavola 3 -	Manovellismo, volano e motorino avviam.	
Tavola 4 -	Teste motore	
Tavola 5 -	Distribuzione	
Tavola 6 -	Apparato refrigerante	
Tavola 7 -	Apparato circolazione e filtraggio olio	
Tavola 8 -	Carburatori e filtro	
Tavola 9 -	Apparato di alimentazione e regolazione Carburante	
Tavola 10 -	Serbatoio carburante con accessori e pompa elettrica	
Tavola 11 -	Accensione e batteria	
Tavola 12 -	Dinamo, ventilatore	
Tavola 13 -	Collettori scarico, marmitte, prolunghe	
Tavola 14 -	Scatola cambio e frizione	
Tavola 15 -	Frizione	
Tavola 16 -	Ingranaggeria cambio	
Tavola 17 -	Comando cambio	
Tavola 18 -	Trasmissione	
Tavola 19 -	Gruppo differenziale	
Tavola 20 -	Bracci ponte e sospensione posteriore	
Tavola 21 -	Ruote, mozzi, semiassi	
Tavola 22 -	Sospensione anteriore e timoneria di sterzo	
Tavola 23 -	Freni	
Tavola 24 -	Comando idraulico freni	
Tavola 25 -	Pedaliera e comando freno	
Tavola 26 -	Organi di guida	
Tavola 27 -	Telaio	
Tavola 28 -	Attrezzi motore	
Tavola 29 -	Attrezzi normali	

List of tables

Table 1 -	Engine crankcase	
Table 2 -	Oil pan	
Table 3 -	Crank mechanism, flywheel, and starter	
Table 4 -	Engine heads	
Table 5 -	Timing	
Table 6 -	Cooling apparatus	
Table 7 -	Oil circulation and filtering apparatus	
Table 8 -	Carburetors and filter	
Table 9 -	Fuel feeding and regulating apparatus	
Table 10 -	Fuel tank with accessories and electric pump	
Table 11 -	Ignition and battery	
Table 12 -	Dynamo and fan	
Table 13 -	Exhaust manifolds, mufflers, lengthening pipes	
Table 14 -	Transmission casing and clutch	
Table 15 -	Clutch	
Table 16 -	Gear wheels	
Table 17 -	Gear control	
Table 18 -	Transmission	
Table 19 -	Differential assembly	
Table 20 -	Axle arms and rear suspension	
Table 21 -	Wheels, hubs, axle shafts	
Table 22 -	Front suspension and steering linkage	
Table 23 -	Brakes	
Table 24 -	Hydraulic brake control	
Table 25 -	Brake pedal and brake control	
Table 26 -	Steering gear	
Table 27 -	Chassis	
Table 28 -	Engine tools	
Table 29 -	Normal tools	

Tavola 1 - Basamento motore

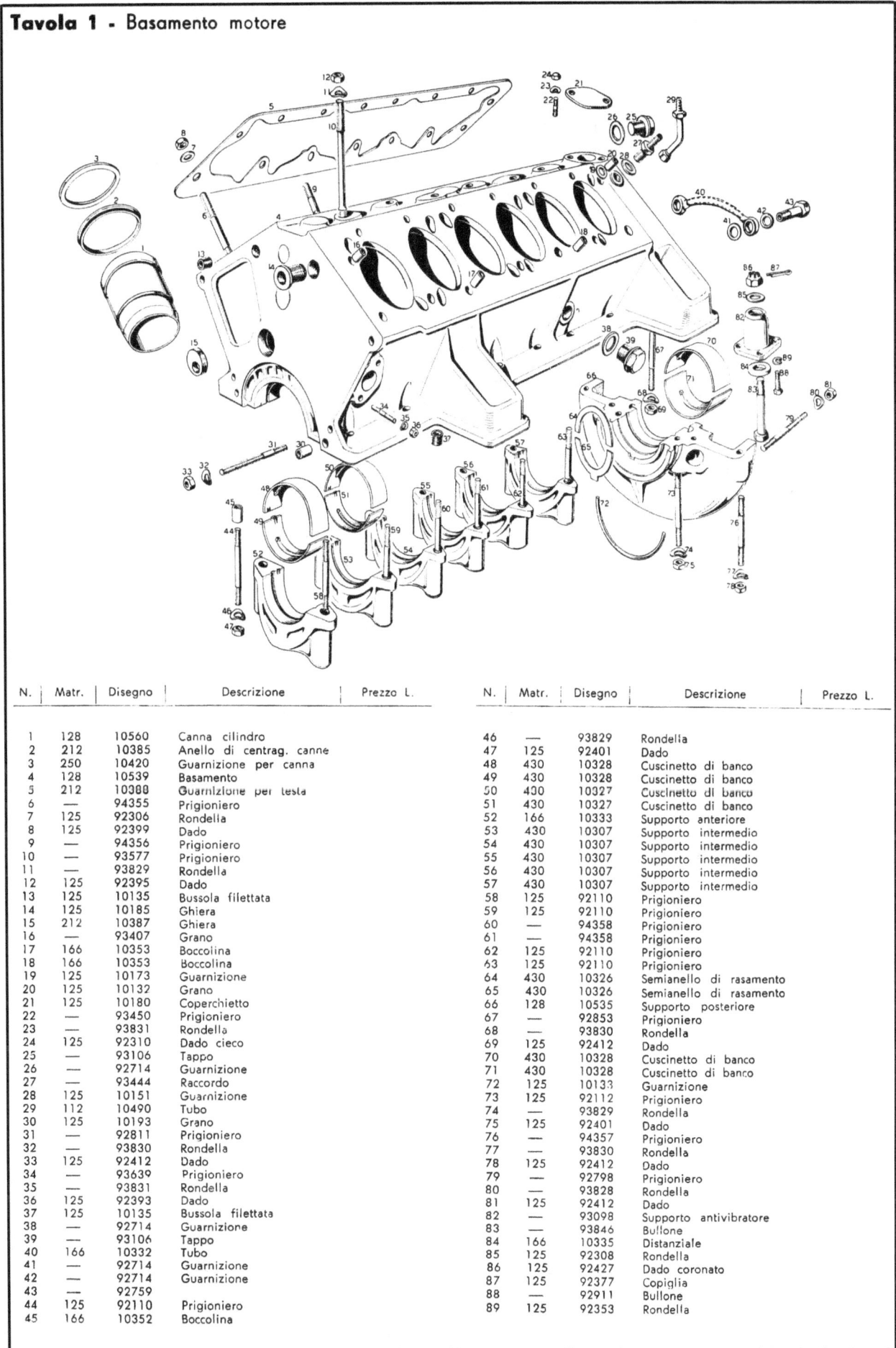

N.	Matr.	Disegno	Descrizione	Prezzo L.	N.	Matr.	Disegno	Descrizione	Prezzo L.
1	128	10560	Canna cilindro		46	—	93829	Rondella	
2	212	10385	Anello di centrag. canne		47	125	92401	Dado	
3	250	10420	Guarnizione per canna		48	430	10328	Cuscinetto di banco	
4	128	10539	Basamento		49	430	10328	Cuscinetto di banco	
5	212	10388	Guarnizione per testa		50	430	10327	Cuscinetto di banco	
6	—	94355	Prigioniero		51	430	10327	Cuscinetto di banco	
7	125	92306	Rondella		52	166	10333	Supporto anteriore	
8	125	92399	Dado		53	430	10307	Supporto intermedio	
9	—	94356	Prigioniero		54	430	10307	Supporto intermedio	
10	—	93577	Prigioniero		55	430	10307	Supporto intermedio	
11	—	93829	Rondella		56	430	10307	Supporto intermedio	
12	125	92395	Dado		57	430	10307	Supporto intermedio	
13	125	10135	Bussola filettata		58	125	92110	Prigioniero	
14	125	10185	Ghiera		59	125	92110	Prigioniero	
15	212	10387	Ghiera		60	—	94358	Prigioniero	
16	—	93407	Grano		61	—	94358	Prigioniero	
17	166	10353	Boccolina		62	125	92110	Prigioniero	
18	166	10353	Boccolina		63	125	92110	Prigioniero	
19	125	10173	Guarnizione		64	430	10326	Semianello di rasamento	
20	125	10132	Grano		65	430	10326	Semianello di rasamento	
21	125	10180	Coperchietto		66	128	10535	Supporto posteriore	
22	—	93450	Prigioniero		67	—	92853	Prigioniero	
23	—	93831	Rondella		68	—	93830	Rondella	
24	125	92310	Dado cieco		69	125	92412	Dado	
25	—	93106	Tappo		70	430	10328	Cuscinetto di banco	
26	—	92714	Guarnizione		71	430	10328	Cuscinetto di banco	
27	—	93444	Raccordo		72	125	10133	Guarnizione	
28	125	10151	Guarnizione		73	125	92112	Prigioniero	
29	112	10490	Tubo		74	—	93829	Rondella	
30	125	10193	Grano		75	125	92401	Dado	
31	—	92811	Prigioniero		76	—	94357	Prigioniero	
32	—	93830	Rondella		77	—	93830	Rondella	
33	125	92412	Dado		78	125	92412	Dado	
34	—	93639	Prigioniero		79	—	92798	Prigioniero	
35	—	93831	Rondella		80	—	93828	Rondella	
36	125	92393	Dado		81	125	92412	Dado	
37	125	10135	Bussola filettata		82	—	93098	Supporto antivibratore	
38	—	92714	Guarnizione		83	—	93846	Bullone	
39	—	93106	Tappo		84	166	10335	Distanziale	
40	166	10332	Tubo		85	125	92308	Rondella	
41	—	92714	Guarnizione		86	125	92427	Dado coronato	
42	—	92714	Guarnizione		87	125	92377	Copiglia	
43	—	92759			88	—	92911	Bullone	
44	125	92110	Prigioniero		89	125	92353	Rondella	
45	166	10352	Boccolina						

Tavola 2 - Coppa olio

N.	Matr.	Disegno	Descrizione	Prezzo L.	N.	Matr.	Disegno	Descrizione	Prezzo L.
1	212	11895	Paraolio laterale destro		22	166	11886	Supportino	
2	212	11894	Paraolio orrizzont. destro		23	—	93087	Bullone	
3	212	11935	Paraolio orrizzon. sinistro		24	125	92516	Rondella	
4	212	11896	Paraolio laterale sinistro		25	125	92405	Dado	
5	125	11120	Guarnizione		26	212	11890	Tubo carico olio	
6	128	11962	Coppa olio		27	375	11814	Guarnizione	
7	125	92262	Bullone		28	—	93630	Prigioniero	
8	—	93830	Rondella		29	125	92353	Rondella	
9	125	92412	Dado		30	125	92393	Dado	
10	125	92266	Bullone		31	166	11863	Corpo tappo	
11	—	93830	Rondella		32	166	11865	Rete	
12	125	92412	Dado		33	166	11864	Parapolvere	
13	125	92266	Bullone		34	125	24124	Anellino	
14	—	93096	Tappo		35	166	11866	Rete paraolio	
15	—	92930	Guarnizione		36	375	11883	Guarnizione	
16	125	92353	Prigioniero		37	212	11887	Coperchio	
17	—	93832	Rondella		38	125	92460	Prigioniero	
18	125	92405	Dado		39	—	93832	Rondella	
19	125	92353	Prigioniero		40	125	92405	Dado	
20	128	11964	Asta livello olio		41	—	92784	Guarnizione	
21	212	11923	Supportino		42	—	92783	Tappo	

Tavola 3 - Manovellismo, volano e motorino avviamento

N.	Matr.	Disegno	Descrizione	Prezzo L.
1			Pistone Borgo 3492	
2			Anello di tenuta Kiklos	
3			Anello di tenuta Kiklos	
4			Anello raschiaolio Kiklos	
5			Anello raschiatoio Kiklos	
6	250	14283	Spinotto	
7	250	14433	Anellino	
8	125	14102	Biella	
9	125	14111	Cuscinetto di biella	
10	125	14102	Biella	
11	125	14130	Boccola	
12	125	92229	Bullone	
13	125	14108	Piastrina	
14	128	12231	Albero motore	
15	275	12157	Vite	
16	—	92987	Piastrina	
17	125	12120/2	Pignone	
18	125	12115	Ingranaggio	
19	340	12199	Volano	
20	—	94129	Grano	
21	125	92230	Bullone	
22	125	12124	Piastrina	
23	166	13158	Motorino d'avviamento	
24	—	93015	Prigioniero	
25	—	93828	Rondella	
26	125	92398	Dado	
27	166	13164	Deflettore	
28	125	92439	Chiodo	
29	128	13187	Fascietta	
30	—	92911	Bullone	
31	125	92353	Rondella	
32	125	92393	Dado	
33	212	13175	Coprimorsetto	

Tavola 4 - Teste motore

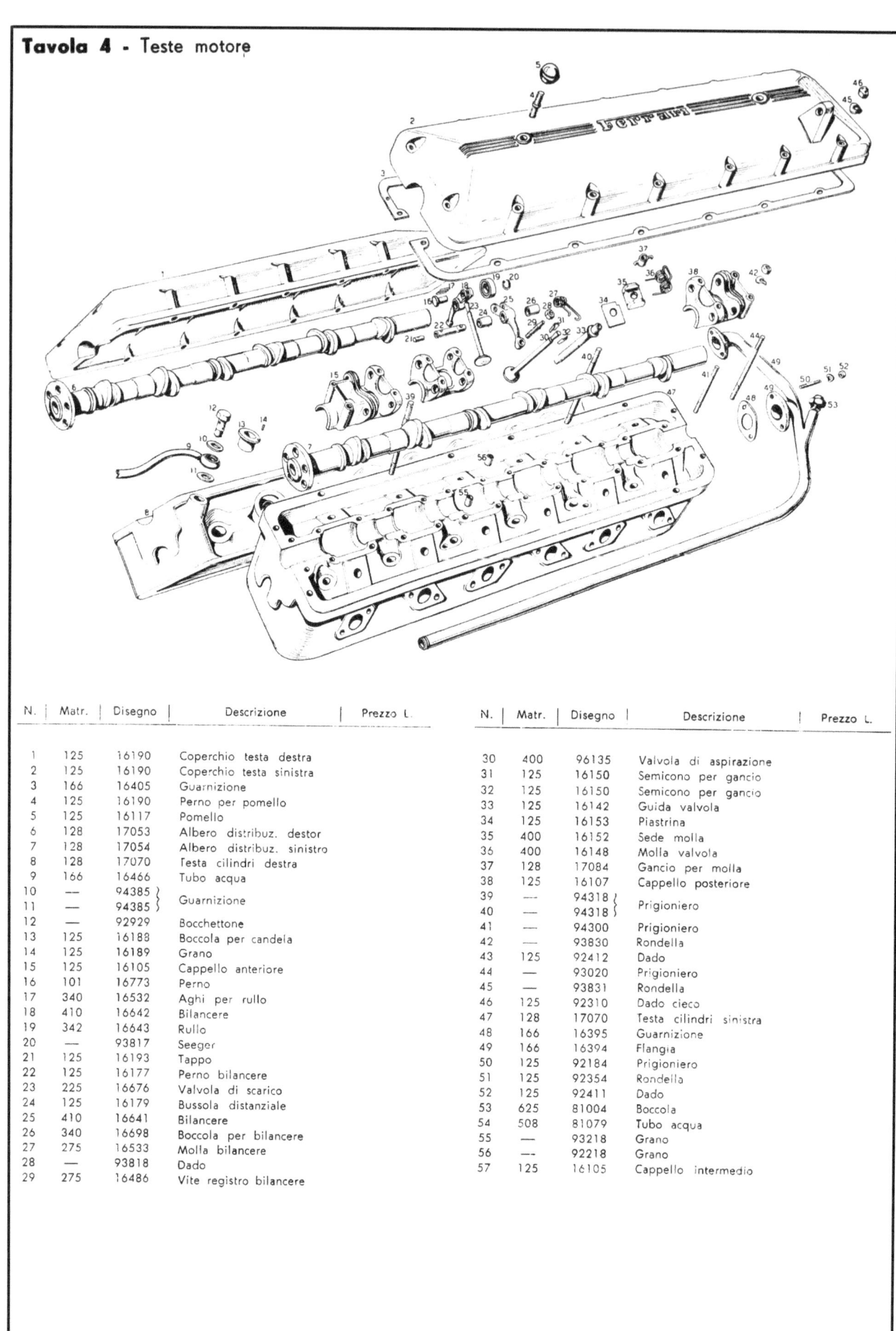

N.	Matr.	Disegno	Descrizione
1	125	16190	Coperchio testa destra
2	125	16190	Coperchio testa sinistra
3	166	16405	Guarnizione
4	125	16190	Perno per pomello
5	125	16117	Pomello
6	128	17053	Albero distribuz. destor
7	128	17054	Albero distribuz. sinistro
8	128	17070	Testa cilindri destra
9	166	16466	Tubo acqua
10	—	94385	Guarnizione
11	—	94385	
12	—	92929	Bocchettone
13	125	16188	Boccola per candela
14	125	16189	Grano
15	125	16105	Cappello anteriore
16	101	16773	Perno
17	340	16532	Aghi per rullo
18	410	16642	Bilancere
19	342	16643	Rullo
20	—	93817	Seeger
21	125	16193	Tappo
22	125	16177	Perno bilancere
23	225	16676	Valvola di scarico
24	125	16179	Bussola distanziale
25	410	16641	Bilancere
26	340	16698	Boccola per bilancere
27	275	16533	Molla bilancere
28	—	93818	Dado
29	275	16486	Vite registro bilancere
30	400	96135	Valvola di aspirazione
31	125	16150	Semicono per gancio
32	125	16150	Semicono per gancio
33	125	16142	Guida valvola
34	125	16153	Piastrina
35	400	16152	Sede molla
36	400	16148	Molla valvola
37	128	17084	Gancio per molla
38	125	16107	Cappello posteriore
39	—	94318	Prigioniero
40	—	94318	
41	—	94300	Prigioniero
42	—	93830	Rondella
43	125	92412	Dado
44	—	93020	Prigioniero
45	—	93831	Rondella
46	125	92310	Dado cieco
47	128	17070	Testa cilindri sinistra
48	166	16395	Guarnizione
49	166	16394	Flangia
50	125	92184	Prigioniero
51	125	92354	Rondella
52	125	92411	Dado
53	625	81004	Boccola
54	508	81079	Tubo acqua
55	—	93218	Grano
56	—	92218	Grano
57	125	16105	Cappello intermedio

Tavola 5 - Distribuzione

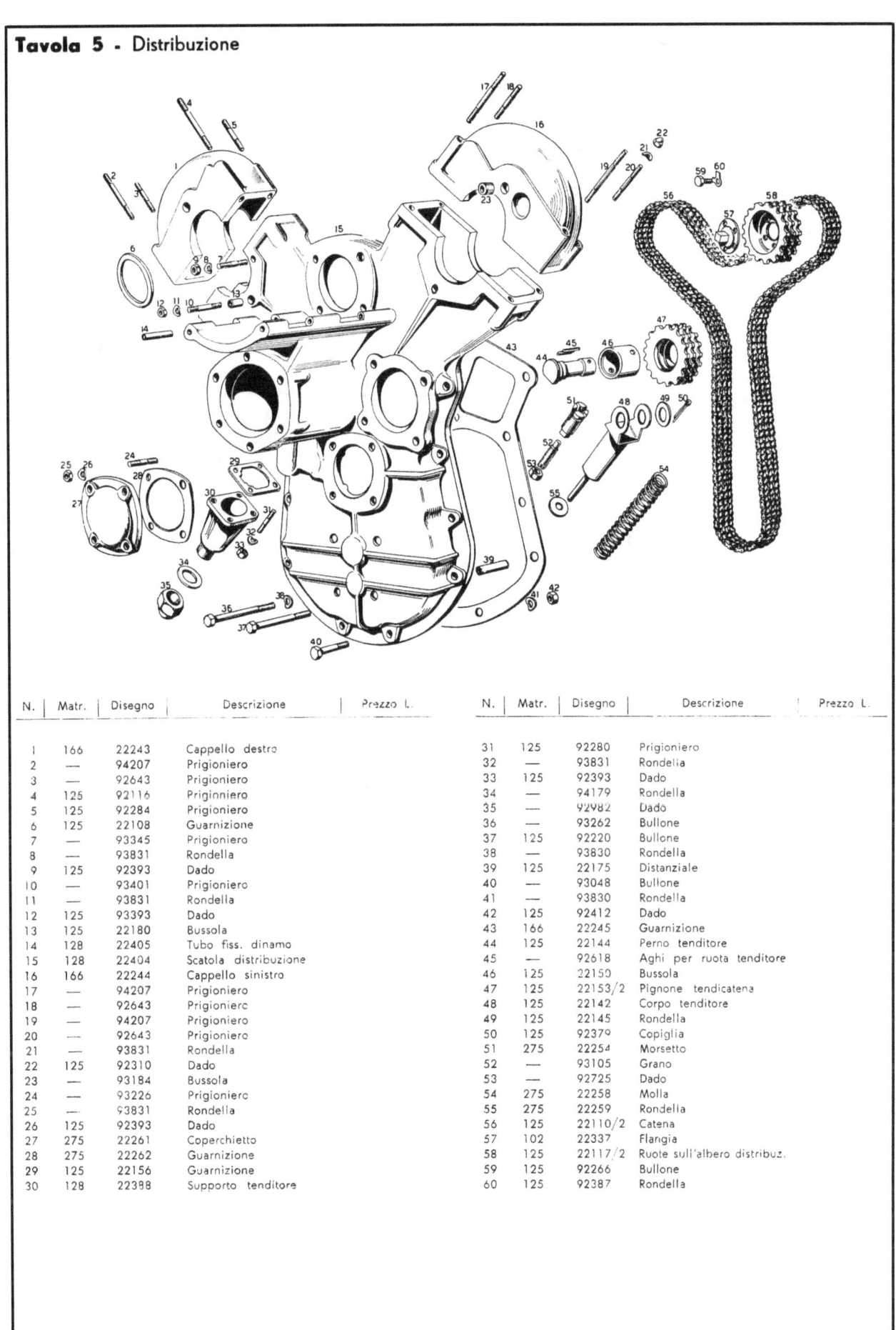

N.	Matr.	Disegno	Descrizione	Prezzo L.	N.	Matr.	Disegno	Descrizione	Prezzo L.
1	166	22243	Cappello destro		31	125	92280	Prigioniero	
2	—	94207	Prigioniero		32	—	93831	Rondella	
3	—	92643	Prigioniero		33	125	92393	Dado	
4	125	92116	Priginniero		34	—	94179	Rondella	
5	125	92284	Prigioniero		35	—	92982	Dado	
6	125	22108	Guarnizione		36	—	93262	Bullone	
7	—	93345	Prigioniero		37	125	92220	Bullone	
8	—	93831	Rondella		38	—	93830	Rondella	
9	125	92393	Dado		39	125	22175	Distanziale	
10	—	93401	Prigioniero		40	—	93048	Bullone	
11	—	93831	Rondella		41	—	93830	Rondella	
12	125	93393	Dado		42	125	92412	Dado	
13	125	22180	Bussola		43	166	22245	Guarnizione	
14	128	22405	Tubo fiss. dinamo		44	125	22144	Perno tenditore	
15	128	22404	Scatola distribuzione		45	—	92618	Aghi per ruota tenditore	
16	166	22244	Cappello sinistro		46	125	22150	Bussola	
17	—	94207	Prigioniero		47	125	22153/2	Pignone tendicatena	
18	—	92643	Prigioniero		48	125	22142	Corpo tenditore	
19	—	94207	Prigioniero		49	125	22145	Rondella	
20	—	92643	Prigioniero		50	—	92379	Copiglia	
21	—	93831	Rondella		51	275	22254	Morsetto	
22	125	92310	Dado		52	—	93105	Grano	
23	—	93184	Bussola		53	—	92725	Dado	
24	—	93226	Prigioniero		54	275	22258	Molla	
25	—	93831	Rondella		55	275	22259	Rondella	
26	125	92393	Dado		56	125	22110/2	Catena	
27	275	22261	Coperchietto		57	102	22337	Flangia	
28	275	22262	Guarnizione		58	125	22117/2	Ruote sull'albero distribuz.	
29	125	22156	Guarnizione		59	125	92266	Bullone	
30	128	22398	Supporto tenditore		60	125	92387	Rondella	

Tavola 6 - Apparato refrigerante

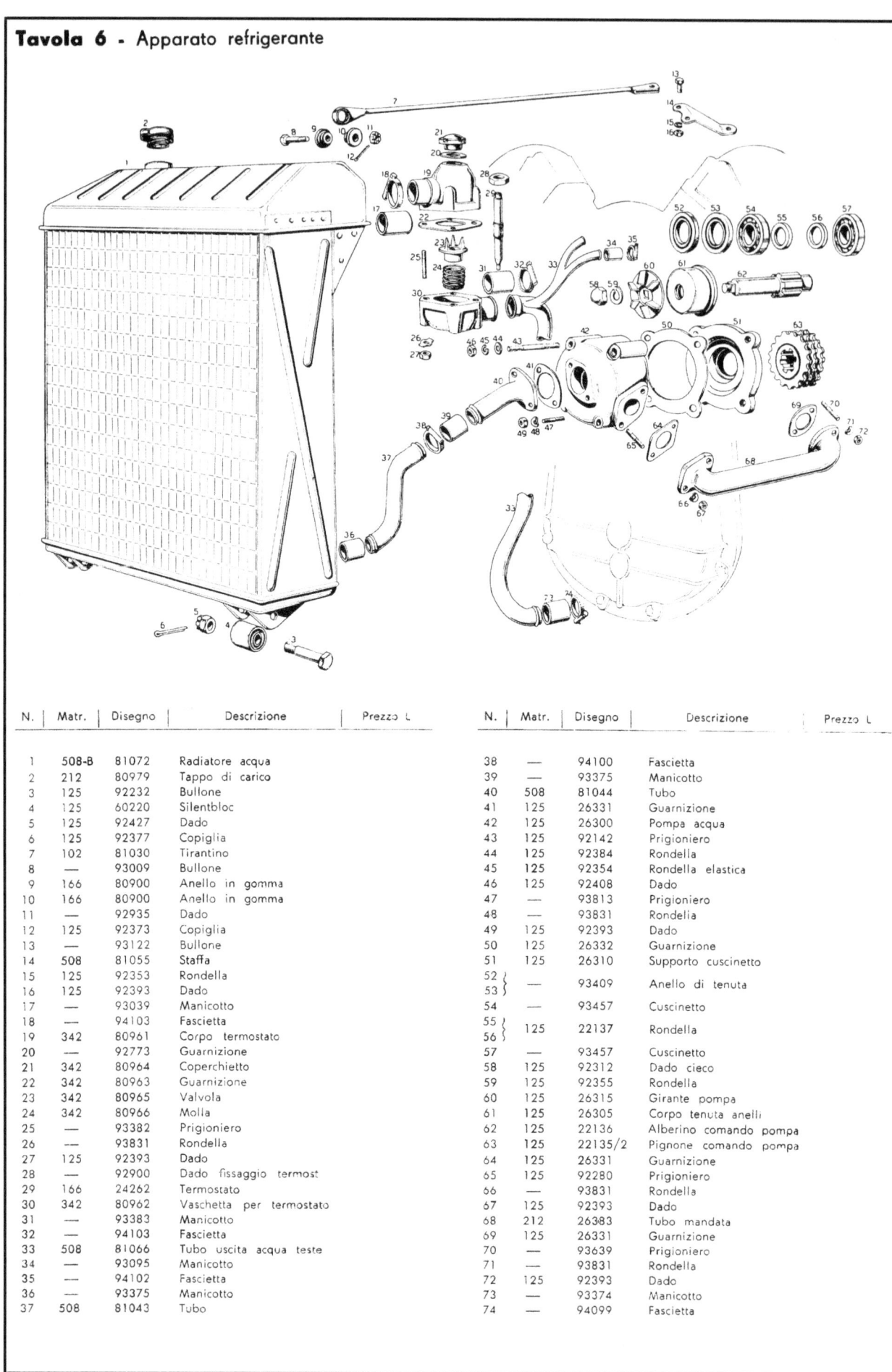

N.	Matr.	Disegno	Descrizione	Prezzo L
1	508-B	81072	Radiatore acqua	
2	212	80979	Tappo di carico	
3	125	92232	Bullone	
4	125	60220	Silentbloc	
5	125	92427	Dado	
6	125	92377	Copiglia	
7	102	81030	Tirantino	
8	—	93009	Bullone	
9	166	80900	Anello in gomma	
10	166	80900	Anello in gomma	
11	—	92935	Dado	
12	125	92373	Copiglia	
13	—	93122	Bullone	
14	508	81055	Staffa	
15	125	92353	Rondella	
16	125	92393	Dado	
17	—	93039	Manicotto	
18	—	94103	Fascietta	
19	342	80961	Corpo termostato	
20	—	92773	Guarnizione	
21	342	80964	Coperchietto	
22	342	80963	Guarnizione	
23	342	80965	Valvola	
24	342	80966	Molla	
25	—	93382	Prigioniero	
26	—	93831	Rondella	
27	125	92393	Dado	
28	—	92900	Dado fissaggio termost.	
29	166	24262	Termostato	
30	342	80962	Vaschetta per termostato	
31	—	93383	Manicotto	
32	—	94103	Fascietta	
33	508	81066	Tubo uscita acqua teste	
34	—	93095	Manicotto	
35	—	94102	Fascietta	
36	—	93375	Manicotto	
37	508	81043	Tubo	

N.	Matr.	Disegno	Descrizione	Prezzo L
38	—	94100	Fascietta	
39	—	93375	Manicotto	
40	508	81044	Tubo	
41	125	26331	Guarnizione	
42	125	26300	Pompa acqua	
43	125	92142	Prigioniero	
44	125	92384	Rondella	
45	125	92354	Rondella elastica	
46	125	92408	Dado	
47	—	93813	Prigioniero	
48	—	93831	Rondella	
49	125	92393	Dado	
50	125	26332	Guarnizione	
51	125	26310	Supporto cuscinetto	
52 / 53	—	93409	Anello di tenuta	
54	—	93457	Cuscinetto	
55 / 56	125	22137	Rondella	
57	—	93457	Cuscinetto	
58	125	92312	Dado cieco	
59	125	92355	Rondella	
60	125	26315	Girante pompa	
61	125	26305	Corpo tenuta anelli	
62	125	22136	Alberino comando pompa	
63	125	22135/2	Pignone comando pompa	
64	125	26331	Guarnizione	
65	125	92280	Prigioniero	
66	—	93831	Rondella	
67	125	92393	Dado	
68	212	26383	Tubo mandata	
69	125	26331	Guarnizione	
70	—	93639	Prigioniero	
71	—	93831	Rondella	
72	125	92393	Dado	
73	—	93374	Manicotto	
74	—	94099	Fascietta	

Tavola 7 - Apparato circolazione e filtraggio olio

N.	Matr.	Disegno	Descrizione	Prezzo L.
1			Filtro FRAM	
2			Tubo ingresso olio al filtro	
3	—	92714	Guarnizione	
4	—	93488	Raccordo	
5	—	92714	Guarnizione	
6	—	92982	Dado cieco	
7			Tubo olio dal filtro FRAM al motore	
8	—	92907	Prigioniero	
9	125	92353	Rondella	
10	125	92393	Dado	
11	128	24525	Tubo olio	
12	128	24510	Tappo	
13			Guarnizione	
14	128	24509	Molla	
15	128	24508	Valvola	
16	166	24267	Dado	
17	—	92897	Guarnizione	
18	—	93100	Dado	
19	—	92897	Guarnizione	
20	166	24268	Registro valvola	
21	166	24266	Molla	
22	128	24507	Corpo valvola	
23	125	24155	Valvola	
24	128	24526	Tubo olio	
25	—	92640	Prigioniero	
26	125	92353	Rondella	
27	125	92393	Dado	
28	166	24270	Guarnizione	
29	—	92639	Prigioniero	
30	—	93831	Rondella	
31	125	92393	Dado	
32	125	92115	Prigioniero	
33	125	92363	Rondella	
34	125	92312	Dado	
35	125	24138	Guarnizione	
36	125	24134	Pipa olio	
37	166	24259	Molla	
38	166	24372	Rete	
39	166	24236	Rete	
40	166	24233	Telaio per filtro esterno	
41			Rete per filtro	
42	166	24242	Rete per filtro	
43	166	24239	Telaio per filtro interno	
44	166	24257	Bullone a colonnetta	
45	125	16397	Guarnizione	
46	166	24235	Rete	
47	166	24371	Rete	
48	166	24241	Rete	
49			Rete per filtro	
50	125	24131	Guarnizione	
51	125	92184	Prigioniero	
52	125	92354	Rondella	
53	125	92408	Dado	
54	128	24551	Pompa olio	
55	—	93218	Grano	
56	125	24110	Ingranaggio	
57	125	24107	Chiavetta	
58	200	24102	Bussola	
59	125	24105	Ingranaggio	
60	200	24111	Bussola	
61	200	24112	Perno	
62	125	24113	Spina	
63	166	24287	Ingranaggio	
64	—	92419	Dado	
65	125	92375	Copiglia	
66	125	92148	Prigioniero	
67	—	93830	Rondella	
68	125	92412	Dado	
69	128	24557	Guarnizione	
70	125	92184	Prigioniero	
71	125	92384	Rondella	
72	125	92354	Rondella	
73	125	92408	Dado	
74	128	24555	Tubo olio	
75	128	24559	Manicotto	
76			Morsetto per fascietta	
77			Copiglia per fascietta	
78	166	18270	Fascietta	
79	128	24554	Tubo olio	
80	125	92528	Bullone	
81	125	92516	Rondella	
82	—	92725	Dado	
83	128	24558	Cavallotto	
84	125	24123	Telaietto filtro	
85	125	24124	Anello	

Tavola 8 - Carburatori e filtro

N.	Matr.	Disegno	Descrizione	Prezzo L.
1	FISPA	9438	Depuratore d'aria Retex	
2	Weber		Coperchio	
3	»		Guarnizione per detto	
4	»		Vite fissaggio coperchio	
5	»		Rondella elastica per detto	
6	»		Centratore	
7	»		Centratore	
8	»		Diffusore	
9	»		Diffusore	
10	»		Rondella alluminio p. valvola spillo	
11	»		Valvola a spillo	
12	»		Corpo carburatore	
13	»		Valvola mandata pompa	
14	»		Rondella per detto	
15	»		Getto pompa	
16	»		Rondella	
17	»		Vite freno	
18	»		Vite freno	
19	»		Pozzetto di emulsione	
20	»		Pozzetto di emulsione	
21	»		Presa aria Starter	
22	»		Getto avviamento	
23	»		Rondella	
24	»		Porta getto massimo	
25	»		Getto max	
26	»		Guarnizione getto massimo	
27	»		Vite fissaggio centratore e diffusore	
28	»		Valvola avviamento	
29	»		Molla avviamento	
30	»		Supporto leva avviamento	
31	»		Vite fissaggio p. detto	
32	»		Perno leva avviamento	
33	»		Coppiglia	
34	»		Leva avviamento	
35	»		Vite fiss. filo comando avviamento	
36	»		Distanziale per comando avviamento	
37	»		Dado per vite fiss. comando avviamento	
38	Weber		Morsetto registro sincronizzazione	
39	»		Vite serraggio morsetto suddetto	
40	»		Cono per morsetto registro sincronizzazione	
41	»		Vite fissaggio coperchio comando leve	
42	»		Coperchio comando leva	
43	»		Leva comando farfalla	
44	»		Piastrina di sicurezza per leva comando farfalla	
45	»		Dado fiss. leva comando leva	
46	»		Vite fiss. centratore e diffusore	
47	»		Vite registro miscela min.	
48	»		Molla p. vite registro miscela min.	
49	»		Boccola p. vite registro andatura minimo	
50	»		Molla p. vite registro andatura minimo	
51	»		Vite registro andatura minimo	
52	»		Vite ispezione foro progressione	
53	»		Settore dentato secondario	
54	»		Settore dentato primario	
55	»		Settore di arresto	
56	»		Porta getto massimo	
57	»		Getto massimo	
58	»		Guarniz. getto massimo	
59	»		Porta getto del minimo	
60	»		Getto del minimo	
61	»		Valvola aspirazione pompa alimentazione	
62	»		Asta comando pompa	
63	»		Registro avviamento	
64	»		Piastrina p. asta comando pompa	
65	»		Molla pompa	
66	»		Pistone pompa	

Tavola 8 - Carburatori e filtro

N.	Matr.	Disegno	Descrizione	Prezzo L.
67	Weber		Galleggiante	
68	»		Perno galleggiante	
69	»		Farfalla	
70	»		Farfalla	
71	»		Vite fissaggio farfalla	
72	»		Boccola albero a farfalla primaria	
73	»		Boccola albero a farfalla secondaria	
74	»		Spina fiss. albero primario su boccola	
75	»		Albero farfalla primaria	
76	»		Albero farfalla secondaria	
77	Weber		Leva comando pompa	
78	»		Piastrina di sicurezza per detto	
79	»		Dado fiss. leva comando pompa	
80	166	18248	Guarnizione	
81	125	92582	Vite	
82	166	18249	Guarnizione	
83	128	18607	Collettore	
84		93044	Prigioniero	
85		93830	Rondella ateco	
86		92631	Dado	

Tavola 9 - Apparato di alimentazione e regolazione carburante

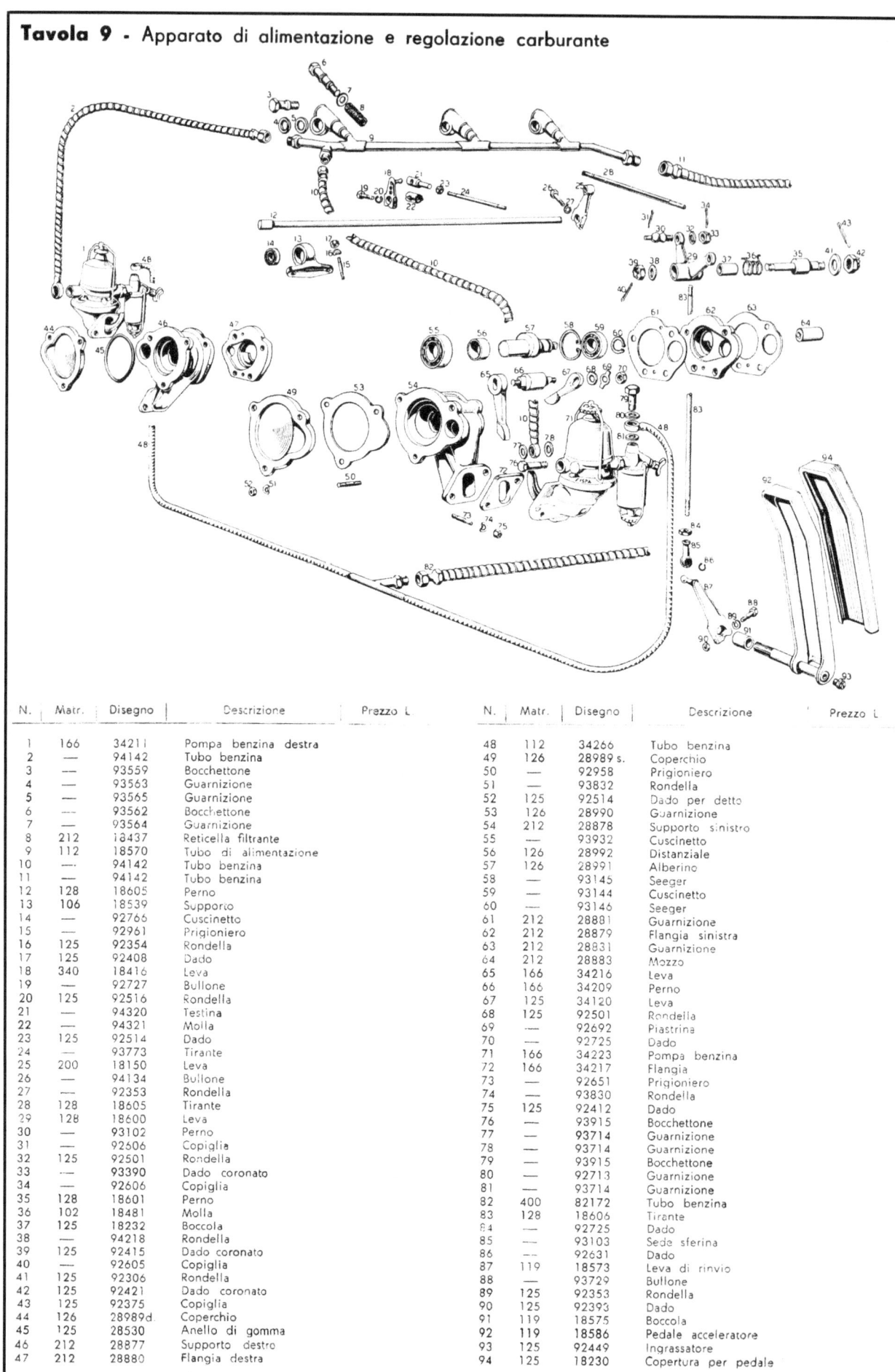

N.	Matr.	Disegno	Descrizione	Prezzo L	N.	Matr.	Disegno	Descrizione	Prezzo L
1	166	34211	Pompa benzina destra		48	112	34266	Tubo benzina	
2	—	94142	Tubo benzina		49	126	28989 s.	Coperchio	
3	—	93559	Bocchettone		50	—	92958	Prigioniero	
4	—	93563	Guarnizione		51	—	93832	Rondella	
5	—	93565	Guarnizione		52	125	92514	Dado per detto	
6	—	93562	Bocchettone		53	126	28990	Guarnizione	
7	—	93564	Guarnizione		54	212	28878	Supporto sinistro	
8	212	18437	Reticella filtrante		55	—	93932	Cuscinetto	
9	112	18570	Tubo di alimentazione		56	126	28992	Distanziale	
10	—	94142	Tubo benzina		57	126	28991	Alberino	
11	—	94142	Tubo benzina		58	—	93145	Seeger	
12	128	18605	Perno		59	—	93144	Cuscinetto	
13	106	18539	Supporto		60	—	93146	Seeger	
14	—	92766	Cuscinetto		61	212	28881	Guarnizione	
15	—	92961	Prigioniero		62	212	28879	Flangia sinistra	
16	125	92354	Rondella		63	212	28831	Guarnizione	
17	125	92408	Dado		64	212	28883	Mozzo	
18	340	18416	Leva		65	166	34216	Leva	
19	—	92727	Bullone		66	166	34209	Perno	
20	125	92516	Rondella		67	125	34120	Leva	
21	—	94320	Testina		68	125	92501	Rondella	
22	—	94321	Molla		69	—	92692	Piastrina	
23	125	92514	Dado		70	—	92725	Dado	
24	—	93773	Tirante		71	166	34223	Pompa benzina	
25	200	18150	Leva		72	166	34217	Flangia	
26	—	94134	Bullone		73	—	92651	Prigioniero	
27	—	92353	Rondella		74	—	93830	Rondella	
28	128	18605	Tirante		75	125	92412	Dado	
29	128	18600	Leva		76	—	93915	Bocchettone	
30	—	93102	Perno		77	—	93714	Guarnizione	
31	—	92606	Copiglia		78	—	93714	Guarnizione	
32	125	92501	Rondella		79	—	93915	Bocchettone	
33	—	93390	Dado coronato		80	—	92713	Guarnizione	
34	—	92606	Copiglia		81	—	93714	Guarnizione	
35	128	18601	Perno		82	400	82172	Tubo benzina	
36	102	18481	Molla		83	128	18606	Tirante	
37	125	18232	Boccola		84	—	92725	Dado	
38	—	94218	Rondella		85	—	93103	Sede sferina	
39	125	92415	Dado coronato		86	—	92631	Dado	
40	—	92605	Copiglia		87	119	18573	Leva di rinvio	
41	125	92306	Rondella		88	—	93729	Bullone	
42	125	92421	Dado coronato		89	125	92353	Rondella	
43	125	92375	Copiglia		90	125	92393	Dado	
44	126	28989d.	Coperchio		91	119	18575	Boccola	
45	—	28530	Anello di gomma		92	119	18586	Pedale acceleratore	
46	212	28877	Supporto destro		93	125	92449	Ingrassatore	
47	212	28880	Flangia destra		94	125	18230	Copertura per pedale	

Tavola 10 - Serbatoio carburante con accessori e pompa elettrica

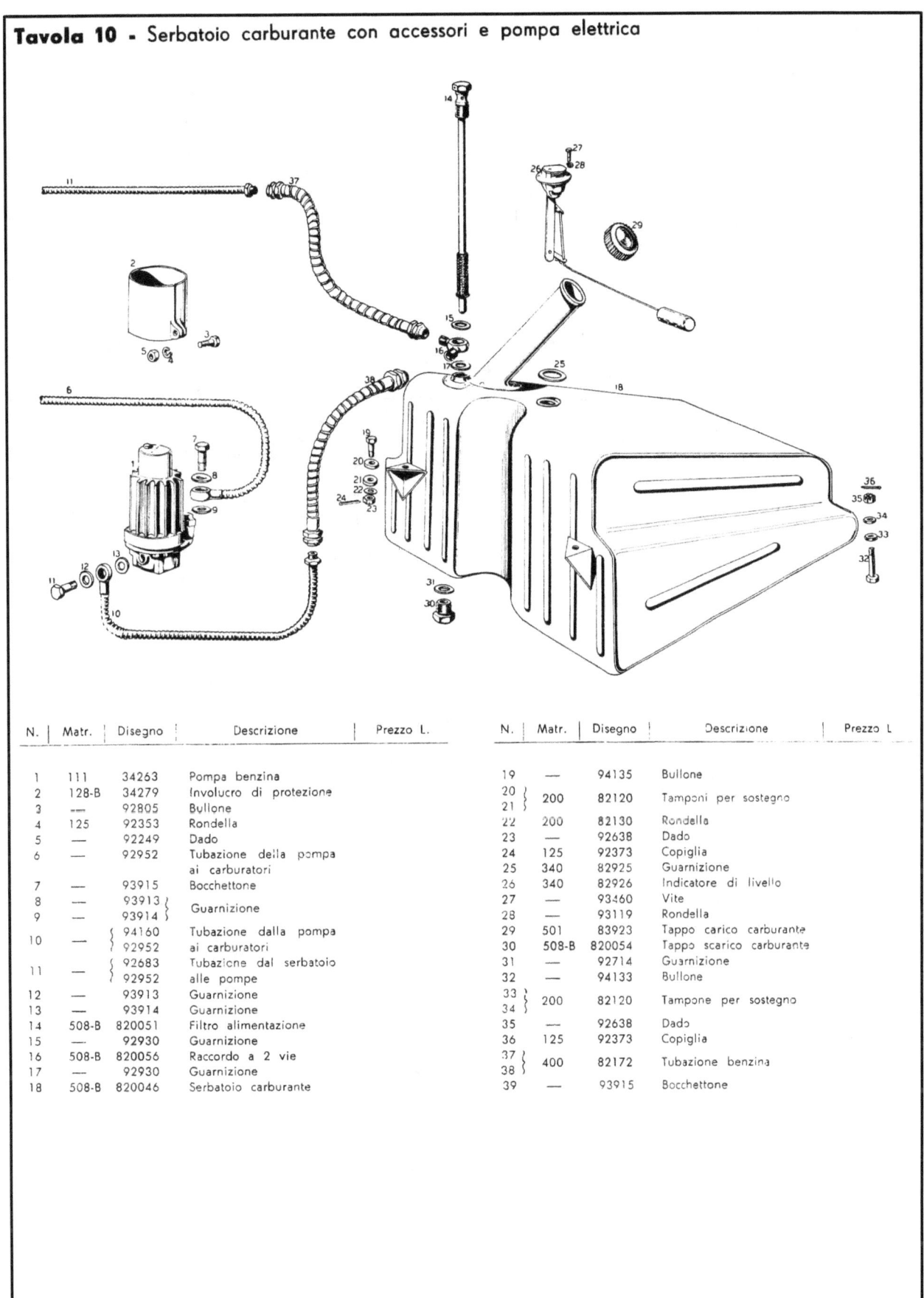

N.	Matr.	Disegno	Descrizione	Prezzo L.
1	111	34263	Pompa benzina	
2	128-B	34279	Involucro di protezione	
3	—	92805	Bullone	
4	125	92353	Rondella	
5	—	92249	Dado	
6	—	92952	Tubazione della pompa ai carburatori	
7	—	93915	Bocchettone	
8	—	93913	Guarnizione	
9	—	93914		
10	—	94160 / 92952	Tubazione dalla pompa ai carburatori	
11	—	92683 / 92952	Tubazione dal serbatoio alle pompe	
12	—	93913	Guarnizione	
13	—	93914	Guarnizione	
14	508-B	820051	Filtro alimentazione	
15	—	92930	Guarnizione	
16	508-B	820056	Raccordo a 2 vie	
17	—	92930	Guarnizione	
18	508-B	820046	Serbatoio carburante	
19	—	94135	Bullone	
20	200	82120	Tamponi per sostegno	
21				
22	200	82130	Rondella	
23	—	92638	Dado	
24	125	92373	Copiglia	
25	340	82925	Guarnizione	
26	340	82926	Indicatore di livello	
27	—	93460	Vite	
28	—	93119	Rondella	
29	501	83923	Tappo carico carburante	
30	508-B	820054	Tappo scarico carburante	
31	—	92714	Guarnizione	
32	—	94133	Bullone	
33	200	82120	Tampone per sostegno	
34				
35	—	92638	Dado	
36	125	92373	Copiglia	
37	400	82172	Tubazione benzina	
38				
39	—	93915	Bocchettone	

Tavola 11 - Accensione e batteria

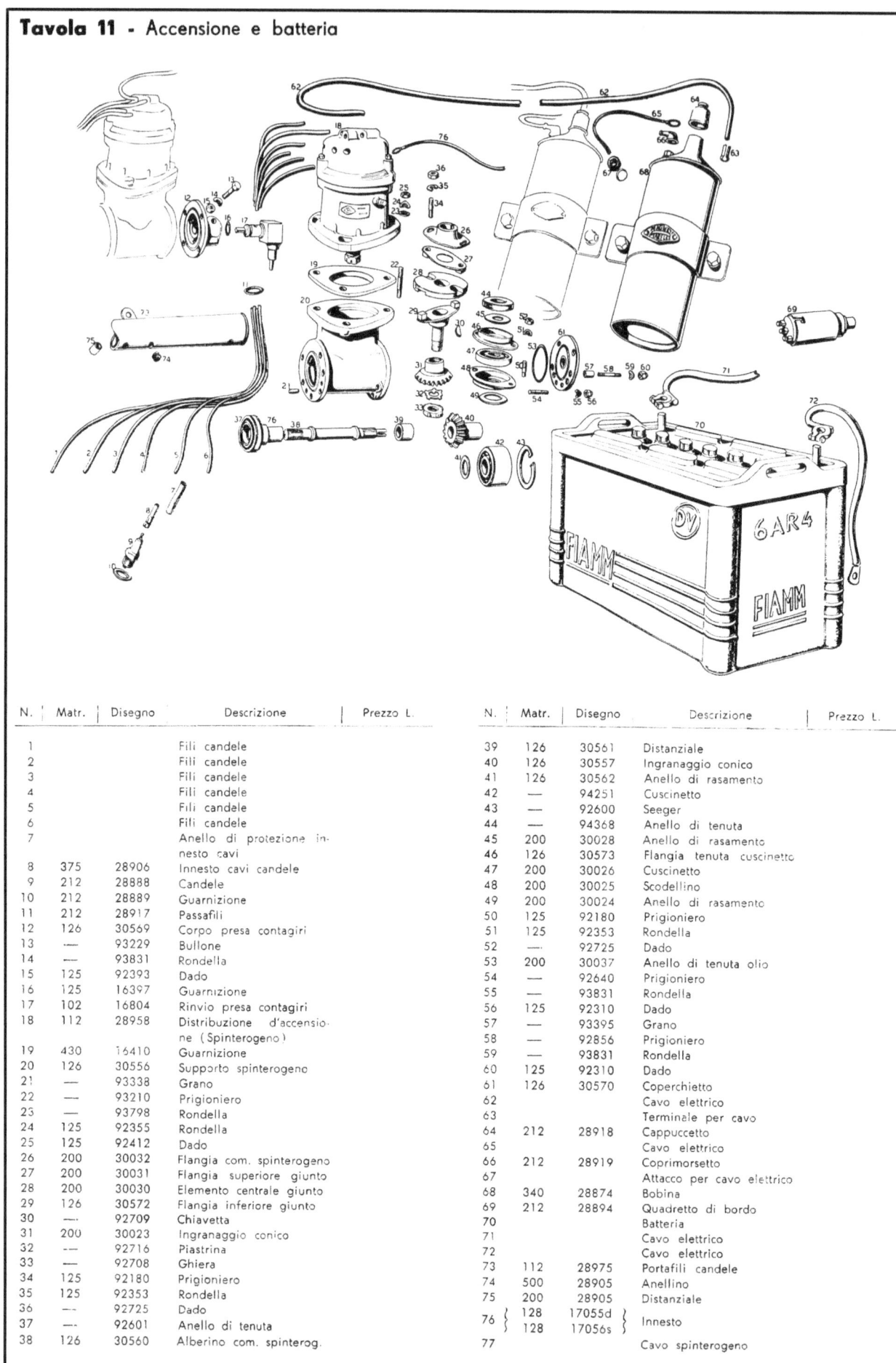

N.	Matr.	Disegno	Descrizione	Prezzo L.
1			Fili candele	
2			Fili candele	
3			Fili candele	
4			Fili candele	
5			Fili candele	
6			Fili candele	
7			Anello di protezione innesto cavi	
8	375	28906	Innesto cavi candele	
9	212	28888	Candele	
10	212	28889	Guarnizione	
11	212	28917	Passafili	
12	126	30569	Corpo presa contagiri	
13	—	93229	Bullone	
14	—	93831	Rondella	
15	125	92393	Dado	
16	125	16397	Guarnizione	
17	102	16804	Rinvio presa contagiri	
18	112	28958	Distribuzione d'accensione (Spinterogeno)	
19	430	16410	Guarnizione	
20	126	30556	Supporto spinterogeno	
21	—	93338	Grano	
22	—	93210	Prigioniero	
23	—	93798	Rondella	
24	125	92355	Rondella	
25	125	92412	Dado	
26	200	30032	Flangia com. spinterogeno	
27	200	30031	Flangia superiore giunto	
28	200	30030	Elemento centrale giunto	
29	126	30572	Flangia inferiore giunto	
30	—	92709	Chiavetta	
31	200	30023	Ingranaggio conico	
32	—	92716	Piastrina	
33	—	92708	Ghiera	
34	125	92180	Prigioniero	
35	125	92353	Rondella	
36	—	92725	Dado	
37	—	92601	Anello di tenuta	
38	126	30560	Alberino com. spinterog.	
39	126	30561	Distanziale	
40	126	30557	Ingranaggio conico	
41	126	30562	Anello di rasamento	
42	—	94251	Cuscinetto	
43	—	92600	Seeger	
44	—	94368	Anello di tenuta	
45	200	30028	Anello di rasamento	
46	126	30573	Flangia tenuta cuscinetto	
47	200	30026	Cuscinetto	
48	200	30025	Scodellino	
49	200	30024	Anello di rasamento	
50	125	92180	Prigioniero	
51	125	92353	Rondella	
52	—	92725	Dado	
53	200	30037	Anello di tenuta olio	
54	—	92640	Prigioniero	
55	—	93831	Rondella	
56	125	92310	Dado	
57	—	93395	Grano	
58	—	92856	Prigioniero	
59	—	93831	Rondella	
60	125	92310	Dado	
61	126	30570	Coperchietto	
62			Cavo elettrico	
63			Terminale per cavo	
64	212	28918	Cappuccetto	
65			Cavo elettrico	
66	212	28919	Coprimorsetto	
67			Attacco per cavo elettrico	
68	340	28874	Bobina	
69	212	28894	Quadretto di bordo	
70			Batteria	
71			Cavo elettrico	
72			Cavo elettrico	
73	112	28975	Portafili candele	
74	500	28905	Anellino	
75	200	28905	Distanziale	
76	128	17055d	Innesto	
76	128	17056s	Innesto	
77			Cavo spinterogeno	

Tavola 12 - Dinamo, ventilatore

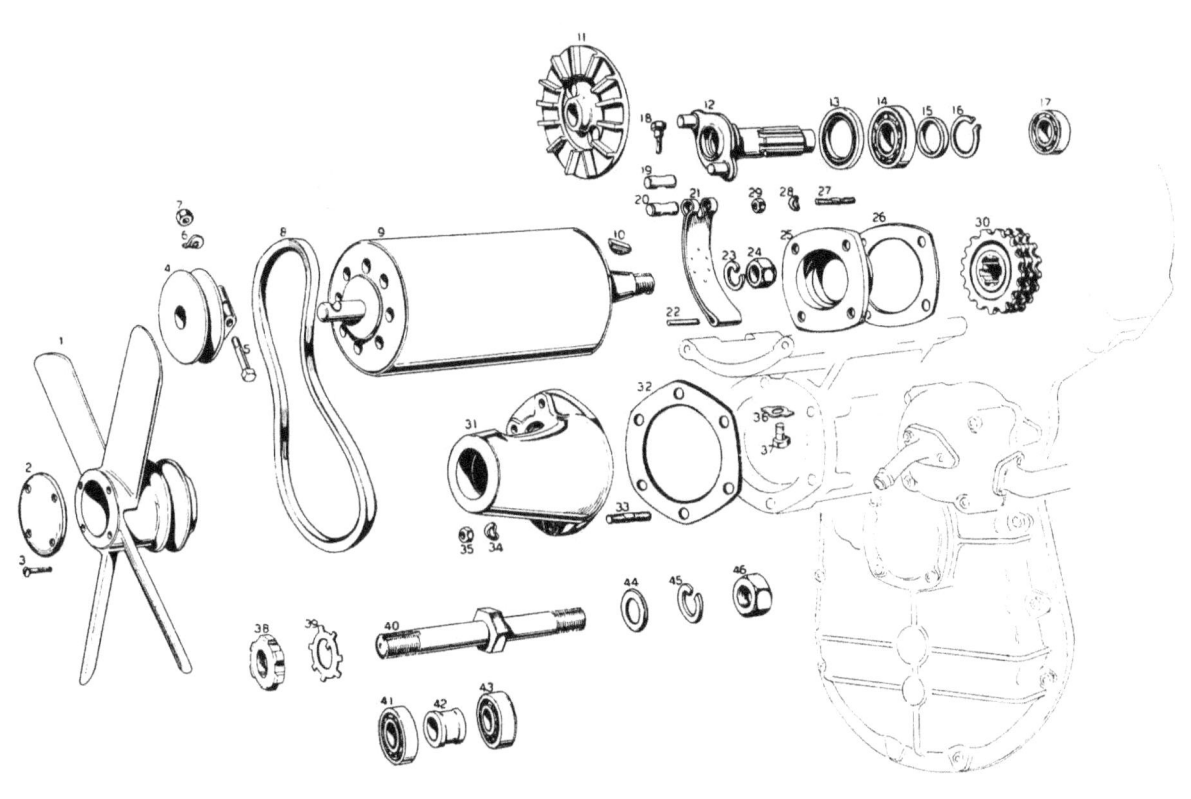

N.	Matr.	Disegno	Descrizione	Prezzo L.
1	513	78173	Ventilatore	
2	513	78178	Coperchietto	
3	—	94280	Vite	
4	513	78174	Puleggia	
5	125	92276	Bullone	
6	—	93830	Rondelle	
7	125	92412	Dado	
8	342	78169	Cinghia trapezioidale	
9	128	30552	Dinamo	
10			Chiavetta trascinamento dinamo	
11	112	30549	Ventola	
12	125	22127	Alberino comando dinamo	
13	—	93454	Anello di tenuta	
14	125	22125	Cuscinetto	
15	125	22126	Distanziale	
16	125	22128	Sceger	
17	—	93457	Cuscinetto	
18	125	92221	Bullone	
19	125	30421	Manicotto	
20	125	30420		
21	166	30467	Staffe chiusura dinamo	
22	128	22405	Tubo fissaggio dinamo	
23			Rondella fisaggio ventola alla dinamo	
24			Dado fissaggio ventola alla dinamo	
25	125	22132	Coperchio	
26	125	22104	Guarnizione	
27	—	92819	Prigioniero	
28	—	93831	Rondelle	
29	125	92393	Dado	
30	125	22120/2	Pignone comando dinamo	
31	128	24520	Coperchio filtro	
32	166	24261	Guarnizione	
33	—	92917	Prigioniero	
34	—	93830	Rondella	
35	125	92412	Dado	
36	125	92353	Piastrina	
37	—	94242	Bullone	
38	—	93121	Ghiera	
39	—	92702	Piastrina	
40	513	78175	Alberino	
41	—	93197	Cuscinetto	
42	513	78177	Distanziale	
43	—	93197	Cuscinetto	
44	513	78180	Rondella	
45	—	94279	Rondella	
46	—	94277	Dado	

Tavola 13 - Collettori scarico, marmitte, prolunghe

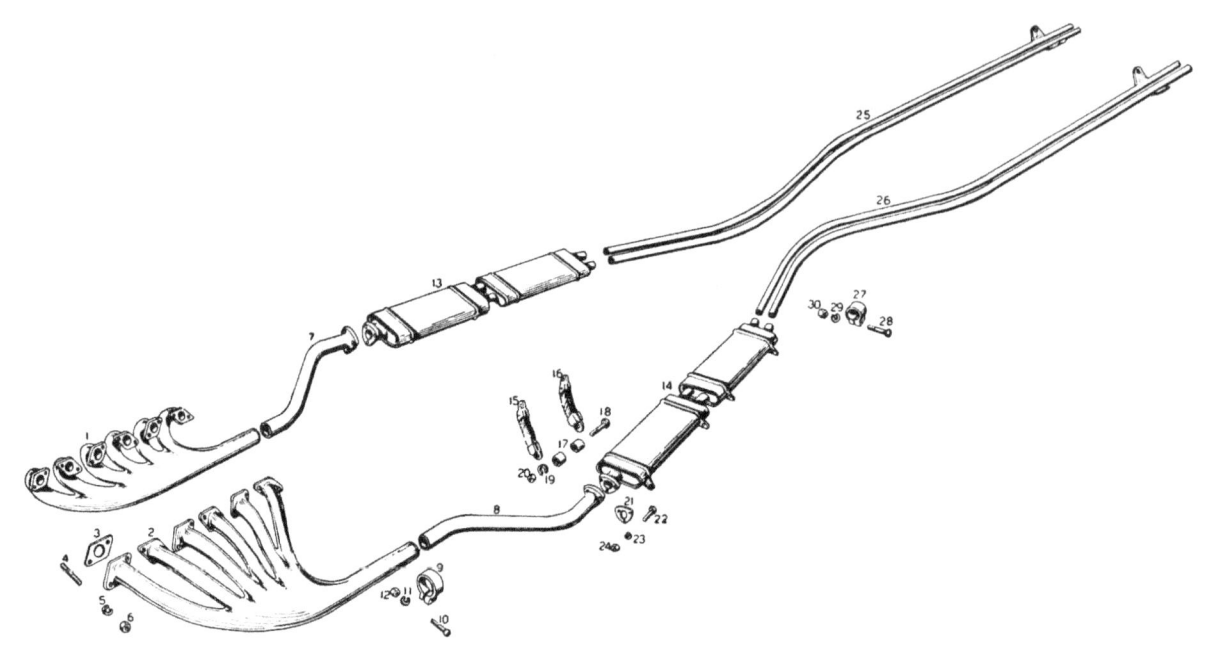

N.	Matr.	Disegno	Descrizione	Prezzo L.
1			Tubo scarico destro	
2			Tubo scarico sinistro	
3	166	16432	Guarnizione tubi di scar.	
4	125	92122	Prigioniero	
5	125	92354	Rondella	
6	125	92454	Dado	
7			Tubo fra collettore e marmitta (destro)	
8			Tubo fra collettore e marmitta (sinistro)	
9	166	20156	Cravatta fissaggio collett.	
10	—	93311	Bullone	
11	125	92352	Rondella	
12	125	92393	Dado	
13	128	20203	Marmitta di scarico destra	
14	128	20203	Marmitta di scarico sinist.	
15	250	20180	Supporto marmitte	
16	250	20180	Supporto marmitte	
17	250	20181	Distanziale	
18	—	93311	Bullone	
19	125	92353	Rondella	
20	125	22393	Dado	
21			Guarnizione per marmitta	
22	—	93311	Bullone	
23	125	92353	Rondella	
24	125	92393	Dado	
25			Tubo uscita della marmit.	
26			Tubo uscita della marmit.	
27	250	20182	Cravatta	
28	—	93311	Bullone	
29	125	92353	Rondella	
30	125	92393	Dado	

Tavola 14 - Scatola cambio e frizione

N.	Matr.	Disegno	Descrizione	Prezzo L.	N.	Matr.	Disegno	Descrizione	Prezzo L.
1	342	50384	Scatola frizione		32	—	93283	Prigionireo lungo	
2	342	50489	Riparo sulla scatola		33	—	93830	Rondella	
3	—	92719	Vite		34	125	92412	Dado	
4	342	53045	Scatola cambio		35	342	53015	Bronzina	
5	—	93344	Prigioniero		36	342	53142	Flangia con manicotto	
6	125	92412	Dado		37	125	92180	Prigioniero	
7	—	93830	Rondella		38	125	92353	Rondella	
8	—	93241	Prigioniero		39	125	92393	Dado	
9	—	93830	Rondella		40	—	92986	Anello di tenuta	
10	125	92412	Dado		41	342	53044	Corpo pompa olio	
11	—	93341	Grano		42	400	50026	Bronzina	
12	—	93343	Grano		43	—	92642	Prigioniero	
13	—	93343	Grano		44	—	93831	Rondella	
14	—	93341	Grano		45	—	93249	Dado	
15	342	53046	Coperchio per scatola		46	430	52937	Coperchio pompa	
16	125	92282	Prigioniero		47	125	92513	Prigioniero	
17	—	93831	Rondella		48	—	93832	Rondella	
18	125	92393	Dado		49	125	92514	Dado	
19	342	53123	Boccola		50	430	52943	Guarnizione	
20	125	53115	Tappo		51	342	53151	Filtro olio	
21	125	53116	Guarnizione		52	342	53093	Flangia	
22	—	93184	Bussola		53	—	93241	Prigioniero medio	
23	—	93834	Vite		54	—	93830	Rondella	
24	342	53041	Coperchio posteriore		55	125	92412	Dado	
25	—	93044	Prigioniero corto		56	—	93333	Bussola	
26	—	93830	Rondella		57	342	53136	Scodellino	
27	125	92412	Dado		58 / 59	342	53135	Tampone	
28	—	93342	Grano		60	342	53136	Scodellino	
29	—	93342	Grano		61	—	94255	Bullone	
30	—	93106	Tappo						
31	—	93332	Guarnizione						

Tavola 15 - Frizione

N.	Matr.	Disegno	Descrizione	Prezzo L.
1	—	92855	Cuscinetto	
2	125	50150	Paraolio	
3	125	50210	Distanziale per cuscinetto supporto albero	
4	125	50160	Anello	
5	400	50009	Mozzo per albero	
6	375	50372	Tamburo parastrappi	
7	514	50572	Disco frizione completo	
8	514	50556	Disco conduttore	
9	513	50579	Spingidisco	
10	400	50018	Vite fissaggio coperchio frizione	
11	125	92354	Rondella	
12	125	92411	Dado	
13	509	50562	Coperchio frizione	
14	513	50595	Tirante per spingidischi	
15	509	50561	Leva comando frizione	
16	509	50563	Perno per leva comando frizione	
17	125	92330	Rondella	
18	125	92373	Copiglia	
19	508	50559	Molla per tirante spingidischi	
20	500	50455	Ghiera tenuta molla tirante	
21	—	93566	Rondella	
22	—	92935	Dado	
23	125	92373	Copiglia	
24	101	50494	Molla supplementare frizione	
25	275	50331	Molla frizione	
26	101	50497	Astuccio molla frizione	
27	511	50537	Distanziale per mozzo	
28	400	50010	Disco tenuta molle parastrappi	
29	400	50011	Molla parastrappi	
30	—	92660	Bullone	
31	125	92353	Rondella	
32	125	92393	Dado	
33	—	92661	Bullone	
34	400	50008	Distanziale per dischi	
35	125	92354	Rondella	
36	—	92841	Dado	
37	400	50002 / 50003	Reggispinta	
38	340	50365	Leva interna comando frizione	
39	400	50026	Bronzina interna per albero	
40	400	50026		
41	125	92612	Spina conica	
42	250	50502	Molla richiamo leva	
43	513	50548	Alberino comando frizione	
44	—	93032	Tappo	
45	125	92448	Ingrassatore	
46	508	67197	Leva	
47	125	92276	Bullone	
48	125	92355	Rondella	
49	125	92397	Dado	
50	501	67105	Perno sferico	
51	125	92359	Rondella	
52	125	92409	Dado	
53	501	67108	Anello	
54	501	67106	Sede sferica	
55	—	93935	Contro dado	
56	508	67131	Manicotto filettato	

Tavola 16 - Ingranaggeria cambio

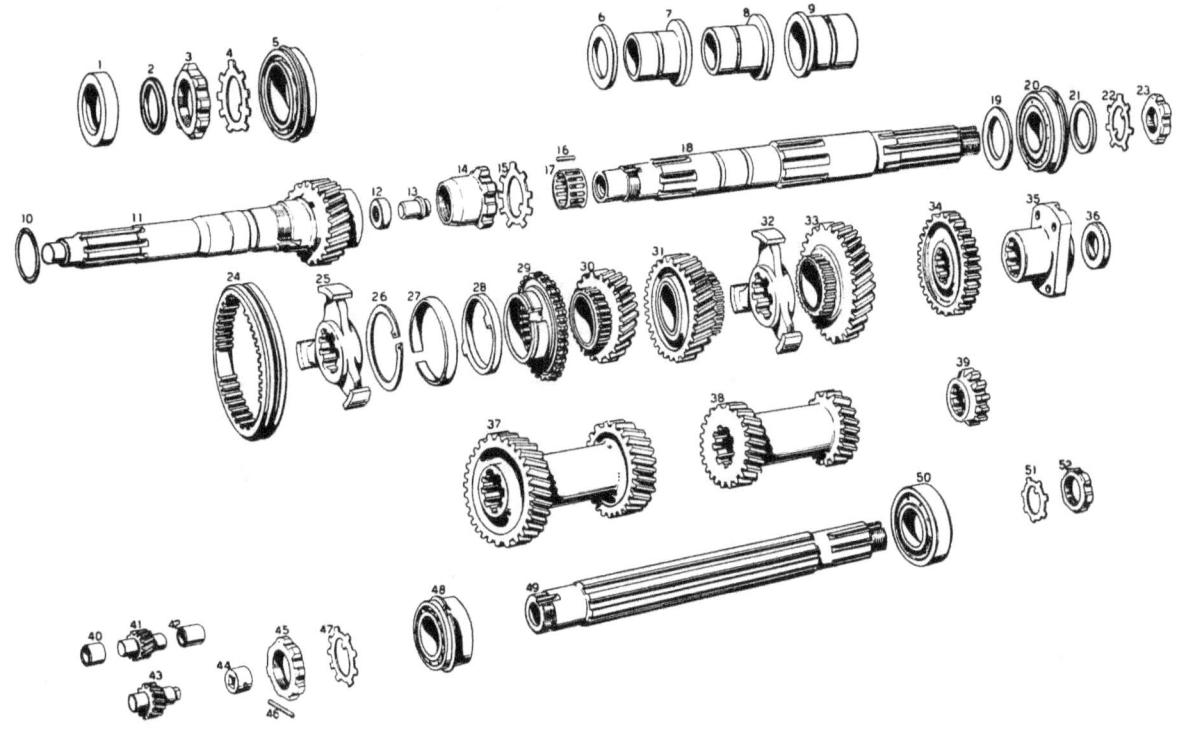

N.	Matr.	Disegno	Descrizione
1	—	92986	Anello di tenuta
2	430	52971	Anello
3	—	93330	Ghiera
4	—	93747	Rondella freno
5	—	93297	Cuscinetto
6	513	53536	Distanziale
7	513	53534	Distanziale 3ª velocità
8	513	53533	Distanziale 2ª velocità
9	513	53531	Distanziale 1ª velocità
10	430	52971	Anello
11	508-B	53750	Albero rinvio
12	—	92968	Anello di tenuta
13	342	53052	Estremità per albero
14	513	53517	Ghiera
15	—	94239	Rondella freno
16, 17	—	94376	Gabbia a rullini
18	508-B	53726	Albero primario
19	513	53557	Distanziale fra cuscinetto e ingran. 1ª
20	—	93297	Cuscinetto
21	342	53092	Distanziale fra cuscinetto e ingr. R.M.
22	—	93748	Rondella freno
23	—	93326	Ghiera
24	513	53511	Manicotto di comando
25	513	53510	Nucleo di guida 3ª e 4ª
26	513	53514	Anello di fermo
27	513	53512	Anello elastico
28	513	53515	Anello di guida
29	513	53513	Corpo di trascinamento
30	508-B	53749	Ingranaggio 3ª velocità
31	508-B	53748	Ingranaggio 2ª velocità
32	513	53509	Nucleo di guida 1ª e 2ª
33	508-B	53747	Ingranaggio 1ª velocità
34	342	53059	Ingranaggio R.M. prim.
35	342	53161	Manicotto
36	342	53095	Rondella
37	508-B	53752	Ingranaggio rinvio e rinvio 3ª
38	508-B	53751	Ingranaggio rinvio 1ª e 2ª
39	342	53060	Ingranaggio R.M. secon.
40	125	53453	Boccola
41	125	52452	Ingranaggio condotto
42	125	52454	Boccola
43	125	52451	Ingranaggio conduttore
44	125	52461	Boccola di trascinamento
45	—	93325	Ghiera
46	125	52455	Spina
47	—	93305	Rondella freno
48	—	93298	Cuscinetto
49	342	53051	Albero secondario
50	—	93380	Cuscinetto
51	—	93306	Rondella freno
52	—	93327	Ghiera

Tavola 17 - Comando cambio

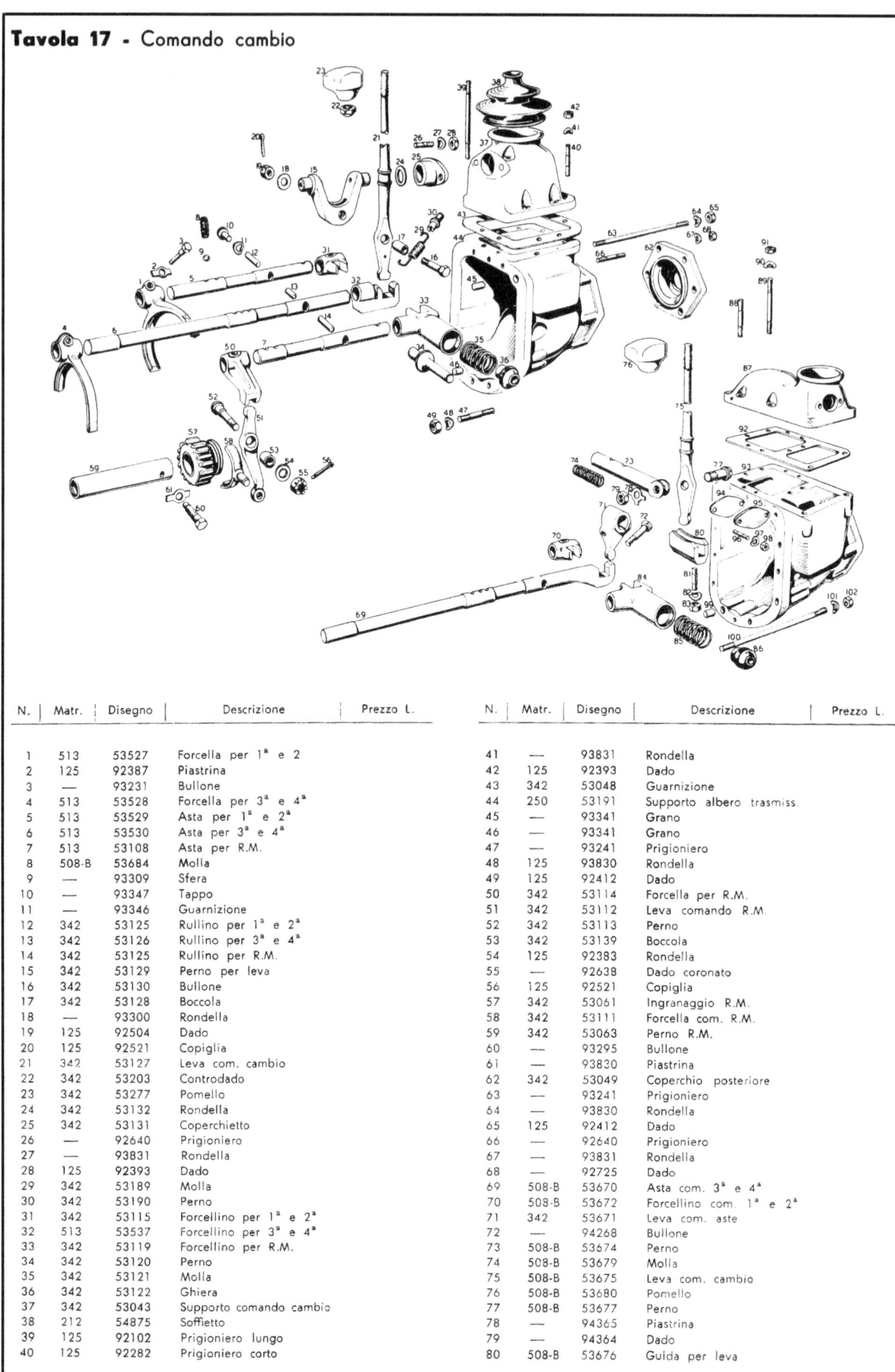

N.	Matr.	Disegno	Descrizione	N.	Matr.	Disegno	Descrizione
1	513	53527	Forcella per 1ª e 2ª	41	—	93831	Rondella
2	125	92387	Piastrina	42	125	92393	Dado
3	—	93231	Bullone	43	342	53048	Guarnizione
4	513	53528	Forcella per 3ª e 4ª	44	250	53191	Supporto albero trasmiss.
5	513	53529	Asta per 1ª e 2ª	45	—	93341	Grano
6	513	53530	Asta per 3ª e 4ª	46	—	93341	Grano
7	513	53108	Asta per R.M.	47	—	93241	Prigioniero
8	508-B	53684	Molla	48	125	93830	Rondella
9	—	93309	Sfera	49	125	92412	Dado
10	—	93347	Tappo	50	342	53114	Forcella per R.M.
11	—	93346	Guarnizione	51	342	53112	Leva comando R.M.
12	342	53125	Rullino per 1ª e 2ª	52	342	53113	Perno
13	342	53126	Rullino per 3ª e 4ª	53	342	53139	Boccola
14	342	53125	Rullino per R.M.	54	125	92383	Rondella
15	342	53129	Perno per leva	55	—	92638	Dado coronato
16	342	53130	Bullone	56	125	92521	Copiglia
17	342	53128	Boccola	57	342	53061	Ingranaggio R.M.
18	—	93300	Rondella	58	342	53111	Forcella com. R.M.
19	125	92504	Dado	59	342	53063	Perno R.M.
20	125	92521	Copiglia	60	—	93295	Bullone
21	342	53127	Leva com. cambio	61	—	93830	Piastrina
22	342	53203	Controdado	62	342	53049	Coperchio posteriore
23	342	53277	Pomello	63	—	93241	Prigioniero
24	342	53132	Rondella	64	—	93830	Rondella
25	342	53131	Coperchietto	65	125	92412	Dado
26	—	92640	Prigioniero	66	—	92640	Prigioniero
27	—	93831	Rondella	67	—	93831	Rondella
28	125	92393	Dado	68	—	92725	Dado
29	342	53189	Molla	69	508-B	53670	Asta com. 3ª e 4ª
30	342	53190	Perno	70	508-B	53672	Forcellino com. 1ª e 2ª
31	342	53115	Forcellino per 1ª e 2ª	71	342	53671	Leva com. aste
32	513	53537	Forcellino per 3ª e 4ª	72	—	94268	Bullone
33	342	53119	Forcellino per R.M.	73	508-B	53674	Perno
34	342	53120	Perno	74	508-B	53679	Molla
35	342	53121	Molla	75	508-B	53675	Leva com. cambio
36	342	53122	Ghiera	76	508-B	53680	Pomello
37	342	53043	Supporto comando cambio	77	508-B	53677	Perno
38	212	54875	Soffietto	78	—	94365	Piastrina
39	125	92102	Prigioniero lungo	79	—	94364	Dado
40	125	92282	Prigioniero corto	80	508-B	53676	Guida per leva

Tavola 17 - Comando cambio

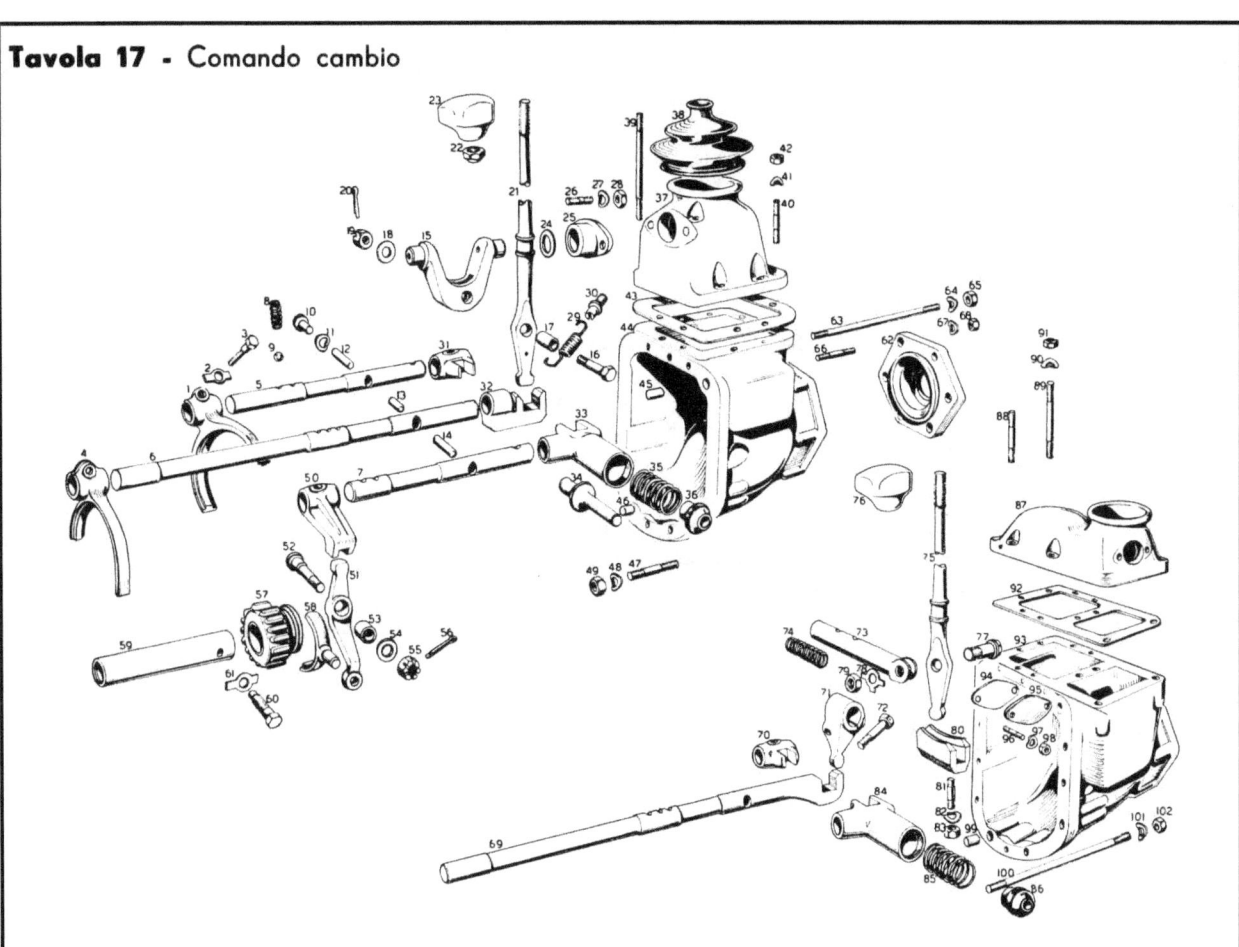

N.	Matr.	Disegno	Descrizione	Prezzo L.	N.	Matr.	Disegno	Descrizione	Prezzo L.
81	—	94348	Prigioniero		92	508-B	53681	Guarnizione	
82	—	93830	Rondella		93	508-B	53668	Supporto albero trasmiss.	
83	125	92412	Dado		94	—	94351	Guarnizione	
84	508-B	53673	Forcellino com. R.M.		95	508-B	53678	Coperchietto	
85	508-B	53700	Molla		96	—	94350	Prigioniero	
86	342	53122	Ghiera		97	—	93832	Rondella	
87	508-B	53669	Coperchio		98	125	92514	Dado	
88	—	94349	Prigioniero corto		99	—	93341	Grano	
89	—	93403	Prigioniero lungo		100	—	93592	Prigioniero	
90	—	93831	Rondella		101	—	93830	Rondella	
91	125	92393	Dado		102	125	92412	Dado	

Tavola 18 - Trasmissione

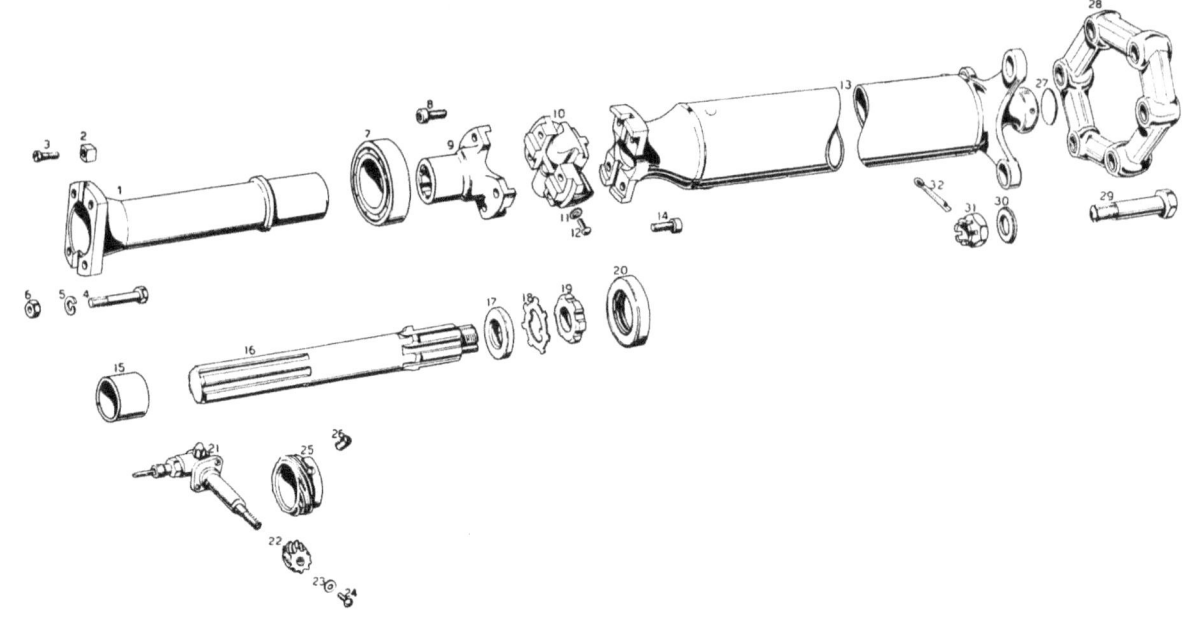

N.	Matr.	Disegno	Descrizione	Prezzo L.
1	250	53192	Manicotto per giunto	
2	342	53185	Chiavetta	
3	—	93518	Vite	
4	125	92278	Bullone	
5	125	92353	Rondella	
6	125	92393	Dado	
7	—	93293	Cuscinetto	
8	—	94186	Vite destra	
9	508	56896	Forcella	
10	400	56105	Giunto cardanico	
11	—	94076	Rondella	
12	—	94075	Vite	
13	508	56895	Albero di trasmissione	
14	—	94187	Vite sinistra	
15	342	53094	Bussola	
16	250	56861	Albero fra giunto e crociera	
17	508	56897	Distanziale	
18	—	92700	Rondella di sicurezza	
19	—	92627	Ghiera	
20	—	92986	Anello di tenuta	
21	102	53326	Giunto per conta Km.	
22	103	53296	Pignone conta Km.	
23	—	93963	Rondella	
24	—	93962	Vite	
25	103	53295	Vite conta Km.	
26	—	93567	Grano filettato	
27	—	94151	Tappo ad espansione	
28	508	56894	Giunto elastico	
29	—	94084	Bullone	
30	—	94085	Rondella	
31	—	93644	Dado	
32	—	93429	Copiglia	

Tavola 19 - Gruppo differenziale

N.	Matr.	Disegno	Descrizione	Prezzo L.	N.	Matr.	Disegno	Descrizione	Prezzo L.
1	508	59017	Flangia per giunto		29	—	94267	Grano di centraggio	
2	125	92302	Rondella		30	—	94268	Bullone	
3	125	58116/1	Ghiera		31	514	59105	Perno porta sotelliti	
4	125	92381	Copiglia		32	514	59111	Sede per sotellitl	
5	—	94076	Rondella		33	514	59110	Boccola	
6	—	94075	Vite		34	514	59107	Sotellite	
7	340	60841	Flangia anteriore		35	125	58115	Spina	
8	125	92192	Prigioniero		36	508-B	59147	Planetario	
9	—	93830	Rondella		37	508-B	59148	Rondella rasamento planetari	
10	—	92631	Dado						
11	508	61178	Scatola ponte		38	508-B	59149	Rondella	
12	125	60117	Tappo per carico olio		39	125	58120	Cuscinetto	
13	—	92779	Guarnizione		40	340	60840	Coperchio per scatola	
14	—	93759	Anello di tenuta		41	125	60105	Grano	
15	—	93165	Cuscinetto a rulli		42	125	60118	Tappo per scarico olio	
16	250	58967	Distanziale conico		43	—	92714	Guarnizione	
17	513	59086	Anello		44	508-B	61315	Sfiato ponte	
18	—	93852	Cuscinetto intermedio		45	—	94385	Guarnizione	
19	513	59084	Distanziale		46	—	92892	Prigioniero corto	
20	513	59085	Distanziale		47	—	93829	Rondella	
21	—	92622	Seeger		48	125	92395	Dado	
22	—	93138	Cuscinetto a rulli		49	—	92891	Prigioniero medio	
23	—	92622	Seeger		50	—	92893	Prigioniero lungo	
24	125	58131	Rondella		51	—	93355	Prigioniero	
25	101	58771	Pignone		52	—	93356	Prigioniero	
26	518	59124	Corona		53	—	92791	Grano di centraggio	
27	508-B	59145	Scatola differenziale		54	125	92355	Rondella	
28	508-B	59146	Coperchio scatola differ.		55	125	92412	Dado	

Tavola 20 - Bracci ponte e sospensione posteriore

N.	Matr.	Disegno	Descrizione	Prezzo L.
1	508-B	61278	Braccio laterale destro	
2	125	92001	Rondella piana	
3	125	92355	Rondella elastica	
4	125	92412	Dado	
5	508	61106	Ammortizzatore destro	
6	508	61106	Ammortizzatore sinistro	
7	—	93328	Bullone	
8	125	92427	Dado	
9	125	92377	Copiglia	
10	—	92990	Silentbloc	
11	—	93550	Bullone	
12	—	93545	Dado	
13	125	92377	Copiglia	
14	508	61081	Biscottino per ammortizzatore	
15	—	93550	Bullone	
16	—	92990	Silentbloc	
17	—	93445	Dado	
18	125	92379	Copiglia	
19	250	58583	Tampone	
20	125	92369	Rondella	
21	—	93547	Dado	
22	125	92375	Copiglia	
23	508-B	61278	Braccio laterale sinistro	
24	—	92937	Cavo d'acciaio	
25	514	61198	Rondella bloccaggio fune	
26	—	93010	Bullone	
27	125	92359	Rondella	
28	125	92401	Dado	
29	—	93543	Bullone	
30	—	93426	Dado	
31	125	92379	Copiglia	
32	508-B	61353	Balestra posteriore	
33	—	92838	Bullone	
34	125	92419	Dado	
35	125	92373	Copiglia	
36	508	61090	Spessore per balestra	
37	508	61079	Staffa inferiore	
38	—	92421	Dado	
39	125	92373	Copiglia	
40			Cavallotto	
41			Bullone	
42			Dado	
43	342	60913	Flangia per cuscinetto	
44	—	92669	Bullone	
45	125	92355	Rondella	
46	125	92412	Dado	
47	508	61084	Biscottino per balestra	
48	—	93543	Bullone	
49	—	93270/a	Silentbloc	
50	—	93426	Dado	
51	125	92379	Copiglia	
52	—	94073	Silentbloc	
53	—	92997	Rondella	
54	—	93644	Dado	
55	125	92381	Copiglia	
56	—	93797/a	Silentbloc	
57	508	61075	Puntone di reazione	

Tavola 21 - Ruote, mozzi, semiassi

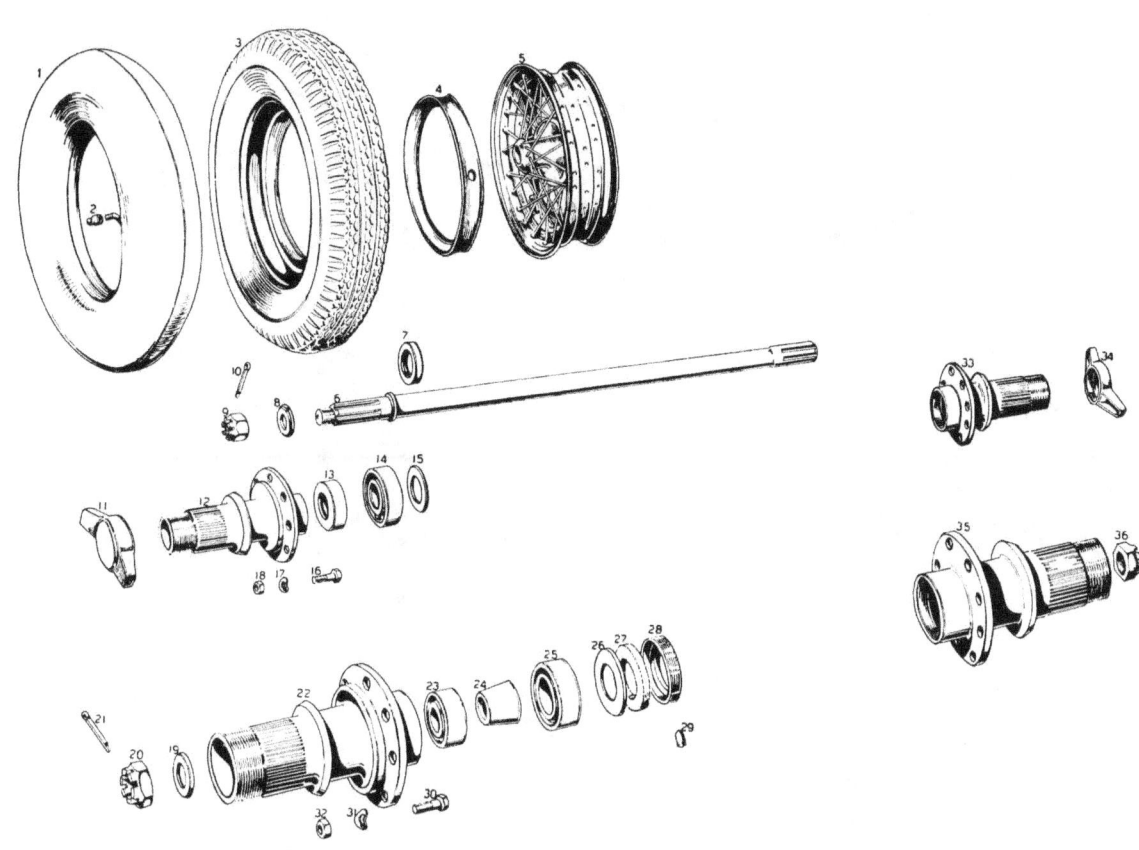

N.	Matr.	Disegno	Descrizione	Prezzo L.
1			Camera d'aria 6.00 x 16	
2			Coprivalvola	
3			Copertura Englebert 6.00 x 16	
4			Flap	
5			Cerchio a raggi 16 x 5½ K-RW 3264	
6	508-B	61276	Semiasse	
7	340	60846	Paraolio	
8	125	60147	Rondella	
9	125	92433	Dado coronato	
10	125	92381	Copiglia	
11	200	70163	Dado a galetto destro	
12	342	70866	Mozzo poster. destro	
13	—	93665	Anello di tenuta	
14	—	93166	Cuscinetto	
15	340	60844	Rondella paraolio	
16	—	93363	Bullone	
17	—	93830	Rondella	
18	125	92412	Dado	
19	—	92913	Rondella	
20	125	92429	Dado per ruota destra	
21	125	92381	Copiglia	
22	166	70856	Mozzo anteriore destro	
23	—	92849	Cuscinetto esterno ruota anteriore	
24	430	64286	Distanziale conico	
25	—	93250	Cuscinetto interno ruota anteriore	
26	166	70859	Rondella	
27	166	70860	Feltro	
28	166	70858	Ghiera	
29	125	70165	Grano	
30	—	93363	Bullone	
31	—	93830	Rondella	
32	125	92412	Dado	
33	342	70865	Mozzo posteriore sinistro	
34	200	70164	Dado a galetto sinistro	
35	166	70857	Mozzo anteriore destro	
36	125	92431	Dado per ruota sinistra	

Tavola 22 - Sospensione anteriore e timoneria di sterzo

N.	Matr.	Disegno	Descrizione	Prezzo L	N.	Matr.	Disegno	Descrizione	Prezzo L
1	519-C	64529	Fuso a snodo destro		39	519-C	64530	Fuso a snodo sinistro	
2	519-C	76269	Leva destra		40	125	92449	Ingrassatore	
3	125	92381	Copiglia		41	125	64125	Boccola	
4	—	94314	Rondella		42	125	64214	Rondella	
5	—	94313	Dado		43	125	64221	Distanziale	
6	508	64457	Ammortizzatore destro		44	513	64512	Perno per fuso	
7	508	64457	Ammortizzatore sinistro		45	508-B	64563	Scodellino per molla	
8	—	93856	Bullone		46	125	92449	Ingrassatore	
9	125	92427	Dado		47	—	94189	Bullone	
10	125	92377	Copiglia		48	513	64510	Boccola	
11	—	—			49	125	64511	Distanziale	
					50	—	93746	Dado	
					51	125	92379	Copiglia	
12	—	92796	Bullone		52	513	64506	Molla	
13	125	92308	Rondella		53	430	64256	Biscottino per ammortizz.	
14	125	92427	Dado		54	508-B	64534	Puntone posteriore	
15	125	92377	Copiglia		55	—	92884	Bullone	
16	508-B	64536	Leve superiori		56	125	92421	Dado	
17	—	92884	Bullone		57	125	92373	Copiglia	
18	125	92421	Dado		58	513	64505	Distanziale	
19	125	92373	Copiglia		59	125	60220	Silentbloc	
20	430	64258	Perno		60	513	64504	Boccola	
21	125	64164	Bussola		61	125	92308	Rondella	
22	125	64177	Rondella		62	125	92427	Dado	
23	125	92449	Ingrassatore		63	125	92377	Copiglia	
24	508-B	64537	Perno		64	—	94179	Rondella	
25	—	94179	Rondella		65	—	94362	Dado	
26	—	94361	Dado		66	125	92381	Copiglia	
27	125	92381	Copiglia		67	513	64528	Perno	
28	125	92429	Dado		68	125	92449	Ingrassatore	
29	125	92385	Copiglia		69	125	64164	Bussola	
30	125	92381	Rondella		70	125	64177	Rondella	
31	342	64310	Nodo per leve		71	513	64507	Supporto per molla	
32	—	93348	Rondella		72	513	64508	Rondella appoggio molla	
33	125	92449	Ingrassatore		73	—	94176	Anello elastico	
34	342	64313	Bussola		74	508-B	64535	Perno	
35	342	64324	Rondella		75	342	64313	Bussola	
36	125	64220	Scodellino		76	342	64324	Rondella	
37	508-B	64548	Ralle superiore		77	508-B	64533	Puntone anteriore	
38	508-B	64549	Ralle inferiore		78	125	60220	Silentbloc	

Tavola 22 - Sospensione anteriore e timoneria di sterzo

N.	Matr.	Disegno	Descrizione	Prezzo L.
79 } 80 }	508-B	64544	Distanziale	
81	513	64503	Rondella	
82	508-B	64543	Biscottino per barra	
83	508-B	76271	Leva rinvio sterzo	
84	430	76214	Coperchietto	
85	125	92449	Ingrassatore	
86	—	93348	Rondella	
87	—	93031	Bullone	
88	125	92353	Rondella	
89	—	92855	Cuscinetto	
90	125	76219	Guarnizione	
91	125	76207	Perno	
92	—	92863	Spina conica	
93	430	76217	Lamierino di tenuta	
94	—	92855	Cuscinetto	
95	508-B	76272	Leva sulla scatola guida	
96	125	92272	Bullone	
97	—	93300	Rondella	
98	125	92421	Dado	
99	125	92373	Copiglia	
100	—	92855	Cuscinetto	
101	508-B	64545	Barra stabilizzatrice	
102	340	64429	Piastra	
103	340	64428	Tampone per barra	
104	—	93280	Bullone	
105	125	92419	Dado	
106	125	92373	Copiglia	
107	—	92796	Bullone	
108	340	64431	Distanziale	
109 } 110 }	340	64430	Gommino	
111	125	92308	Rondella	
112	125	92427	Dado	
113	125	92377	Copiglia	
114	340	76250	Tirante centrale	
115	125	92413	Dado	
116	125	76148	Estremità tirante	
117	125	76140	Perno sferico	
118	—	94281	Dado	
119	125	92373	Copiglia	
120	125	76155	Scodellino	
121 } 122 }	125	76146	Calotta sferica	
123	125	76160	Rondella freno	
124	125	76150	Coperchietto	
125	—	93348	Rondella	
126	125	92449	Ingrassatore	
127	501	76257	Tirante sulle ruote	
128	519-C	76270	Leva sinistra	
129	125	76122	Linguetta	

Tavola 23 - Freni

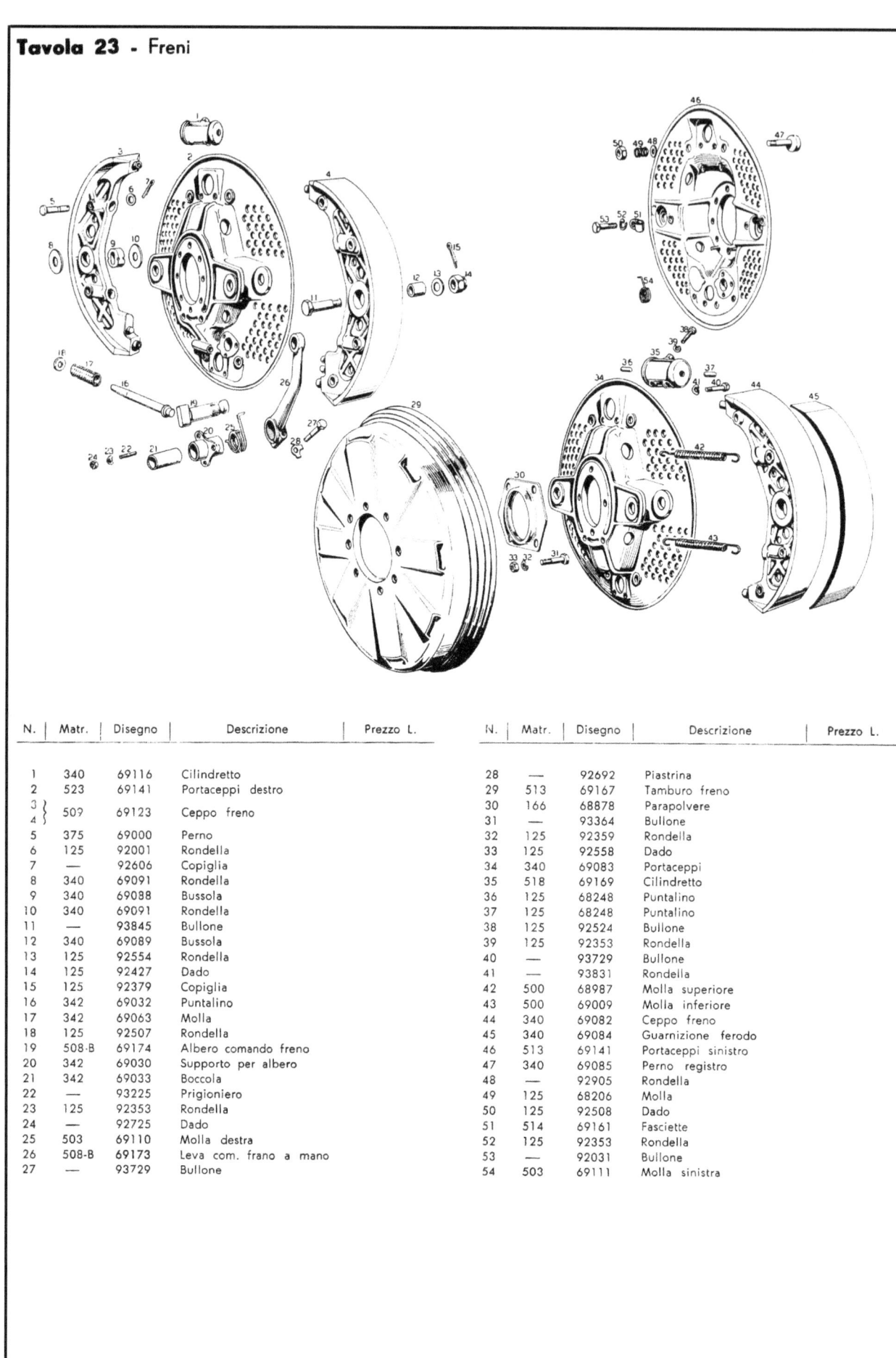

N.	Matr.	Disegno	Descrizione	Prezzo L.	N.	Matr.	Disegno	Descrizione	Prezzo L.
1	340	69116	Cilindretto		28	—	92692	Piastrina	
2	523	69141	Portaceppi destro		29	513	69167	Tamburo freno	
3	509	69123	Ceppo freno		30	166	68878	Parapolvere	
4					31	—	93364	Bullone	
5	375	69000	Perno		32	125	92359	Rondella	
6	125	92001	Rondella		33	125	92558	Dado	
7	—	92606	Copiglia		34	340	69083	Portaceppi	
8	340	69091	Rondella		35	518	69169	Cilindretto	
9	340	69088	Bussola		36	125	68248	Puntalino	
10	340	69091	Rondella		37	125	68248	Puntalino	
11	—	93845	Bullone		38	125	92524	Bullone	
12	340	69089	Bussola		39	125	92353	Rondella	
13	125	92554	Rondella		40	—	93729	Bullone	
14	125	92427	Dado		41	—	93831	Rondella	
15	125	92379	Copiglia		42	500	68987	Molla superiore	
16	342	69032	Puntalino		43	500	69009	Molla inferiore	
17	342	69063	Molla		44	340	69082	Ceppo freno	
18	125	92507	Rondella		45	340	69084	Guarnizione ferodo	
19	508-B	69174	Albero comando freno		46	513	69141	Portaceppi sinistro	
20	342	69030	Supporto per albero		47	340	69085	Perno registro	
21	342	69033	Boccola		48	—	92905	Rondella	
22	—	93225	Prigioniero		49	125	68206	Molla	
23	125	92353	Rondella		50	125	92508	Dado	
24	—	92725	Dado		51	514	69161	Fasciette	
25	503	69110	Molla destra		52	125	92353	Rondella	
26	508-B	69173	Leva com. frano a mano		53	—	92031	Bullone	
27	—	93729	Bullone		54	503	69111	Molla sinistra	

Tavola 24 - Comando idrauli freni

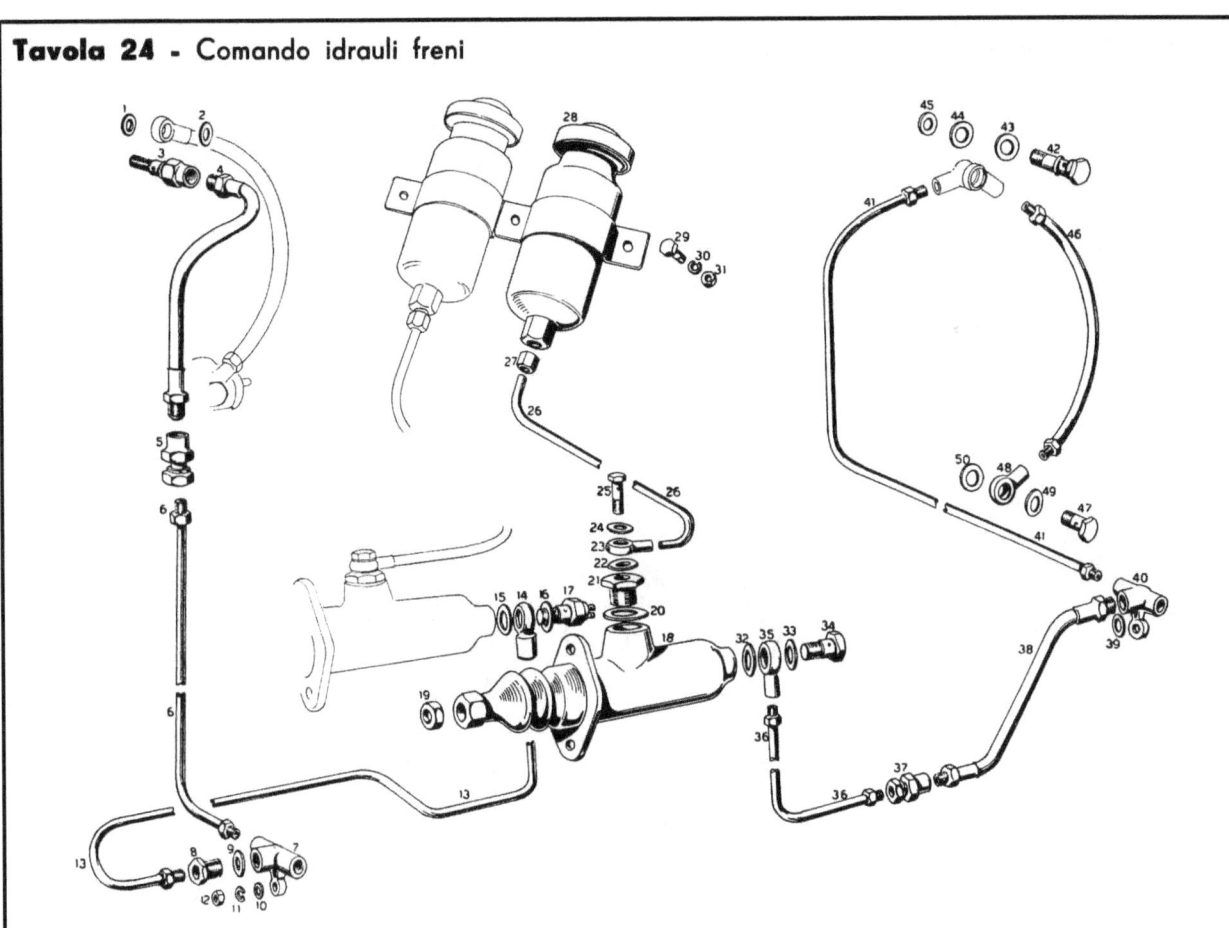

N.	Matr.	Disegno	Descrizione	Prezzo L.
1	—	93901	Guarnizione interna	
2	—	93079	Guarnizione esterna	
3	—	93903	Raccordo entrata cilindretti	
4	125	68246	Tubo comando freni	
5	—	93913	Raccordo a due vie anteriore	
6	—	93912	Raccordo e tubo per olio	
7	—	93911	Raccordo a tre vie anteriore	
8	—	94392	Riduttore per raccordo	
9	—	93926	Guarnizione	
10	125	92001	Rondella	
11	125	92355	Rondella elastica	
12	125	92397	Dado	
13	—	92940	Tubo	
14	—	93077	Femmina	
15	—	93893	Guarnizione	
16	—	93079	Guarnizione	
17	102	69103	Interruttore per Stop	
18	508-B	67225	Pompa comando freni	
19	Lockheed	987	Dado	
20	Lockheed	1427	Guarnizione	
21	—	94366	Raccordo entrata pompa	
22	—	94385	Guarnizione	
23	125	92575	Femmina per raccordo	
24	—	94385	Guarnizione	
25	125	92576	Bocchettone	
26	—	92940	Tubo	
27	—	93912	Raccordo	
28	103	69117	Serbatoio alimentazione freni	
29	—	93031	Bullone	
30	125	92353	Rondella	
31	125	92393	Dado	
32	—	93893	Guarnizione interna	
33	—	93894	Guarnizione esterna	
34	—	93967	Bocchettone	
35	—	93891	Femmina	
36	—	92940	Tubo	
37	—	93913	Raccordo a 2 vie posteriore	
38	125	68246	Tubo comando freni	
39	—	93926	Guarnizione	
40	—	93911	Raccordo a 3 vie posteriore	
41	—	92940	Tubo conduttore olio	
42	—	93900	Bocchettone	
43 44	—	93079	Guarnizione esterna	
45	—	93901	Guarnizione interna	
46	—	92940	Tubo conduttore olio	
47	—	93902	Bocchettone	
48	—	93077	Femmine	
49	—	93901	Guarnizione interna	
50	—	93079	Guarnizione esterna	

Tavola 25 - Pedaliera e comando freno

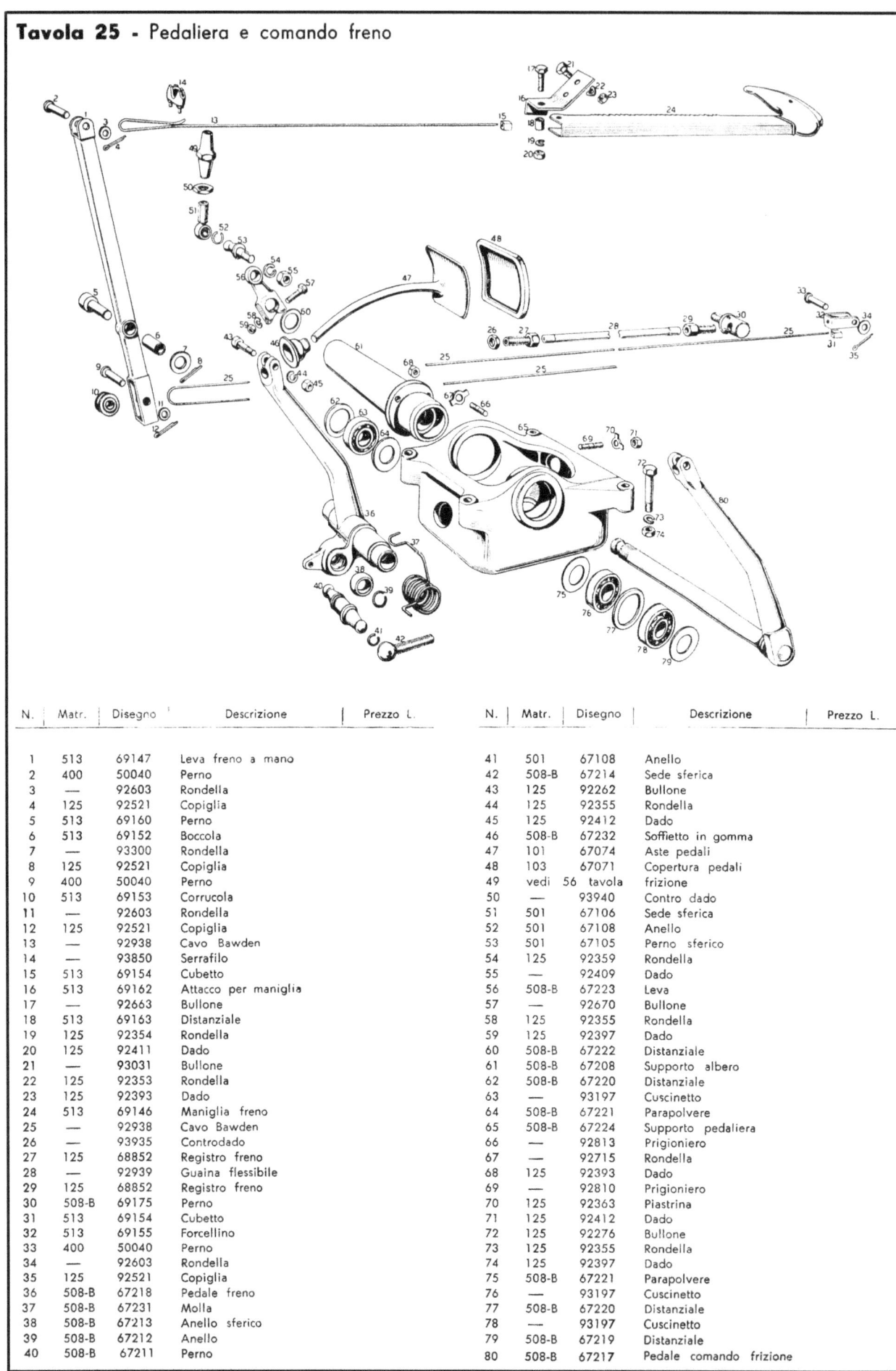

N.	Matr.	Disegno	Descrizione	Prezzo L.	N.	Matr.	Disegno	Descrizione	Prezzo L.
1	513	69147	Leva freno a mano		41	501	67108	Anello	
2	400	50040	Perno		42	508-B	67214	Sede sferica	
3	—	92603	Rondella		43	125	92262	Bullone	
4	125	92521	Copiglia		44	125	92355	Rondella	
5	513	69160	Perno		45	125	92412	Dado	
6	513	69152	Boccola		46	508-B	67232	Soffietto in gomma	
7	—	93300	Rondella		47	101	67074	Aste pedali	
8	125	92521	Copiglia		48	103	67071	Copertura pedali	
9	400	50040	Perno		49	vedi	56 tavola	frizione	
10	513	69153	Corrucola		50	—	93940	Contro dado	
11	—	92603	Rondella		51	501	67106	Sede sferica	
12	125	92521	Copiglia		52	501	67108	Anello	
13	—	92938	Cavo Bawden		53	501	67105	Perno sferico	
14	—	93850	Serrafilo		54	125	92359	Rondella	
15	513	69154	Cubetto		55	—	92409	Dado	
16	513	69162	Attacco per maniglia		56	508-B	67223	Leva	
17	—	92663	Bullone		57	—	92670	Bullone	
18	513	69163	Distanziale		58	125	92355	Rondella	
19	125	92354	Rondella		59	125	92397	Dado	
20	125	92411	Dado		60	508-B	67222	Distanziale	
21	—	93031	Bullone		61	508-B	67208	Supporto albero	
22	125	92353	Rondella		62	508-B	67220	Distanziale	
23	125	92393	Dado		63	—	93197	Cuscinetto	
24	513	69146	Maniglia freno		64	508-B	67221	Parapolvere	
25	—	92938	Cavo Bawden		65	508-B	67224	Supporto pedaliera	
26	—	93935	Controdado		66	—	92813	Prigioniero	
27	125	68852	Registro freno		67	—	92715	Rondella	
28	—	92939	Guaina flessibile		68	125	92393	Dado	
29	125	68852	Registro freno		69	—	92810	Prigioniero	
30	508-B	69175	Perno		70	125	92363	Piastrina	
31	513	69154	Cubetto		71	125	92412	Dado	
32	513	69155	Forcellino		72	125	92276	Bullone	
33	400	50040	Perno		73	125	92355	Rondella	
34	—	92603	Rondella		74	125	92397	Dado	
35	125	92521	Copiglia		75	508-B	67221	Parapolvere	
36	508-B	67218	Pedale freno		76	—	93197	Cuscinetto	
37	508-B	67231	Molla		77	508-B	67220	Distanziale	
38	508-B	67213	Anello sferico		78	—	93197	Cuscinetto	
39	508-B	67212	Anello		79	508-B	67219	Distanziale	
40	508-B	67211	Perno		80	508-B	67217	Pedale comando frizione	

Tavola 26 - Organi di guida

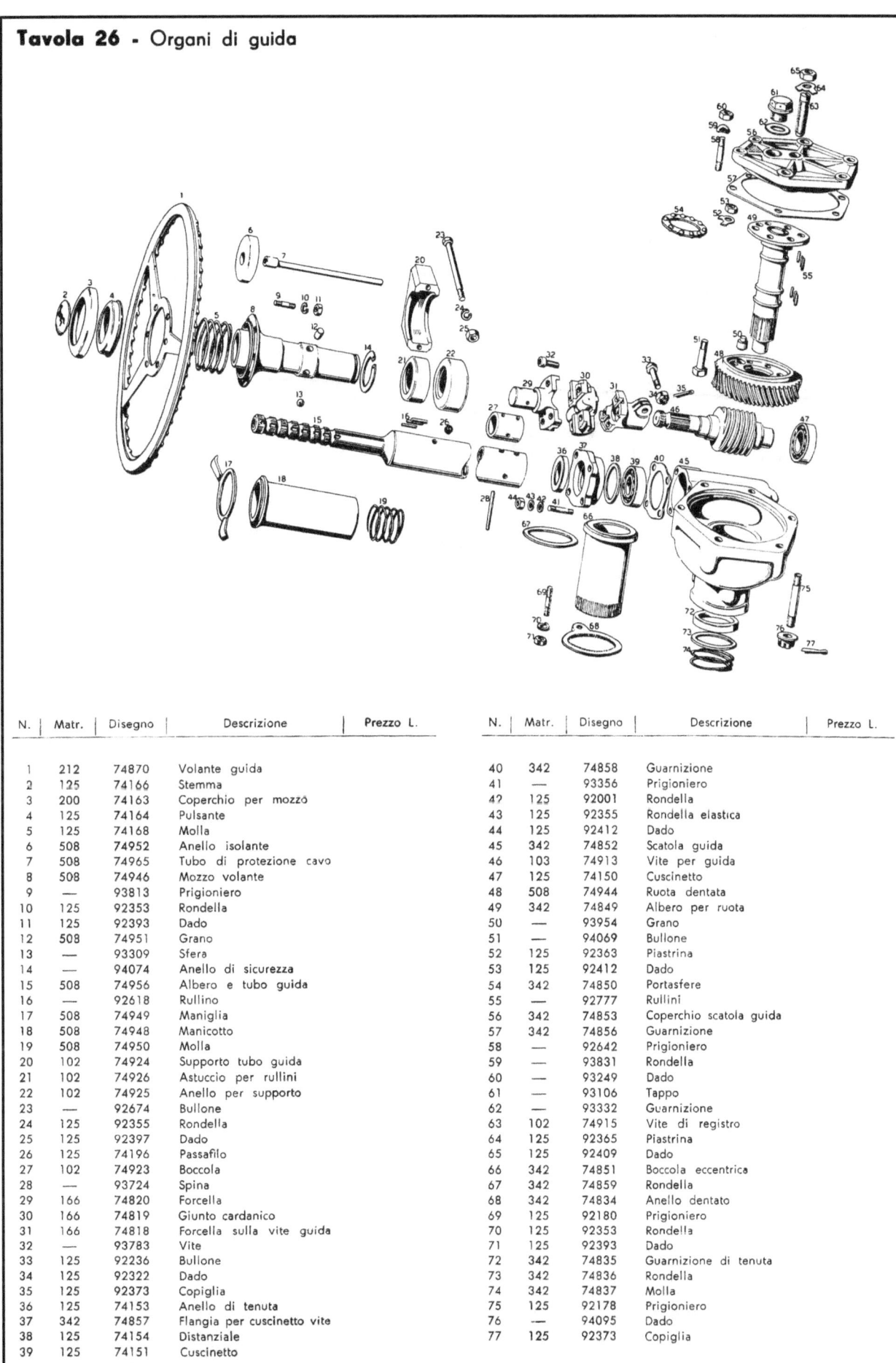

N.	Matr.	Disegno	Descrizione	Prezzo L.
1	212	74870	Volante guida	
2	125	74166	Stemma	
3	200	74163	Coperchio per mozzo	
4	125	74164	Pulsante	
5	125	74168	Molla	
6	508	74952	Anello isolante	
7	508	74965	Tubo di protezione cavo	
8	508	74946	Mozzo volante	
9	—	93813	Prigioniero	
10	125	92353	Rondella	
11	125	92393	Dado	
12	508	74951	Grano	
13	—	93309	Sfera	
14	—	94074	Anello di sicurezza	
15	508	74956	Albero e tubo guida	
16	—	92618	Rullino	
17	508	74949	Maniglia	
18	508	74948	Manicotto	
19	508	74950	Molla	
20	102	74924	Supporto tubo guida	
21	102	74926	Astuccio per rullini	
22	102	74925	Anello per supporto	
23	—	92674	Bullone	
24	125	92355	Rondella	
25	125	92397	Dado	
26	125	74196	Passafilo	
27	102	74923	Boccola	
28	—	93724	Spina	
29	166	74820	Forcella	
30	166	74819	Giunto cardanico	
31	166	74818	Forcella sulla vite guida	
32	—	93783	Vite	
33	125	92236	Bullone	
34	125	92322	Dado	
35	125	92373	Copiglia	
36	125	74153	Anello di tenuta	
37	342	74857	Flangia per cuscinetto vite	
38	125	74154	Distanziale	
39	125	74151	Cuscinetto	
40	342	74858	Guarnizione	
41	—	93356	Prigioniero	
42	125	92001	Rondella	
43	125	92355	Rondella elastica	
44	125	92412	Dado	
45	342	74852	Scatola guida	
46	103	74913	Vite per guida	
47	125	74150	Cuscinetto	
48	508	74944	Ruota dentata	
49	342	74849	Albero per ruota	
50	—	93954	Grano	
51	—	94069	Bullone	
52	125	92363	Piastrina	
53	125	92412	Dado	
54	342	74850	Portasfere	
55	—	92777	Rullini	
56	342	74853	Coperchio scatola guida	
57	342	74856	Guarnizione	
58	—	92642	Prigioniero	
59	—	93831	Rondella	
60	—	93249	Dado	
61	—	93106	Tappo	
62	—	93332	Guarnizione	
63	102	74915	Vite di registro	
64	125	92365	Piastrina	
65	125	92409	Dado	
66	342	74851	Boccola eccentrica	
67	342	74859	Rondella	
68	342	74834	Anello dentato	
69	125	92180	Prigioniero	
70	125	92353	Rondella	
71	125	92393	Dado	
72	342	74835	Guarnizione di tenuta	
73	342	74836	Rondella	
74	342	74837	Molla	
75	125	92178	Prigioniero	
76	—	94095	Dado	
77	125	92373	Copiglia	

Tavola 27 - Telaio

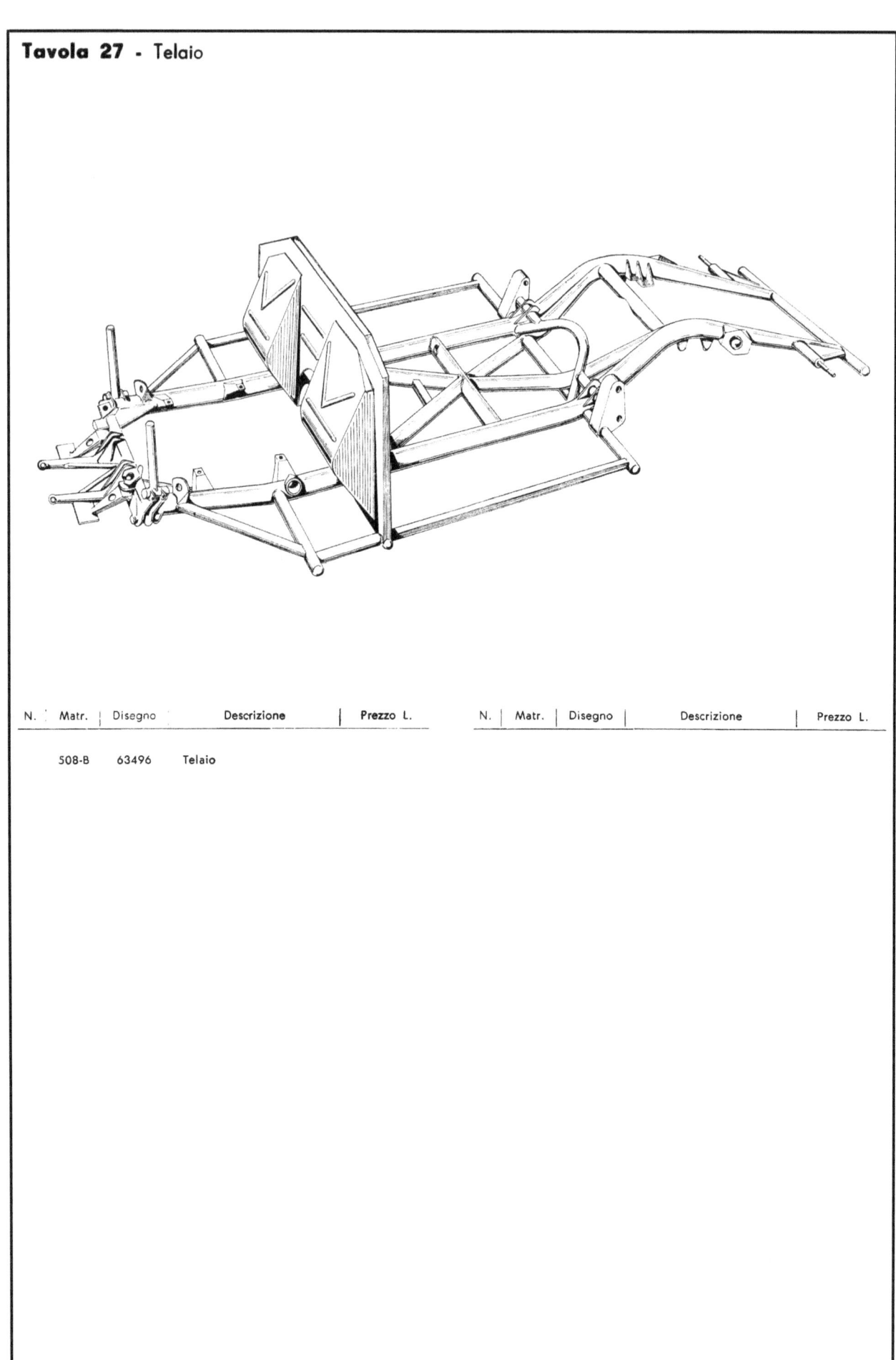

N.	Matr.	Disegno	Descrizione	Prezzo L.	N.	Matr.	Disegno	Descrizione	Prezzo L.
	508-B	63496	Telaio						

Tavola 28 - Attrezzi motore

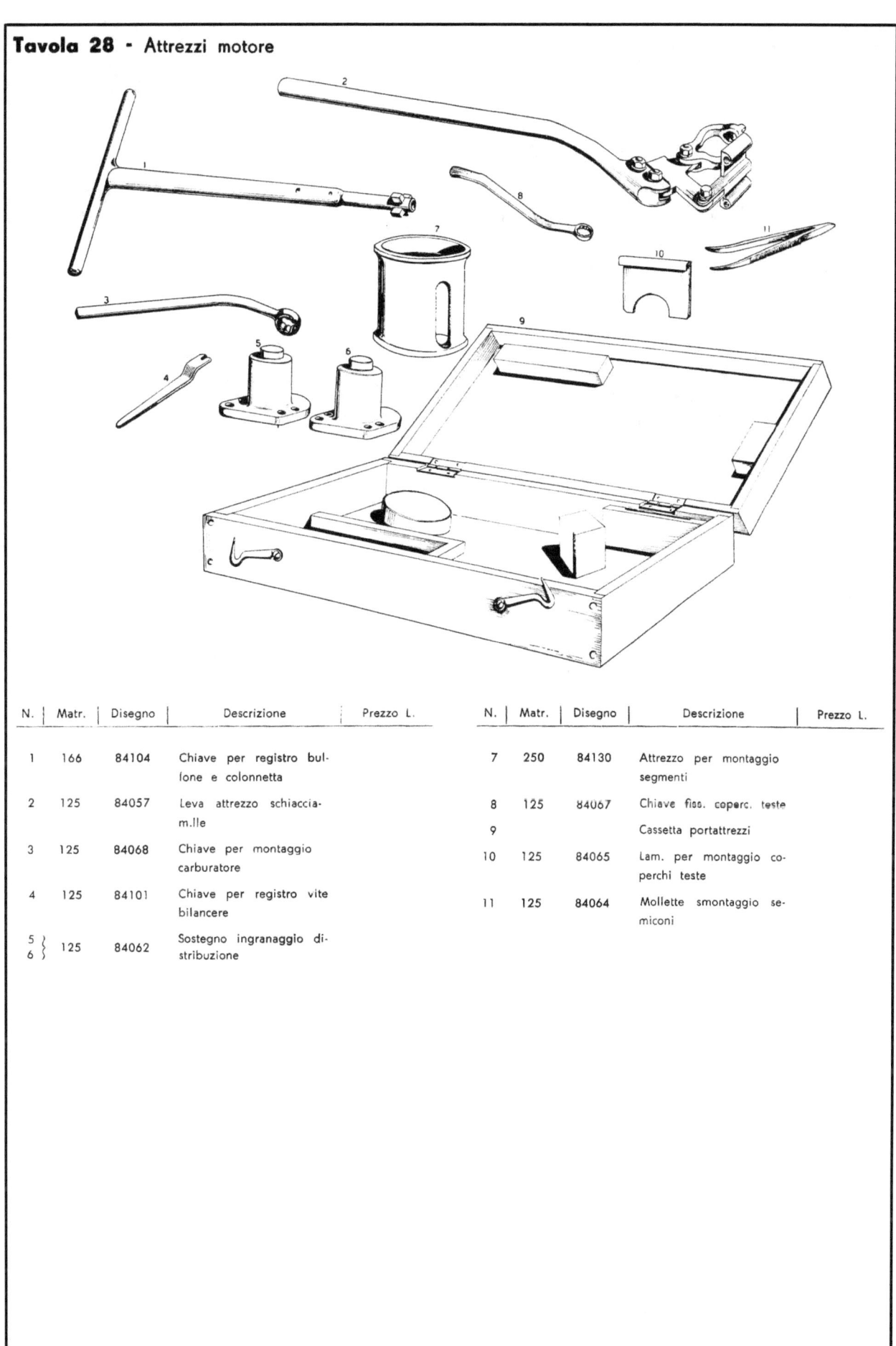

N.	Matr.	Disegno	Descrizione	Prezzo L.
1	166	84104	Chiave per registro bullone e colonnetta	
2	125	84057	Leva attrezzo schiaccia-m.lle	
3	125	84068	Chiave per montaggio carburatore	
4	125	84101	Chiave per registro vite bilancere	
5 6	125	84062	Sostegno ingranaggio distribuzione	
7	250	84130	Attrezzo per montaggio segmenti	
8	125	84067	Chiave fiss. coperc. teste	
9			Cassetta portattrezzi	
10	125	84065	Lam. per montaggio coperchi teste	
11	125	84064	Mollette smontaggio semiconi	

Tavola 29 - Attrezzi normali

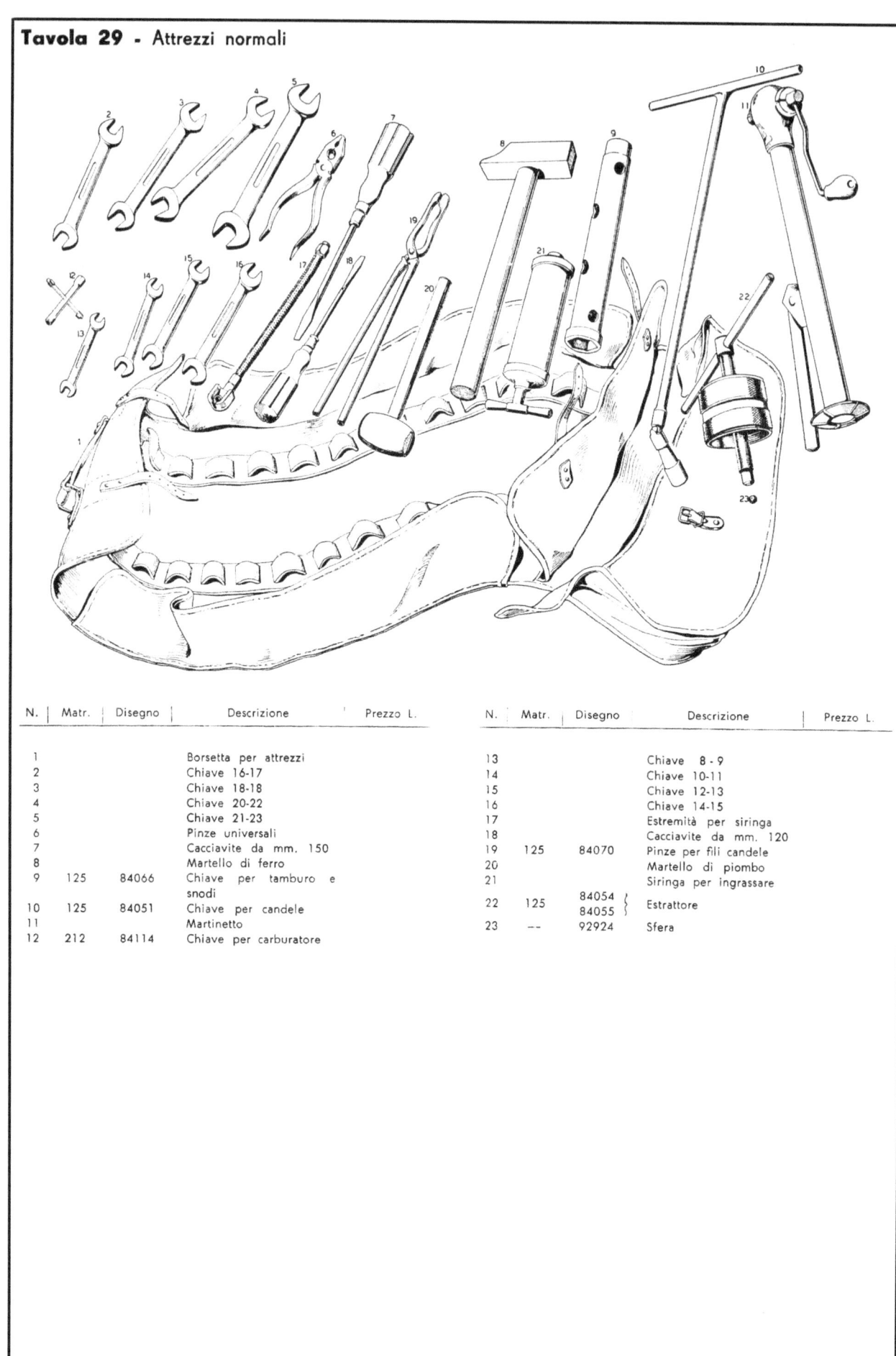

N.	Matr.	Disegno	Descrizione	Prezzo L.
1			Borsetta per attrezzi	
2			Chiave 16-17	
3			Chiave 18-18	
4			Chiave 20-22	
5			Chiave 21-23	
6			Pinze universali	
7			Cacciavite da mm. 150	
8			Martello di ferro	
9	125	84066	Chiave per tamburo e snodi	
10	125	84051	Chiave per candele	
11			Martinetto	
12	212	84114	Chiave per carburatore	
13			Chiave 8-9	
14			Chiave 10-11	
15			Chiave 12-13	
16			Chiave 14-15	
17			Estremità per siringa	
18			Cacciavite da mm. 120	
19	125	84070	Pinze per fili candele	
20			Martello di piombo	
21			Siringa per ingrassare	
22	125	84054 / 84055	Estrattore	
23	--	92924	Sfera	

PREFACE

TRADEMARKS & COPYRIGHT

Ferrari ® is the registered trademark of Ferrari S.p.A. This publication is not sponsored by or endorsed by the trademark owner. We recognize that some words, model names and designations, for example, mentioned herein are the property of the trademark holder. We use them for identification purposes only. This is not an official publication however; it may include non-copyright works of the trademark holder.

INTRODUCTION

Welcome to the world of digital publishing ~ the book you now hold in your hand was printed using the latest state of the art digital technology. The advent of print-on-demand has forever changed the publishing process, never has information been so accessible and it is our hope that this book serves your informational needs for years to come. If this is your first exposure to digital publishing, we hope that you are pleased with the results. Many more titles of interest to the classic automobile and motorcycle enthusiast, collector and restorer are available via our website at www.VelocePress.com. We hope that you find this title as interesting as we do.

NOTE FROM THE PUBLISHER

The information presented is true and complete to the best of our knowledge. All recommendations are made without any guarantees on the part of the author or the publisher, who also disclaim all liability incurred with the use of this information.

INFORMATION ON THE USE OF THIS PUBLICATION

This manual is an invaluable resource for those interested in performing their own maintenance. However, in today's information age we are constantly subject to changes in common practice, new technology, availability of improved materials and increased awareness of chemical toxicity. As such, it is advised that the user consult with an experienced professional prior to undertaking any procedure described herein. While every care has been taken to ensure correctness of information, it is obviously not possible to guarantee complete freedom from errors or omissions or to accept liability arising from such errors or omissions. Therefore, any individual that uses the information contained within, or elects to perform or participate in do-it-yourself repairs or modifications acknowledges that there is a risk factor involved and that the publisher or its associates cannot be held responsible for personal injury or property damage resulting from the use of the information or the outcome of such procedures.

WARNING!

One final word of advice, this publication is intended to be used as a reference guide, and when in doubt the reader should consult with a qualified technician.

ferrari

250 gt/e pininfarina coupé 2+2

operating, maintenance and service handbook

sefac

Ferrari

INDEX

General specification — page 2

Operating instructions — page 11

Routine maintenance — Lubrication — page 26

General — Engine servicing — page 32

Chassis components servicing — page 55

Electrical equipment — page 79

Tool kit — page 89

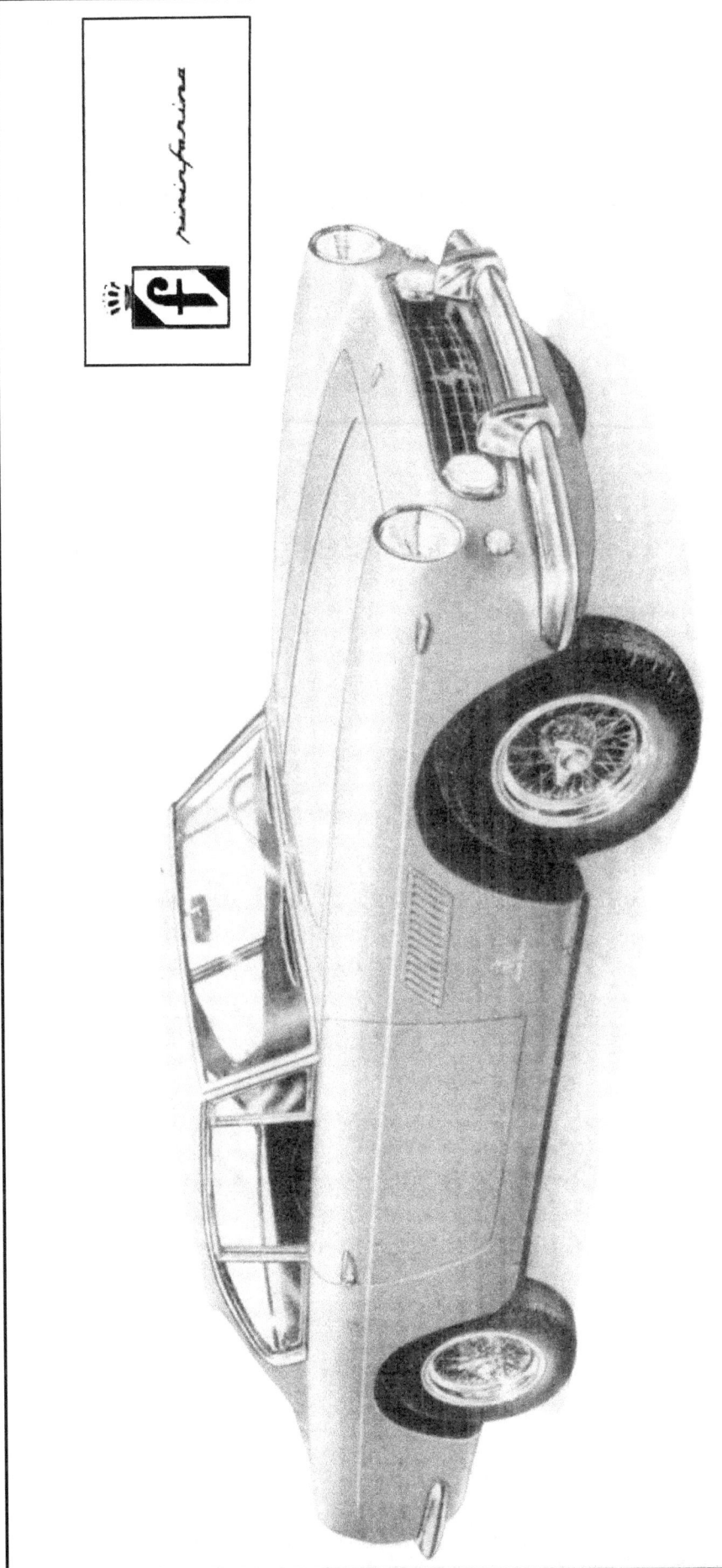

Fig. 1 - Ferrari 250 GT/E Coupé Pininfarina 2+2.

In his book 'Ferrari Operating Maintenance and Service Handbooks' Dick Merritt makes the following statement with regard to the **250 GT/E manual:**

"At long last a well-illustrated, detailed and comprehensive owner's manual was published that was comparable to those provided by the large automotive companies. However, the spare parts catalogue was deleted but the prior volume was still generally applicable in many areas. The 250 GT/E 2+2 manual was intended to cover all V-12 models built for customers between about 1959 and 1963."

Foreword

— The 250 GT Ferrari is a high performance car, built to the exacting standards of an advanced design. It deserves and requires skilled attention.

— The manual includes a comprehensive description of the various features of the car and we recommend that it be consulted before servicing, or work of any kind, is attempted.

— For maintenance operations, or work that would involve special equipment, we suggest that our Concessionaires be contacted.

— Should repairs or new parts become necessary, only genuine Ferrari spares may be used. These are obtainable from our Concessionaires.

— The factory trained staff available at our Concessionaires are always at the disposal of Ferrari owners for information or advice.

Replenishing   page 3

	Litres	Gallons/Pints	
WATER	11	2	3
FUEL	90	19	7
OIL	Kilograms.		
Sump	9	—	15
Filters	1	—	2
Gearbox & Overdrive	4.6	—	6
Rear axle	1.8	—	5
Steering box	0.4	—	1

First Part
Identification data of motor-car

page 4

Identification Numbers

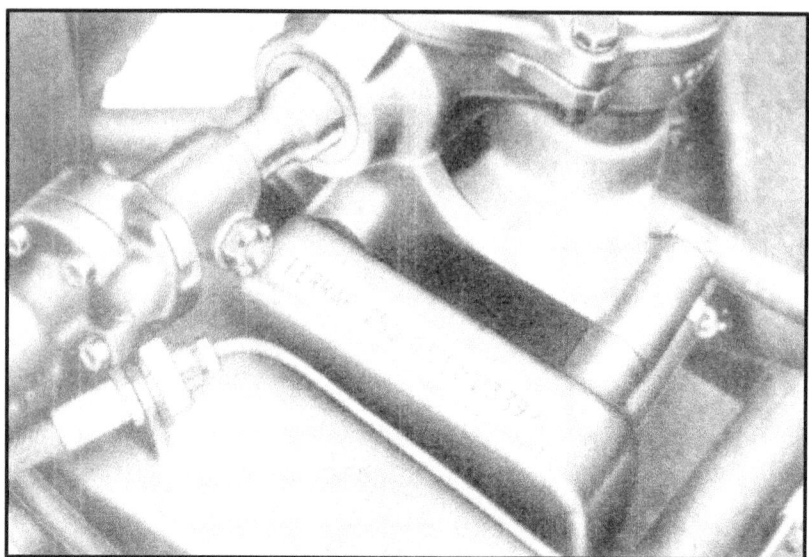

Fig. 2 - Chassis number. Nearside of front cross member.

Fig. 3 - Engine number. Timing casing and Flywheel bell housing.

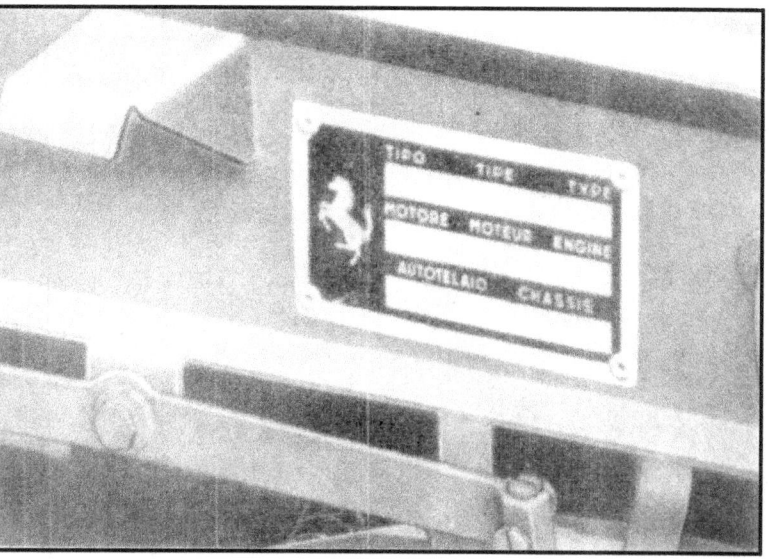

Fig. 4 - General data plate. Bulkhead.

Main features

ENGINE

Cylinders	12
Arrangement	V 60
Bore	73 mm
Stroke	58.8 mm
Total displacement	2953.211 cc
Compression ratio	9.2 to 1
Max. power at 7000 r.p.m.	235 bhp net

CHASSIS

Wheel base	m. 2.600	8'6"
Max. length	m. 4.700	15'5"
Max. width	m. 1.710	5'10"
Min. height from the ground (loaded)	m. 0.145	5"
Max. height (loaded)	m. 1.340	4'5"
Front track (loaded)	m. 1.395	4'7"
Rear track	m. 1.387	4'6"
Min. turning circle	m. 12.2	40'1"
Weight empty	kg. 1310	25.7 cwt.
Overall weight full load (4 persons)	kg. 1695	33.2 cwt.
High octane fuel consumption (normal) for 100 Km.	Litres 16	17.7 mpg.
Oil consumption (normal) engine cruising speed for 100 Km.	grs. 100	
Maximum speed	km. 230	143 mph.
Tyres (front and rear)	185 × 15 - 6.50/6.70 × 15	
Front tyre pressure ⎱ Pirelli	Kg/cm. 1.7/2	29 lbs/sq.ins.
Rear tyre pressure ⎰ Cinturato	Kg/cm. 2.1/2.3	33 lbs/sq.ins.
Electric Installation	12 volts.	

page 5

Main features

PERFORMANCE

Maximum speeds in gears

MAXIMUM SPEEDS AT 7000 r.p.m.					
ratio	1st.	2nd.	3rd.	4th.	4th. at 1000 r.p.m.
7/32	74 KMH 46 MPH	110 KMH 68 MPH	150 KMH 93 MPH	188 KMH 116 MPH	26.857 KMH 17 MPH
8/34	79 KMH 49 MPH	119 KMH 74 MPH	160 KMH 99 MPH	202 KMH 125 MPH	28.857 KMH 18 MPH

5th. automatic overdrive is fitted - exclusively - with ratio 7/32 and provides a max. speed of 230 KMH. 143 MPH.

HILL CLIMBING

	1st.	2nd.	3rd.	4th.	overdrive
gradient in %	47	29	19	12	4
speed in KMH and MPH	60 KMH 37 MPH	92 KMH 57 MPH	122 KMH 76 MPH	153 KMH 94 MPH	185 KMH 115 MPH

Maximum range, without refuelling

at normal speed on road : about 500 Km/300 miles.

Instruments and controls

page 7

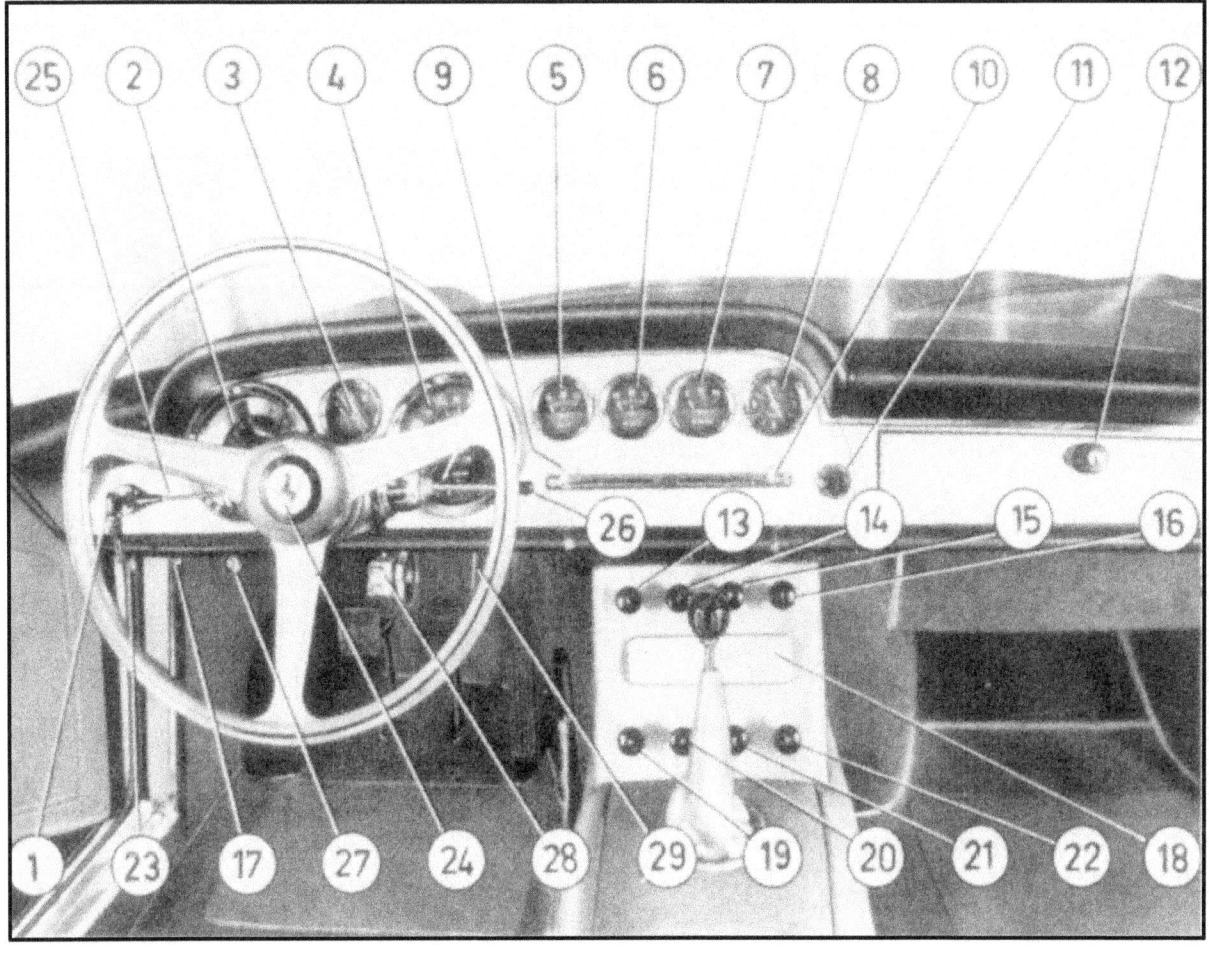

Fig. 5 - Drives and various controls.

1. **Ignition lock switch**	By turning the key clockwise, the first trip (90°) completes the panel light, de-mister, blower and windscreen wiper circuits, should the separate controls for these circuits be left on. The second trip (180°) completes the ignition and dynamo warning light circuits. The starter is operated by depressing the key in the second trip (180°) position.
2. **Revolution Counter**	Reads to 8,000 r.p.m. Each division equals 250 r.p.m. Numbered every 500 r.p.m.
3. **Oil pressure gauge**	Minimum pressure at 700-800 r.p.m. - 35-40 lbs sq.in. Minimum pressure at 7000 r.p.m. - 55-60 lbs sq.in.

Instruments and controls (continued.)

page 8

4. **Speedometer**	Reads to 180 mph Each division equals 5 mph Numbered every 10 mph
5. **Oil Temperature gauge**	Maximum Temperature 110-115° C or 230-235° F.
6. **Water temperature gauge**	Maximum Temperature 90-95° C or 190-195° F
7. **Fuel level Indicator**	Shows quantity of fuel in the tank. The Red warning light comes on when there are only 2½ to 3 gallons left.
8. **Clock**	—
9. **Heater Temperature control**	To increase the temperature, move the control lever to the right.
10. **Heater Air control**	To increase the flow of fresh air move the control lever to the right.
11. **Lighter**	Push the knob in, towards the dashboard. The Lighter then works automatically, springing out when ready for use.
12. **Glove pocket**	Press the catch to open. This catch has its own key.
13. **Lights switch Marked 'L'**	Draw the knob out from the dashboard. If lever 25 is forwards, this merely switches the side lights on. Flicking lever 25 back towards the steering wheel, switches the headlamps on, but with the beams dipped. Rotating the knob 'L' a quarter turn clockwise, and then drawing it out a further knotch, switches the headlamps on. The beams will be at dipped with lever 25 to the rear; flicking this lever forward towards the dashboard, sets the lights onto full beam.

Instruments and controls (continued.) page 9

14. **Panel Lights.** Switch marked 'P'	This is a Rheostat switch. Rotate the knob clockwise to switch on. Further rotation dims the lights.
15. **Fog light switch 'F'**	Draw the knob out to switch on.
16. **Inside light switch 'I'**	Draw the knob out to switch on.
17. **Windshield washing pushknob (*)**	Pressing this knob with the foot squirts water onto the windscreen.
18. **Radio-set**	
19. **Windscreen wiper switch, marked with a 'W'**	Turn the knob clockwise to operate. The first position operates the blades at half speed, the second at full speed.
20. **Petrol pump switch marked 'A'**	Draw the knob out to operate the pump. A blue warning light, marked Autoflux and situated in the revolution counter, shows when this pump is operating.
21. **Electric fan and heating switch 'D'**	Draw the knob out to operate.
22. **Rear electric fan switch 'B'**	Draw the knob out to operate.
23. **- Socket**	
24. **- Warning horn push button**	
25. **Indicator and Dipping switch**	This lever works in two planes: Vertically to operate the Turn Indicators and horizontally to operate the headlamp dipping. The latter operation was described with switch number 13. Flick the lever down to operate the offside flashers, indicating a right-hand turn, and up for a lefthand turn.

(*) **N.B.** This knob has been moved since the diagram was drawn.

Instruments and controls (continued.) page 10

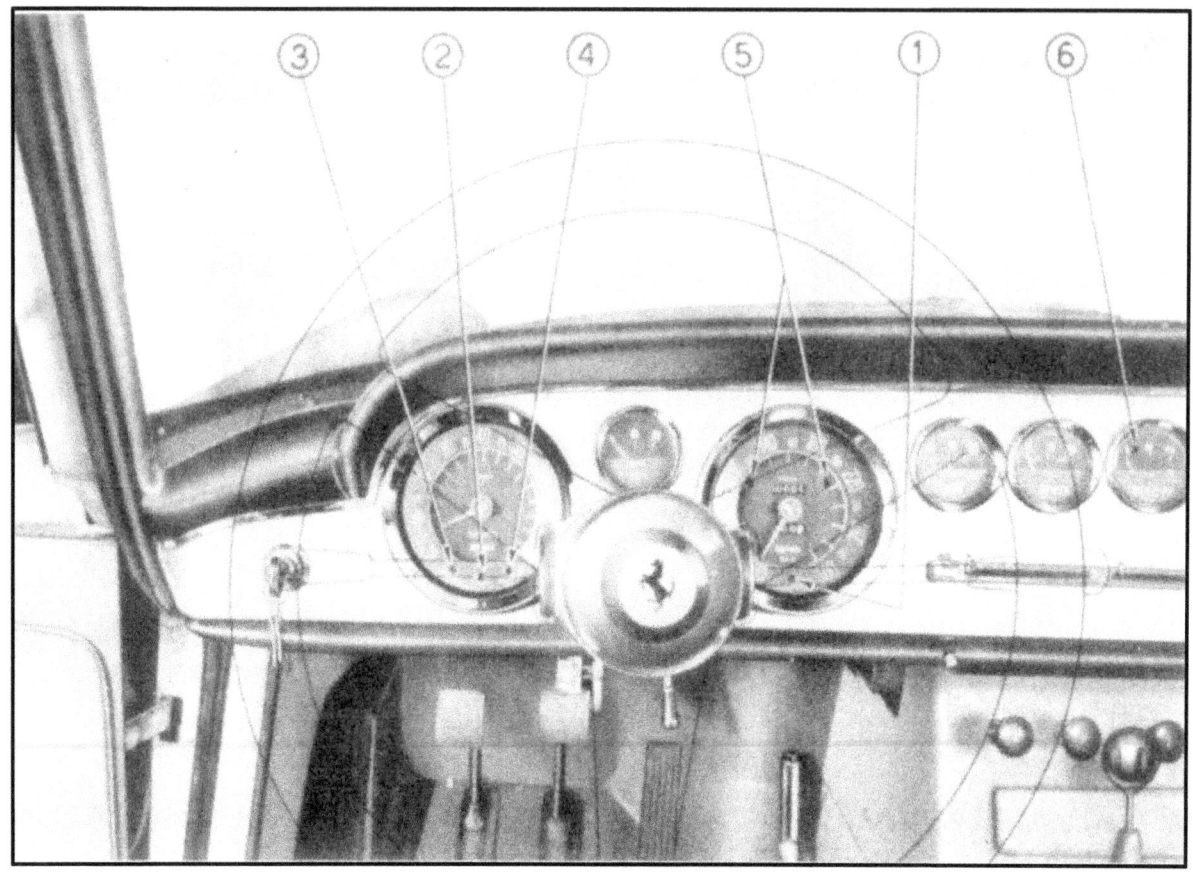

Fig. 6 - Various driving aids.
1) green warning for side lights; 2) dynamo and ignition warning (red); 3) orange warning for heating and electric fan; 4) Blue warning for electric fuel pump; 5) Red warning for Indicator flashers; 6) Red warning for fuel level.

26.	**Overdrive switch**	Flick the lever forwards to engage overdrive.
27.	**Starter knob**	See page 14.
28.	**Radiator blind control**	Turn the handwheel clockwise to raise the blind. Pull the release catch, situated on top of the control, to the rear to lower the blind.
29.	**Bonnet catch.**	Draw the lever up to open.
(*)	30. **Choke**	Pull out to operate.
	31 & 32. **Air duct controls**	Pull out to increase the fresh air flow.
	33 & 34. **Dashboard ventilator controls**	Turn to increase the fresh air flow.
	35 & 36. **Car interior heater doors**	Pull open to allow heated air to enter the car interior.

(*) Not shown on diagram.

Second Part
Running instructions

Running-in

Although the engine has been thoroughly bench-tested before being installed, it is still necessary to run the car in for the first 2000 miles. The following speeds are the maximum allowed:

Distances in miles	Maximum speeds in MPH and Km/h allowed			
	First	Second	Third	Fourth
Up to 1000	30 mph 50 km/h	40 mph 70 km/h	55 mph 95 km/h	80 mph 130 km/h
From 1000 to 2000	40 mph 70 km/h	55 mph 95 km/h	75 mph 120 km/h	90 mph 150 km/h

Also, when starting:

1. Do not operate the starter for longer than three seconds at a time.
2. Use the electric petrol pump for starting from cold. The pump should be switched off when it has finished ticking, before attempting to use the starter.
3. Allow the engine to run at 2,000 rpm for at least 1 minute, 2-3 mins: in cold weather, before moving off.

When driving:

1. Never accelerate hard.
2. Never use the maximum speeds in the above table as cruising speeds.
3. From time to time, release the accelerator for a second or two.
4. Avoid heavy or long braking, at least for the first 1000 miles.

Running instructions

RUNNING-IN

Engine oil changes

The engine oil should be changed at the following intervals:

1st. change after 500 miles
2nd. » » 1500 miles
3rd. » » 2500 miles
Thereafter every 250 miles.

Gearbox and rear axle

The oil should be changed at 2,500 miles.

Cylinder head nuts

These must be checked for tightness at 500 miles (correct torque 62-66 lbs/ft).

Steering adjustments

After the first 3,000 miles, check the play in the sector shaft and adjust if necessary - see page 64.

CHECKS

Before use, check.

Running instructions
page 13

1. Check the water level in the radiator
2. Check the sump oil level
3. Check the tyre pressure
4. Check the level of the brake reservoir.

Fuel

98/100 Octane fuel only to be used.

Oil

The sump oil level should be kept up to the maximum line on the dipstick - measured before running the engine.

Water

The correct level is 1" below the bottom of the filler neck. The level should never be allowed to drop more than 2" below the bottom of the filler neck.

To check the level when the engine is hot, or overheating, cover the radiator cap with a rag and twist anti-clockwise by a quarter turn: allow the pressure to escape and then unscrew. If it is found necessary to replenish, pour water in slowly, with the engine ticking over.

Tyres

Check the tyres are not wearing unevenly at least every fortnight.

Running instructions

Starting

COLD START

Check the gear lever is in neutral.

Draw out the choke, if the weather is very cold. This should be pushed in slowly after starting.

Turn on the electrical petrol pump, switching off when it ceases pumping.

Depress the ignition key, releasing it as soon as the engine fires.

It eases starting to depress the clutch pedal, but never press the accelerator until the engine has started.

Should the engine prove difficult to start, stop trying to start for a minute or two, to save the battery.

Should the engine still not start, the battery may be low, the plugs may be dirty, or the contact breaker points incorrectly set, or the coils faulty.

A fuse may be blown or the slow running jets may be blocked.

Never rev-up until the oil is warm.

Check that the oil pressure at tick-over is not below 35 lbs.

Check that the dynamo warning light goes out as soon as the engine reaches 1000 rpm.

WARM START

No choke will be necessary - press down on the accelerator slowly, releasing it gradually as soon as the engine fires.

Never pump the accelerator repeatedly.

Running instructions

Fig. 7 - Gear positions.

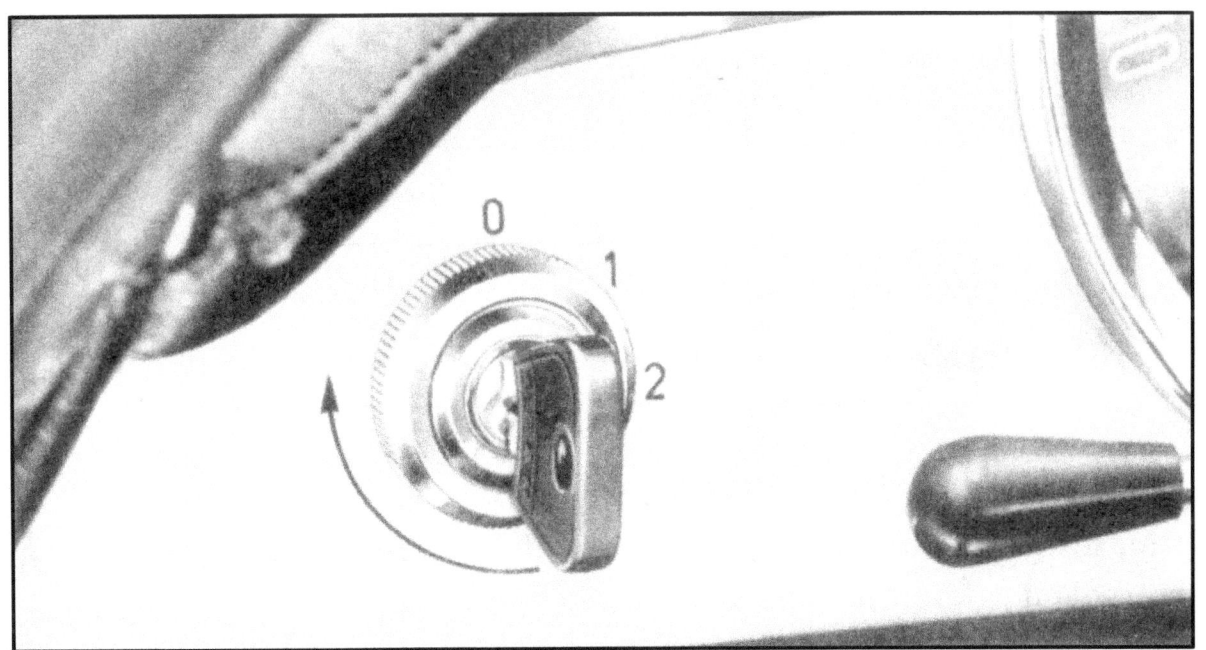

Fig. 8 - Ignition switch positions.

Running instructions

Driving pointers

1. Never exceed 7000 rpm.

2. Try to form a habit of glancing at the oil, water and ammeter gauges occasionally.

3. Should the oil pressure gauge read less than 55-60 lbs/sq in. at maximum rpm with warm oil, the engine must be stopped immediately and the cause investigated.

4. Never accelerate hard before the oil has reached its working temperature of 130° F/60° C.

5. Never drive with the foot resting on the clutch pedal, and do not keep the clutch depressed for long periods in traffic.

Wintry conditions

Shell antifreeze is recommended for use in the following quantities:

Temperature	Antifreeze
About − 8° C	2 Litre or 3 ½ pts.
» −15° C	3.1 » or 5 ½ pts.
» −25° C	4.5 » or 8 pts.

If antifreeze has not been mixed with the coolant, it is important that the coolant is drained immediately after use.

Diagrams on page 17 show where the drain cocks are situated.

Running instructions — page 17

Draining the coolant

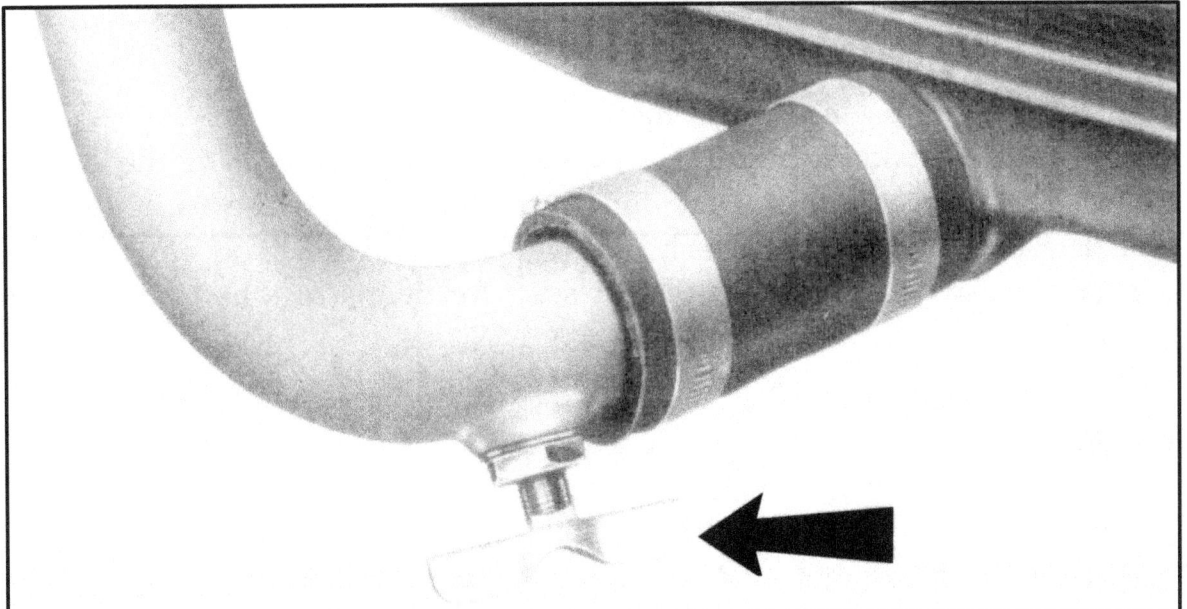

Fig. 9 - Radiator drain cock.

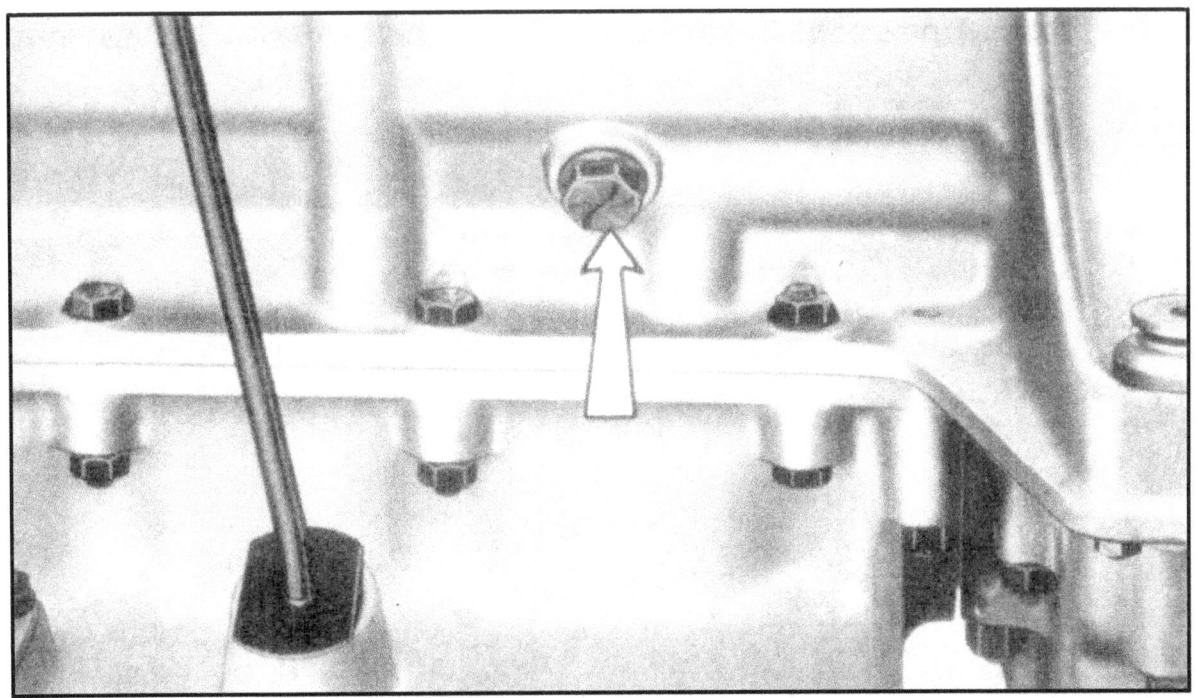

Fig. 10 - Crankcase drain cock.

Running instructions

Heating and ventilation

The car heating and ventilation equipment is situated at the centre of the dashboard and comprises:

1. A water radiator inside the heater box.
2. A fresh air intake between the windscreen and the rear of the bonnet.
3. A cable operated throw cock for warm water from the radiator.
4. A demister fan to draw fresh air over the heater.
5. There is also a fan behind the rear seat, for demisting the rear window.

Hot weather

Fresh air may be induced by:

1. Moving the facia mounted air control lever to the right and opening the heater doors - situated either side of the heater box - see fig. 11 - item 6.
2. Turning the facia ventilator controls to permit a full air flow.
3. Pulling knobs 7 & 8 diagram 11, to admit fresh air around the passenger's and driver's feet.
4. The air flow produced by action No. 1 may be increased by switching on the fan - though this is not effective above 40 mph.

Mild weather

De-misting.
Leave the heater doors closed but move the facia mounted air control lever to the right. The use of the fan will accelerate de-misting.

Cold weather

Heating, de-misting and de-frosting.
Move the heater temperature control lever fully to the right, but the air control lever only partially to the right.

Running instructions
page 19

Ventilation and heating - continued

Open the heater doors and switch on the fan - marked 'D'.

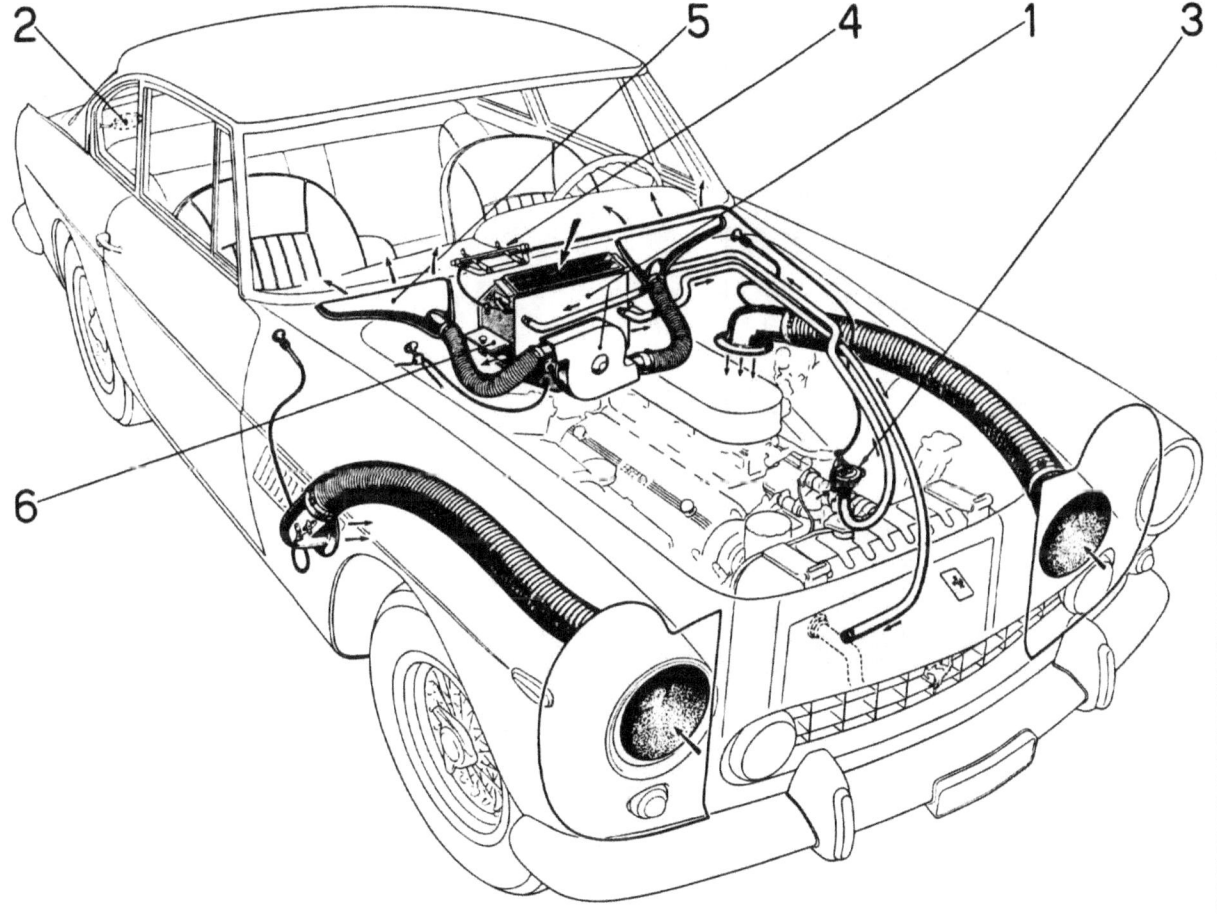

Fig. 11 - Ventilation and heating installation.

1) Ventilator and heating motor unit; 2) rear ventilator motor unit; 3) warm water cock; 4) controls group; 5) de-mist warm air inflow; 6) heater doors.

Running instructions

Front seats adjustment

Front seats may be adjusted backwards and forwards by pulling up on Bar 1 (Fig. 12).

The rake of the seat backrests may be adjusted by rotating cam 1. Fig. 13 - there are two of these cams per seat and they must both be turned when altering the rake.

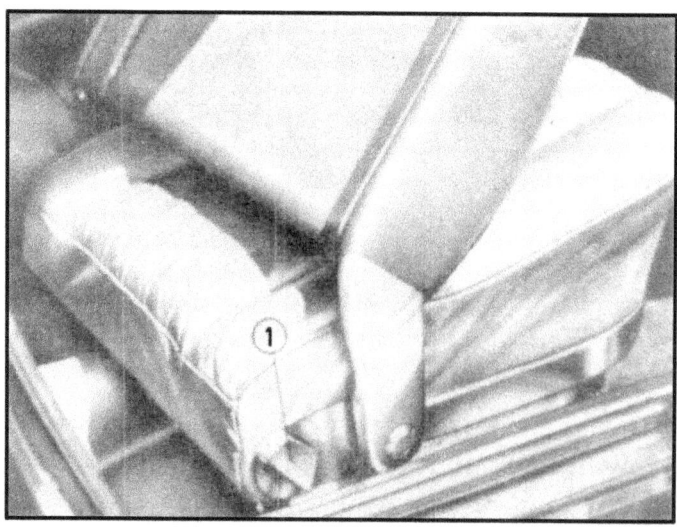

Fig. 12 - Front seats adjustment : 1) lever.

Fig. 13 - Rake : 1) rotating cam.

Running instructions

Operating the windows

To raise or lower the side windows, turn handle 1) fig. 14.

Swivelling quarter lights are on the front doors and are controlled by handwheels (2).

Fig. 14 - 1) Handle to raise side window; 2) quarter light knob; 3) door lever.

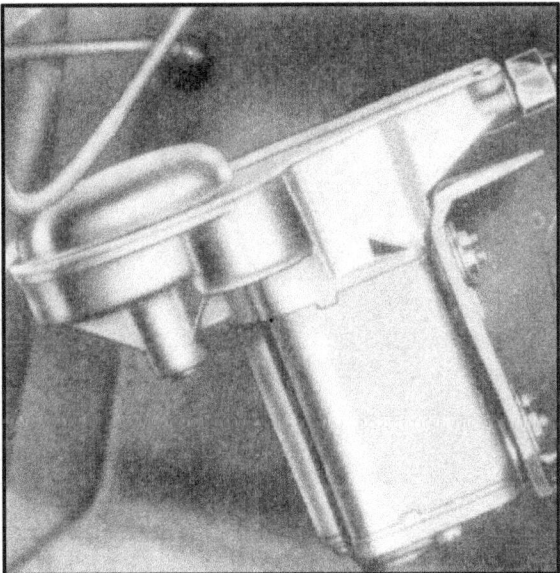

Fig. 15 - Windscreen wiper motor.

Windscreen wiper

To remove the motor, disconnect the battery, break the connection to the motor, remove the motor cover plate, and disconnect the flexible drive.

Undo the mounting nuts.

When assembling, make sure the flexible drive is clean and greased.

Running instructions page 22

Opening the bonnet

The bonnet is hinged at the front end, and is opened by pulling up lever 29 (fig. 5), pushing the safety catch 1 (fig. 16) forward, and lifting by the rear edge. Two spiral springs hold the bonnet open, though a small stay is also provided to prop the bonnet open, say, in a wind. To close, it is sufficient to lower the bonnet for the first 10-12 inches, and then let it fall.

Running instructions   page 23

Opening the boot

Press the barrel of the boot lock and lift the lid.

There is a small stay, similar to the one on the bonnet, fitted at the bottom left hand corner of the lid.

The spare wheel, the jack and the tool kit are located in the boot.

Fig. 17 - Boot.

Running instructions   page 24

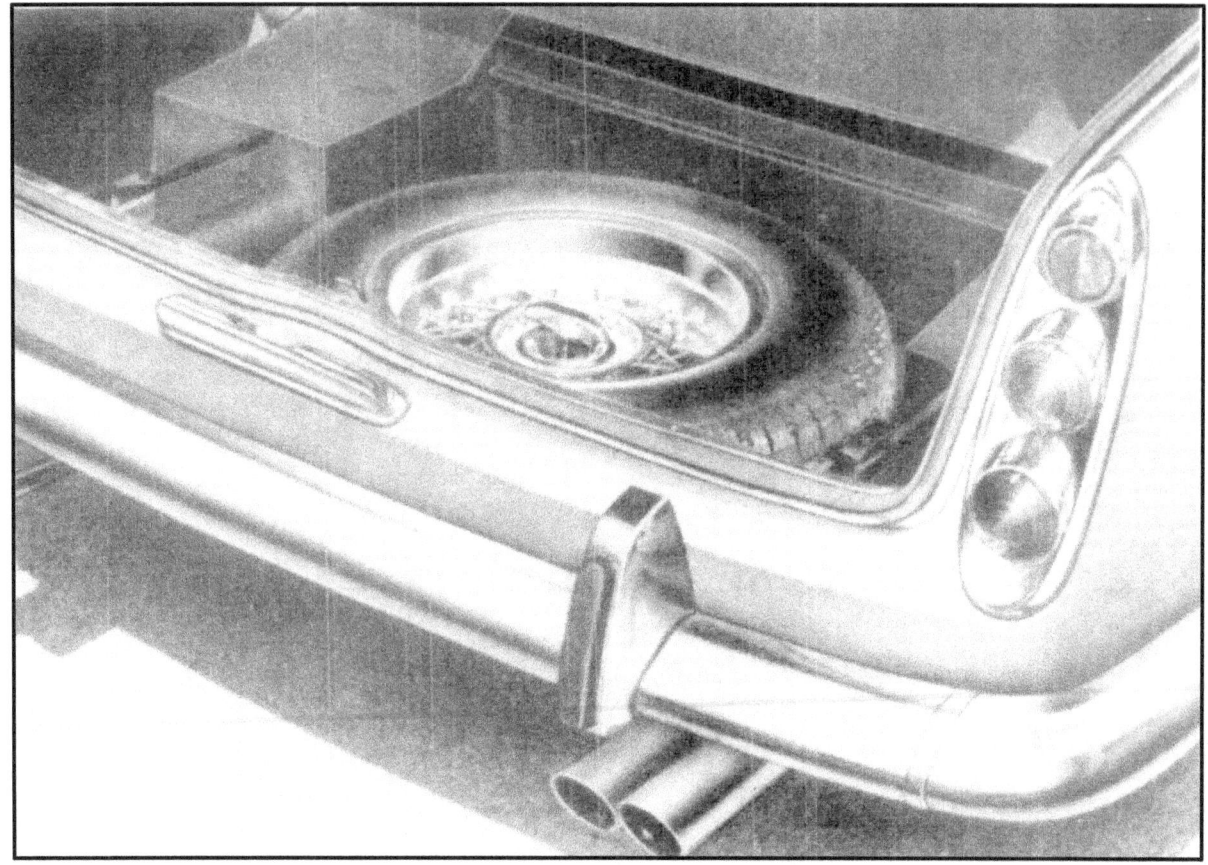

Fig. 18 - Housing the spare wheel in the boot.

Jacking up the car.

Remove the chromed plug, insert the jack and wind - see fig. 19.

To remove the wheels

Offside   - Tap the hub caps clockwise
Nearside - Tap the hub caps anti-clockwise.

Running instructions　　　　　　　　　　　　　page 25

Fig. 19 - Jacking-up the car.

Washing the car

1. We would suggest this is done on a proper washdown so that the paint is not damaged.

2. Never wash the car under a full sun or when the coachwork is still warm.

3. We would suggest that the brakes be applied lightly once or twice immediately after a washdown, to dry out the pads.

Third part
Routine maintenance

page 26

Lubrication

Each 300 miles	1) Check the engine oil level	see page 28
Each 2500 miles	2) Change the engine oil and filters	» » 28
	3) Check the oil level in the gear box and overdrive	» » 58
	4) Check the oil level in the rear axle	» » 60
	5) Check the oil level in the steering box	» » 64
	6) Grease the front wheel suspension arm pivots	» » 61
	7) Grease the steering drag link joints	» » 65
	8) Grease the universal joint and the sliding coupling of the propeller shaft	» » 59
	9) Grease the clutch drive shaft	» » 55
Each 5000 miles	10) Change the oil in the gear box and the overdrive	» » 58
	11) Change the oil in the rear axle	» » 60
	12) Top up the level of the brake fluid supply tank	» » 69
	13) Grease the front wheel bearings	» » 66
	14) Lubricate the wheel hubs	» » 66
	15) Lubricate door hinges and bonnet locks	» » 25
	16) Wash the rear leaf springs with oil	» » 62

NOTE: 1. In winter, or very wet weather, carry out items 6, 7, and 8 more frequently.
2. See Fig. 20 for location of filler plugs, grease nipples etc.

Routine maintenance

Lubrication

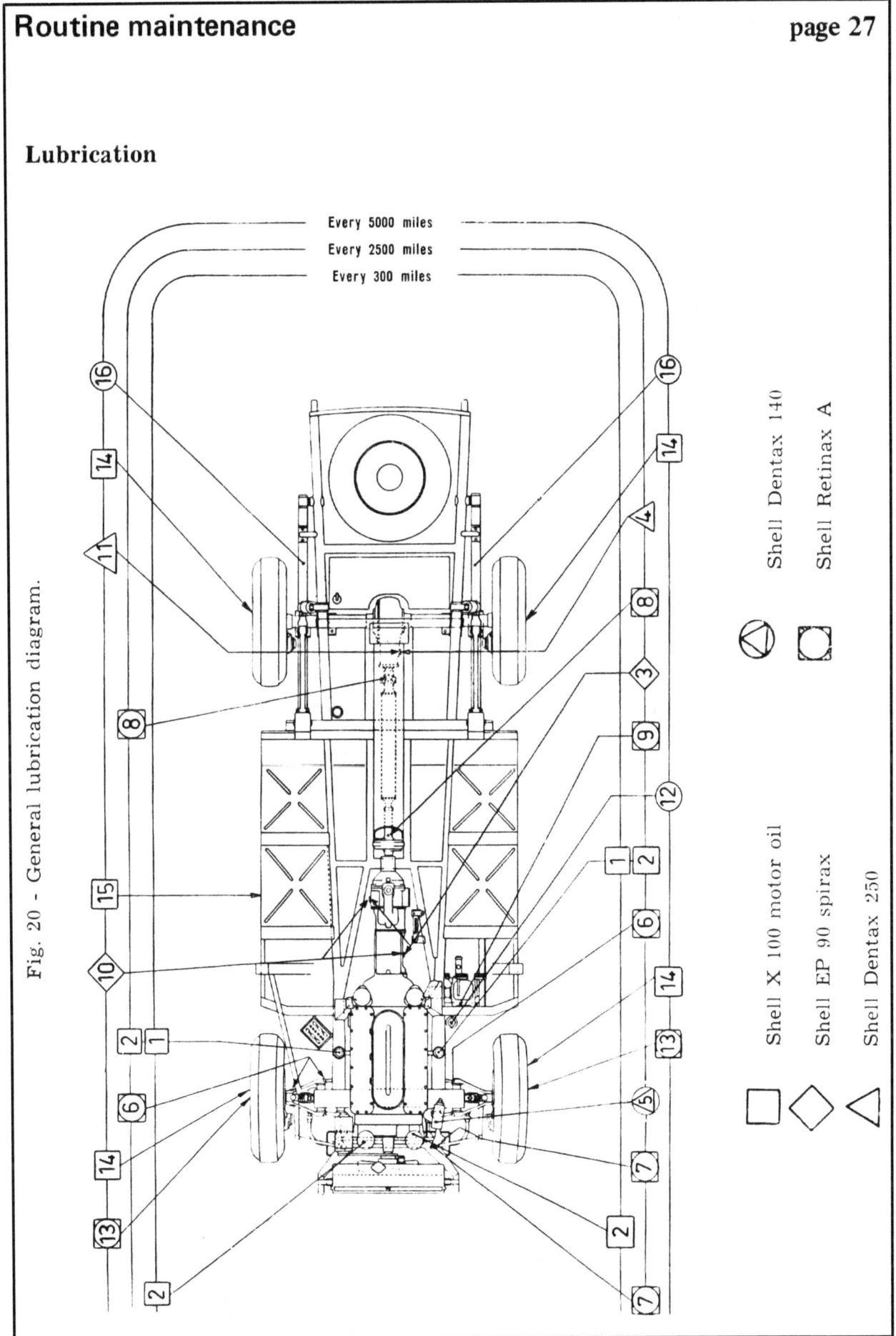

Fig. 20 - General lubrication diagram.

Routine maintenance page 28

Lubrication

Engine lubrication is by a gear pressure pump mounted in the engine timing case, and the oil is filtered by a fine straining filter PH3, and a second partial filter PB50.

The oil level should not be allowed to drop below the minimum level on the dipstick, nor filled above the maximum. The level should be checked before starting the engine, and every 300 miles.

With a new car, or overhauled engine, oil changes should be made as indicated in page 12.

The oil pressure may be regulated by an adjustable cap on the pressure relief valve, but should the pressure drop below the minimum permissible (see page 7) it is best that a skilled mechanic adjust the relief valve.

Never allow the engine to run with the pressure below normal.

Max. oil pressure - 7000 RPM	85 psi
Min. oil pressure at 7000 RPM	55-60 psi
Min. oil pressure at 700-800 RPM	35-40 psi

Routine maintenance

LUBRICATION

Every 2500 miles

Change the cartridge bodies of both filters using the special tool to remove them from their seats. This is most important in the interest of long engine life.

Be sure there are no oil leaks after the change.

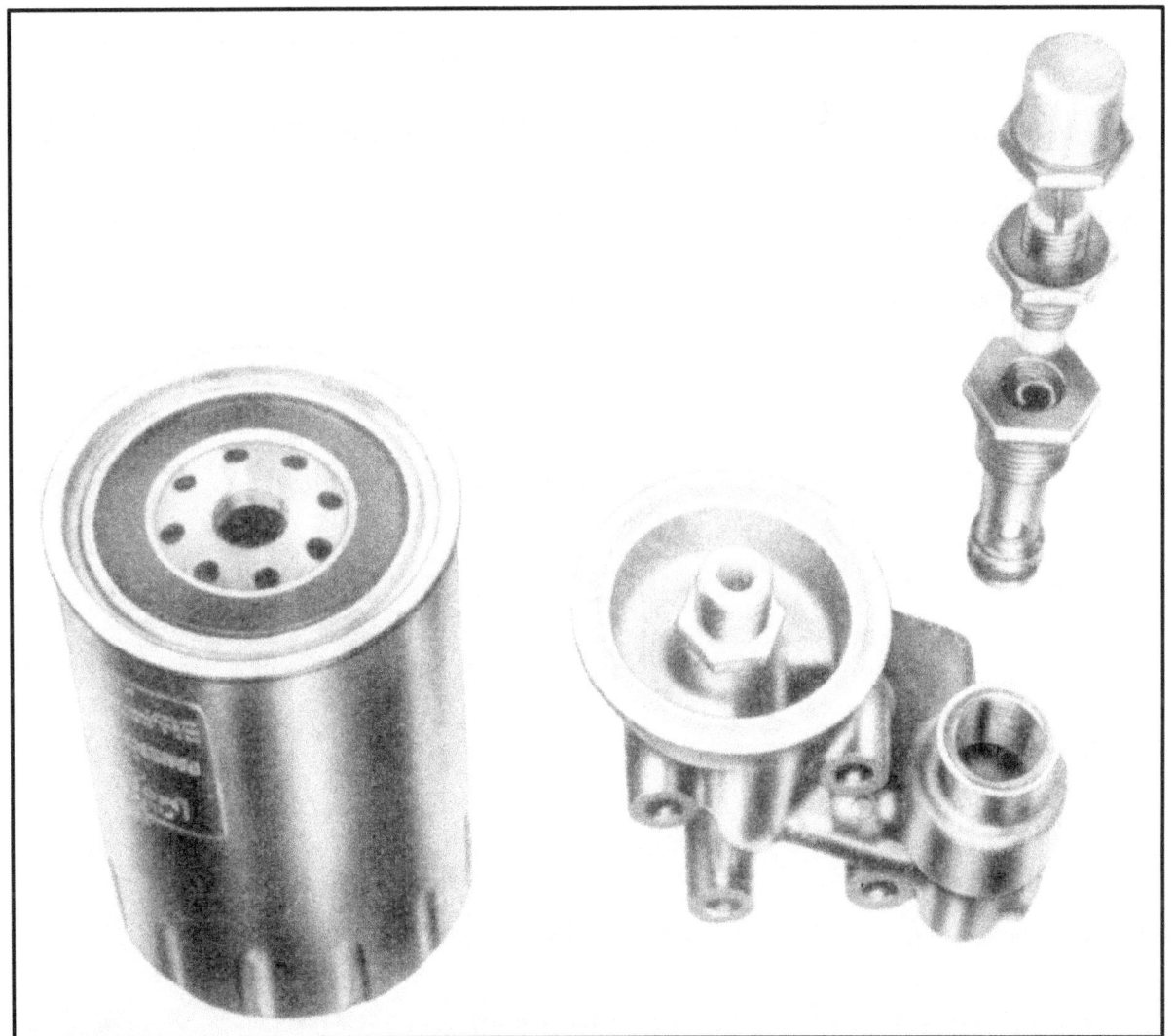

Fig. 21 - Oil filter.

Routine maintenance   page 30

LUBRICATION

Changing from a non-detergent to a detergent oil

A detergent oil will clean the deposits, left in various parts of the engine by a non-detergent oil, which may clog the filters and cause damage to the big-end and main bearings. It is advisable to carry out the following procedure.

1) Draining the oil:

    Warm engine to working temperature

    Drain the oil

    Remove filters, wash them with petrol and blow them through with compressed air.

2) Fill with new oil

3) Change the oil, as above, after **300 miles,** but fit new filters

4) Thereafter change the oil every **2500 miles.**

Routine maintenance

LUBRICATION — LUBRICANTS TO BE USED

ENGINE	In Summer	with temperature over +15°C Shell X 100 40 or Shell X 100 Multigrade 20W/40
	Middle season	with temperature from —5°C up to +15°C Shell X 100 30 or Shell X 100 Multigrade 20W/40
	In Winter	with temperature below —5°C. Shell X 100 20W or Shell X 100 Multigrade 10W/30

WARNING: IN RESTORING THE OIL LEVEL IN THE SUMP **NEVER USE** OIL OF A DIFFERENT TYPE OR QUALITY

GEARBOX AND OVERDRIVE	Shell Spirax E P 90
REAR AXLE	Shell Dentax 250
STEERING BOX	Shell Dentax 140
BRAKE FLUID SUPPLY TANK	Shell Donax B SAE 70 R3 Dunlop Racing Brake Fluid (Castrol).
FRONT-WHEEL SUSPENSION ARMS STUB AXLE PINS UNIVERSAL JOINT STEERING TIE ROD KNUCKLES	Shell Retinax A
FRONT WHEEL BEARINGS	Shell Alvania Grease 3 or Shell Retinax DX
COOLING SYSTEM	Shell Anti-Freeze

Routine maintenance   page 32

GENERAL

Before using the car	1) Check the radiator level	page.	13
	2) Check the engine oil level	»	28
	3) Check the tyre pressures	»	76
	4) Check the brake fluid level	»	69
Every 300 miles	5) Check the radiator level	»	53
	6) Check the tyre pressures	»	76
Every 1500 miles	7) Check the level of the electrolyte in the batteries	»	80
Every 2500 miles	8) Check the tension of the dynamo driving belt	»	54
	9) Clean the carburettor air filters	»	45
	10) Check the foot brake pedal adjustment	»	73
	11) Change the tyres around	»	78
	12) Check, and if necessary, clean and adjust the contact breaker points	»	47
	13) Inject two or three drops of oil into the dynamo	»	79
Every 5000 miles	14) Change the spark plugs	»	50
	15) Check the valve clearance	»	35
	16) Check the timing chain tension	»	38
	17) Change the disc brake pads and bleed the system	»	71
	18) Check the operation of the shock absorbers and their bushes for wear	»	63
	19) Check the starter motor brushes and commutator	»	79
	20) Adjust the clutch pedal travel	»	55
	21) Adjust the play in the steering gear	»	64
Every 10,000 miles	22) Check the front wheel 'toe out' and camber	»	66
	23) Clean the petrol filter	»	39
	24) Check the carburettors and controls	»	40

N. B. Should at any time the front suspension suffer a severe shock, toe out and camber must be checked. In this case the joints should be replaced.

Routine maintenance

page 33

GENERAL

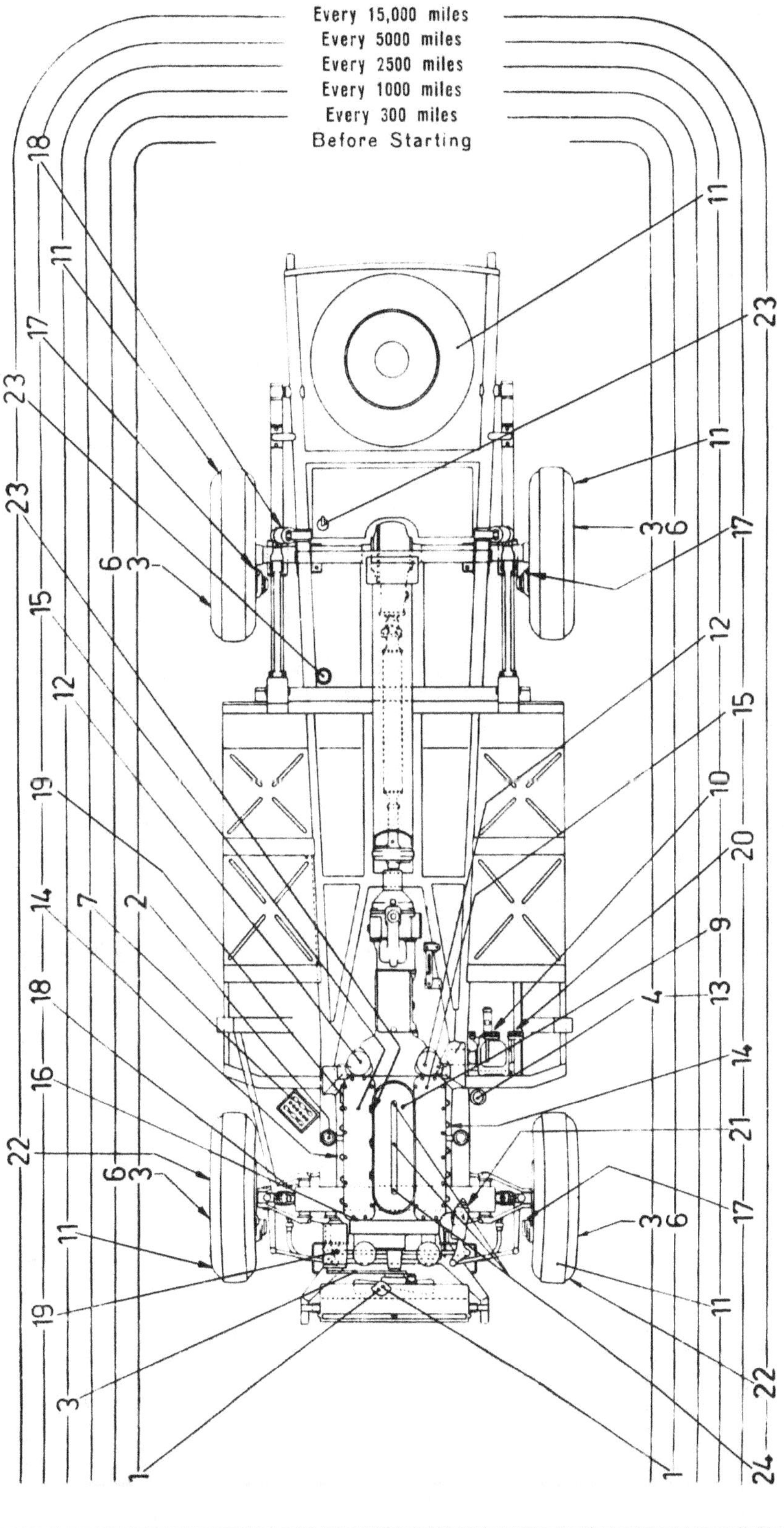

Fig. 22 - Routine maintenance operations diagram.

Every 15,000 miles
Every 5000 miles
Every 2500 miles
Every 1000 miles
Every 300 miles
Before Starting

Fourth part
Engine servicing

Timing system

Each cylinder head has a single centrally set camshaft, driven, at the front end, by chain.

There are two valves per chamber set at 60°.

The valve rockers are fitted with adjustable tappets and roller cam followers.

VALVE TIMING DATA

Inlet	Opens Closes	27° before TDC 65° after BDC
Exhaust	Opens Closes	74° before BDC 16° after TDC
Valve clearance with cold engine	Inlet exhaust	(mm. 0.15) .006" (mm. 0.20) .008"

Engine servicing
page 35

Valve clearance adjustment

The valve clearance should be set with a cold engine, using the proper tools. The clearance between the valve stem and tappet should be .006" inlet and .008" exhaust.

When the clearances are set, place the steel or brass shim, provided in the tool kit, behind the timing housing cover, fit the rocker cover down on its gasket and remove the shim before tightening the cover nuts. This is to prevent the rocker cover catching, and distorting the 'O' ring in the rear of the timing housing.

Fig. 23 - Adjusting the valve clearance.

Engine servicing — page 36

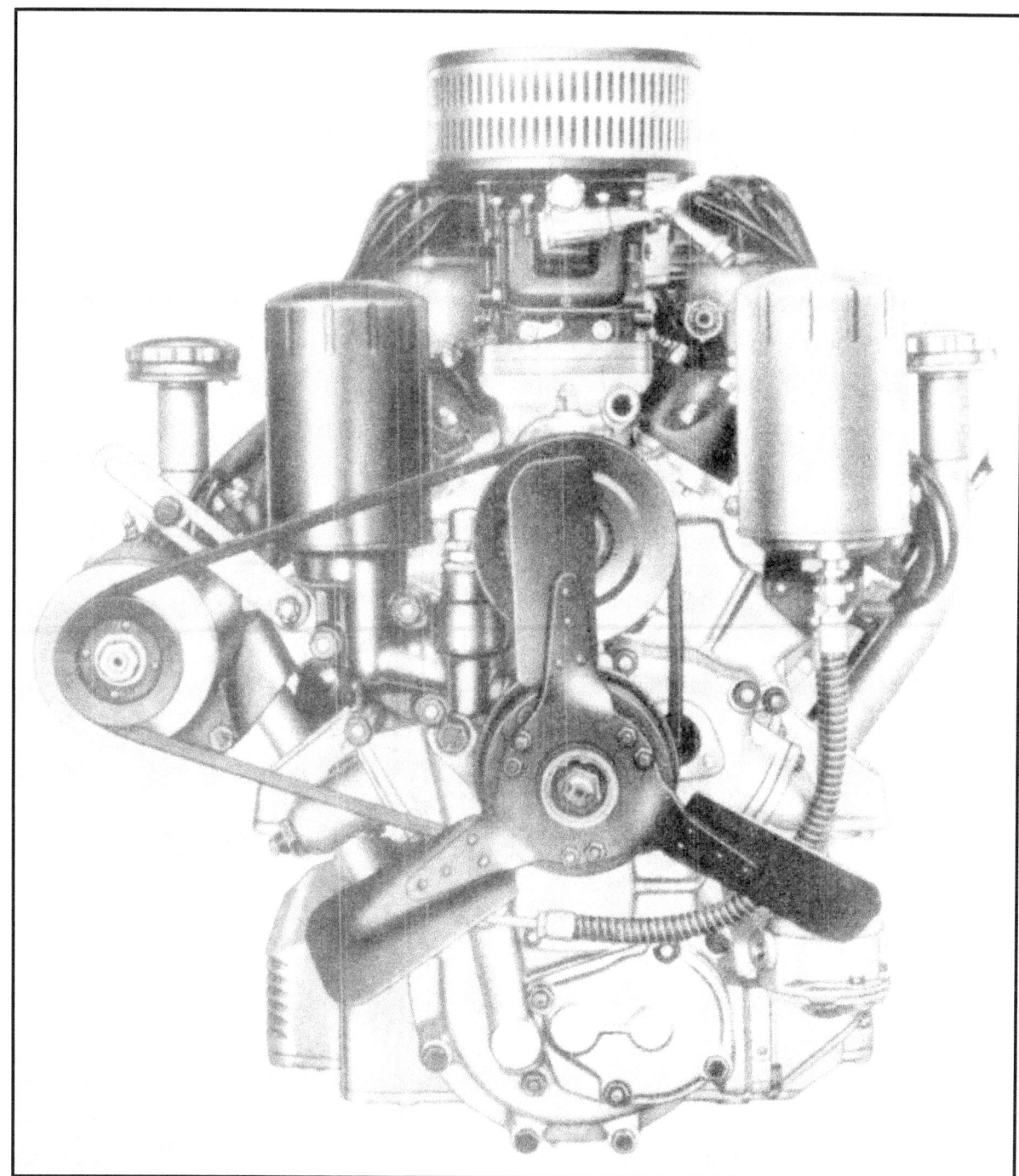

Fig. 24 - Front view of the engine.

Engine servicing   page 37

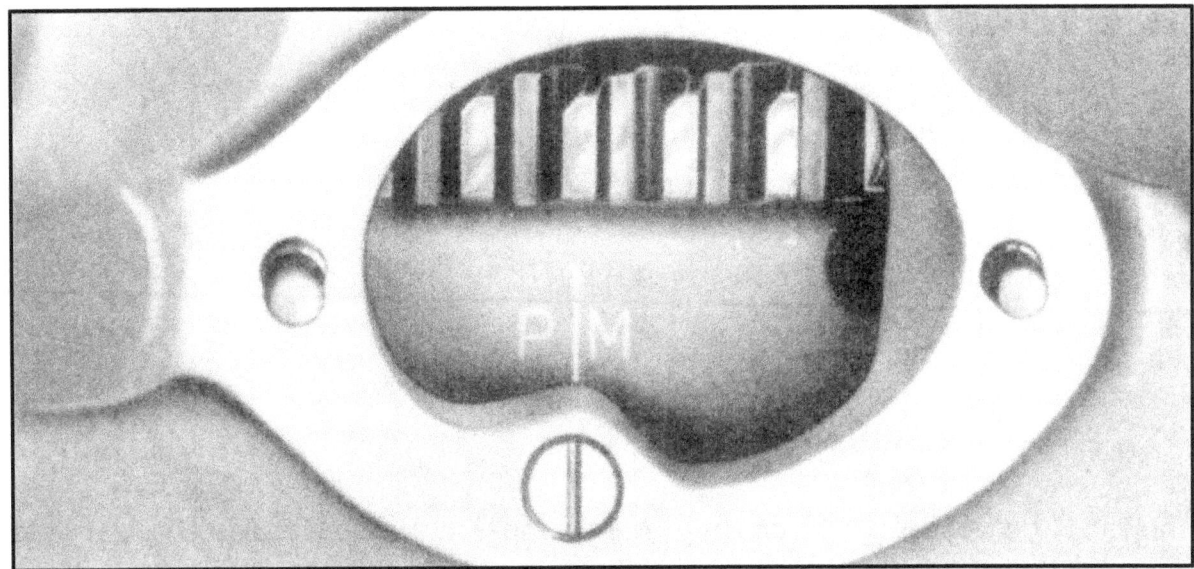

Fig. 25 - Reference points engraved on the flywheel (PMS).

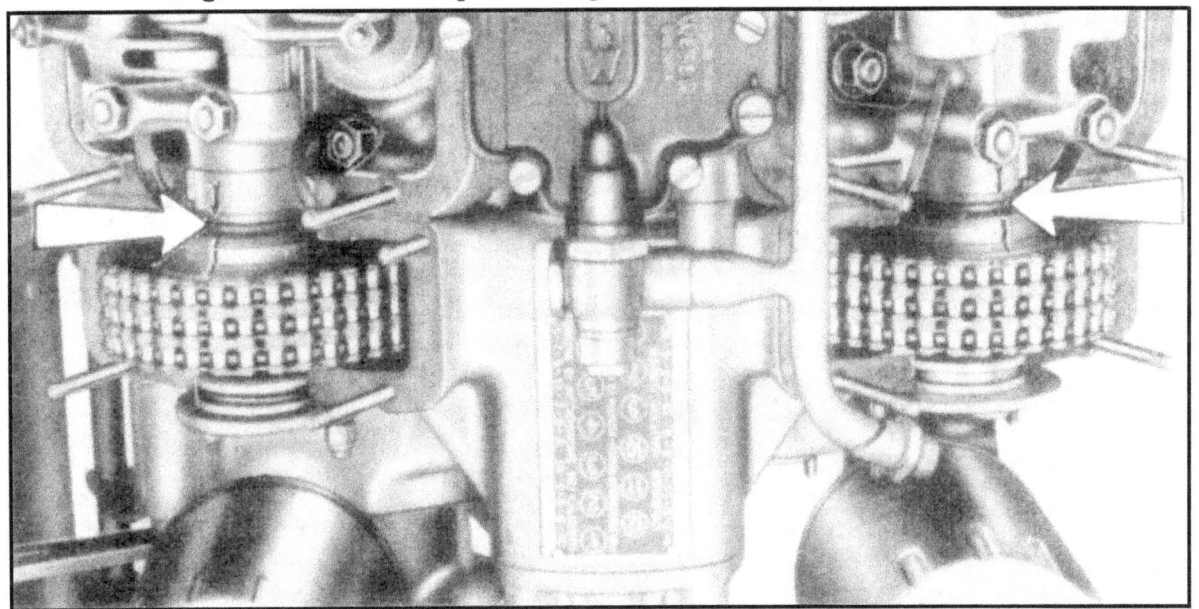

Fig. 26 - Reference points engraved on camshaft timing wheels and on camshaft bearing caps.

Checking the engine timing

Turn the engine until No. 1 piston is at TDC, and both valves are closed. Remove the inspection plate on the flywheel casing. The mark PM 1/6 should be exactly opposite the centre of a set screw on the casing, which serves as a datum point. Remove both rocker covers. The scribe marks on the camshafts and timing wheels should now be co-incident with the arrows stamped on the front camshaft bearing casings. See Figs. 25 & 26.

N.B. Should the engine have to be stripped, set up as above and note the various markings, as they can become obscured.

Engine servicing

Timing chain

Should it be necessary to adjust the timing chain tension, slacken lock-nut (1) Fig. 27.

This slackens the grip of the casing onto the chain tensioner and allows the tensioner to take up tension automatically, as it is spring loaded.

Screw up pin (2) Fig. 27, until it is felt to bear against the tensioner, tighten its lock-nut, and then tighten lock-nut (1) to 62-66 lbs/ft.

WARNING

Should it be necessary to change one or more cylinder head gaskets, make sure lock nut (1) is tightened to 62-66 lbs/ft, after 300 miles have been completed.

Fig. 27 - Tensioner casing lock-nut (1) Adjuster pin (2).

Engine servicing

Fuel pumps

Fuel is pumped to the carburettors by a mechanical pump, with a diaphram-type **Fispa Sup. 150,** and fitted with a wire gauze filter (Fig. 28) also by an auxiliary electrical pump, type **Fispa PBE 10** (Fig. 29).

Fuel starvation could be caused by

1. The pump filter clogging.
2. Inlet or delivery valves or seats, dirty or worn. If so, wash in petrol and replace worn parts.
3. Worn or torn diaphram.

It is possible to check on the diaphram by seeing if petrol drips from the pump air vent.

Fig. 28 - Mechanic fuel pump.

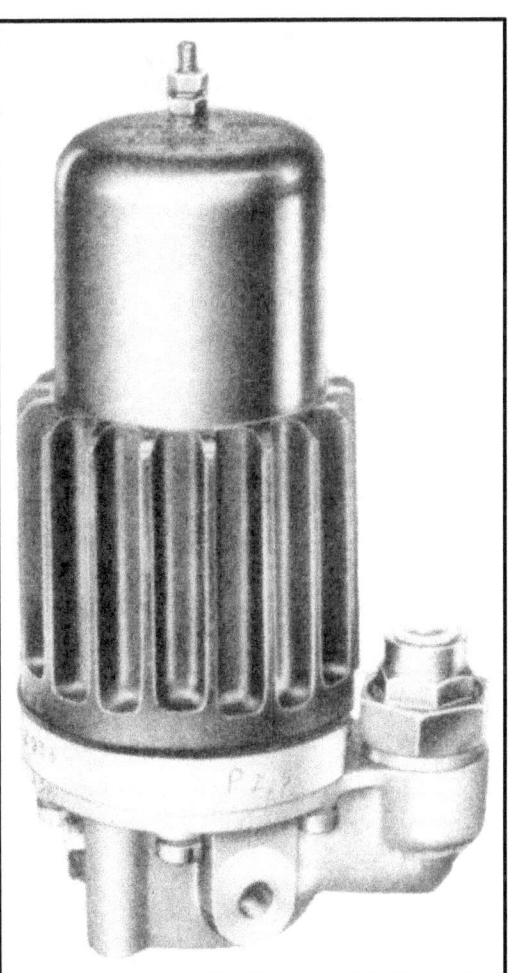

Fig. 29 - Auxiliary electric pump.

Engine servicing

page 40

CARBURETTORS

Carburation is by three double choke 40 DCL/6 **Weber** carburettors.

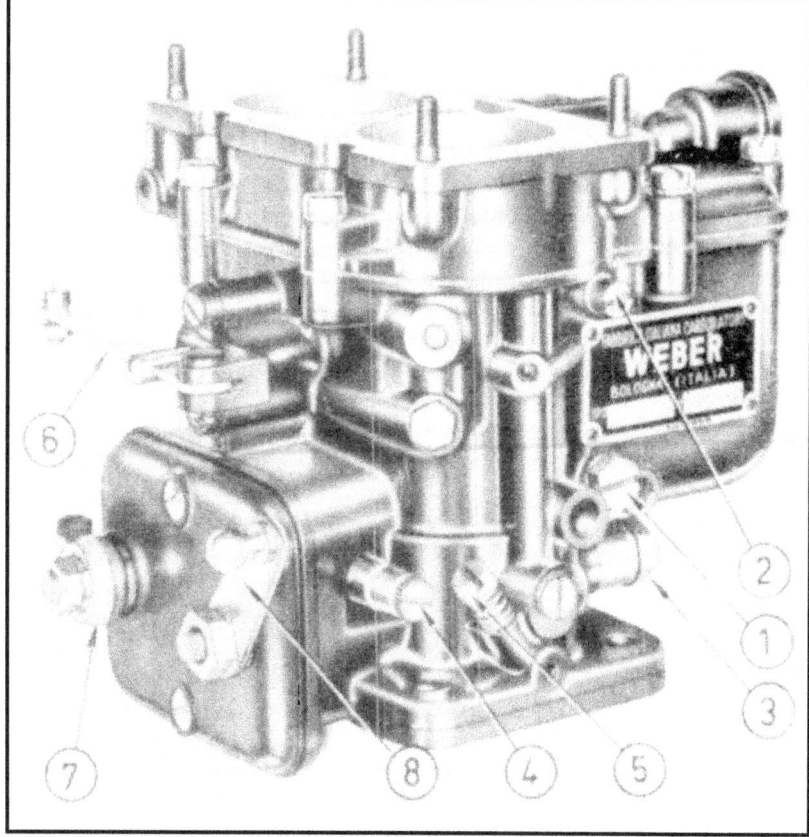

Fig. 30 - Carburettor Weber 40 DCL/6 - seen from the offside.

1) main jet ;
2) slow running jet ;
3) pickup pump drive ;
4) adjustment screw for min. opening of throttle;
5) idling mixture adjustment screw ;
6) choke lever ;
7) synchronisation clamp for second throttle ;
8) driving lever ;
9) throttle clamp bolt.

ADJUSTMENT DATA

Diffusers	mm. 27		Center squares	mm. 2.50
Main jets	mm. 1.50		Air brake jets	mm. 1.80
Slow running jets	mm. 0.60		Needle valve seat	mm. 1.75
Pump jets	mm. 0.60		Starting jet	mm. 1.40
Pump stroke	mm. 3		Sump F/8 with 20 holes	

Float level - 3 mm between top of float and cover.

Engine servicing

page 41

CARBURETTORS

Never try to tune the carburettors.

The operation described below should only be attemped by trained personnel ; the description itself is only intended as a guide and does not include sufficient detail to tune the carburettors properly.

Tuning should only be necessary if the engine hesitates on pickup, or is irregular or tends to stop when idling, and should be done with a warm engine and after a check has been made on the ignition, and cylinder compressions.

BALANCING THE CARBURETTORS

Equipment required

1. Synchro tester.
2. Screwdriver.
3. 8 mm box spanner.

Procedure

1. Remove air cleaners complete.
2. Release the clamp bolts on the accelerator linkage on the front two carburettors - bolts situated on the near side.

Engine servicing page 42

3. Release the throttle clamps (9) Fig. 30 on all carburettors.

4. Place the synchro tester in the offside intake of the rear carburettor, and adjust the valve in the centre of the tester so that the float is half way up the gauge glass, and coincident with one of the scribe marks. The gauge glass must be vertical. The valve in the centre of the tester must not be moved again, throughout the remaining adjustments.

5. Place the tester in the near side intake of the same carburettor.

6. By means of the throttle adjusting screw - located in the near side of the carburettor, opposite No. 4 Fig. 30. Adjust the throttle opening until the float on the testers is in the same position as before.

N. B. If the float is higher up the gauge glass than in the first instance, when the tester is inserted, unscrew the throttle adjusting screw $1/8$ turn, remove the tester, tap the butterfly closed with a screwdriver, and replace tester.

Remember, only when the float has to be moved **down** the gauge glass must the operation described just above be completed, as the butterfly valve will not move by itself when the throttle adjusting screw is **unscrewed** - applicable to near-side intakes only.

Engine servicing

7. Repeat placing the tester in the intakes of the middle and then the front carburettors, dealing with the offside intakes first, and always adjusting the tester float to the same scribe mark on the gauge glass.

8. Repeat the operation, starting on the offside intake of the carburettor and finishing on the nearside of the front carburettor, arriving at a final engine tick-over of 750 RPM.

9. Assuming all throttle openings are now the same, i.e. balanced, tighten up on all the throttle clamp bolts (9) Fig. 30 taking care not to disturb the nut adjacent to clamp (7) Fig. 30.

10. Tighten the remaining two clamp bolts on the accelerator linkage of the front two carburettors.

11. Slow running mixture adjustment.
    Screw in the idling mixture adjustment screw (5) Fig. 30 on the offside of the rear carburettor. This cuts out the two cylinders served by this intake - slowly screw out again until the engine is heard to pick up on all 12 cylinders - unscrew by a further $1/8$ turn. Complete this operation on the remaining five screws.

12. Refit air cleaners.

Engine servicing
page 44

Adjustment of carburettors by synchroniser

Fig. 31 - Synchroniser for carburettors adjustment.

The carburettors will be correctly tuned when, on a road test, with a warm engine and in top gear, the car accelerates cleanly over 1000 RPM. If a popping noise is heard in the exhaust on the overrun from 6000 RPM in second gear, richen the idling mixture a little.

Engine servicing

Air cleaner

Each carburettor is equipped with an air cleaner of special fabric and circular in shape.

The three cleaners are contained in one housing the cover of which is easily removed by unscrewing the three wing nuts on the top.

Each 2500 miles

Take care of the filter elements when removing them from the housing : wash them in petrol ; blow them through with compressed air (from the inside outwards) and then wet them with engine oil.

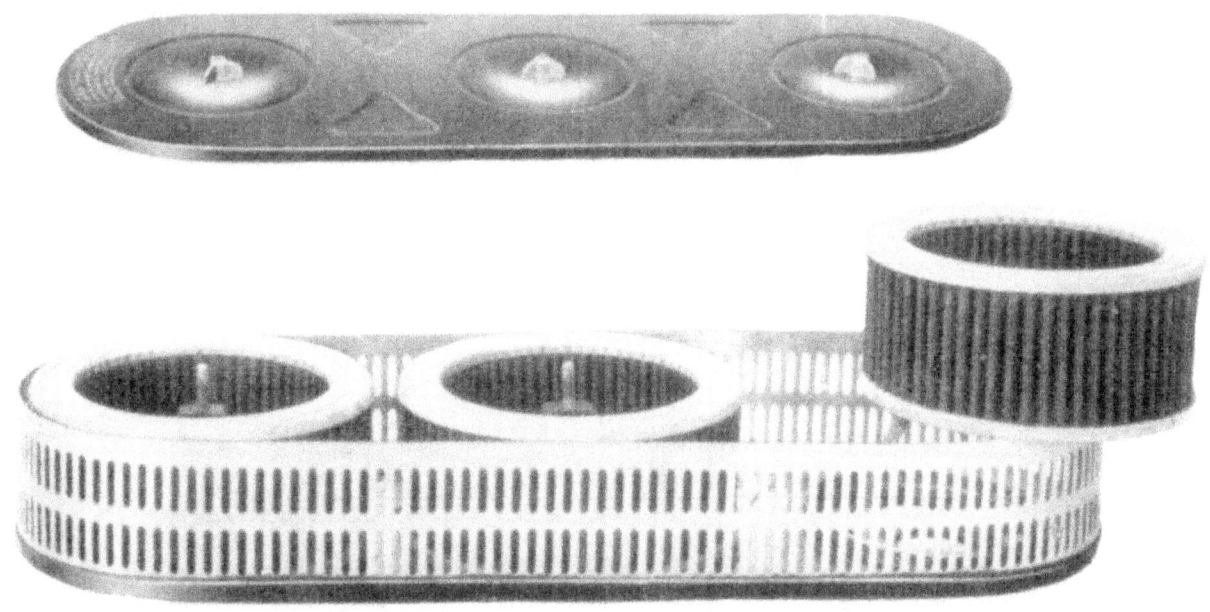

Fig. 32 - Air cleaner.

Engine servicing

page 46

Ignition

A 12v battery supplies current to two coils and two distributors (one for each bank of cylinders).

Each distributor has two sets of contacts and an automatic advance device which works on a variable curve designed to give maximum engine power throughout the rev range.

Firing order

| 1 - 7 - 5 - 11 - 3 - 9 - 6 - 12 - 2 - 8 - 4 - 10 |

No. 1 cylinder is the front cylinder on the offside bank, No. 7 the rear on the nearside.

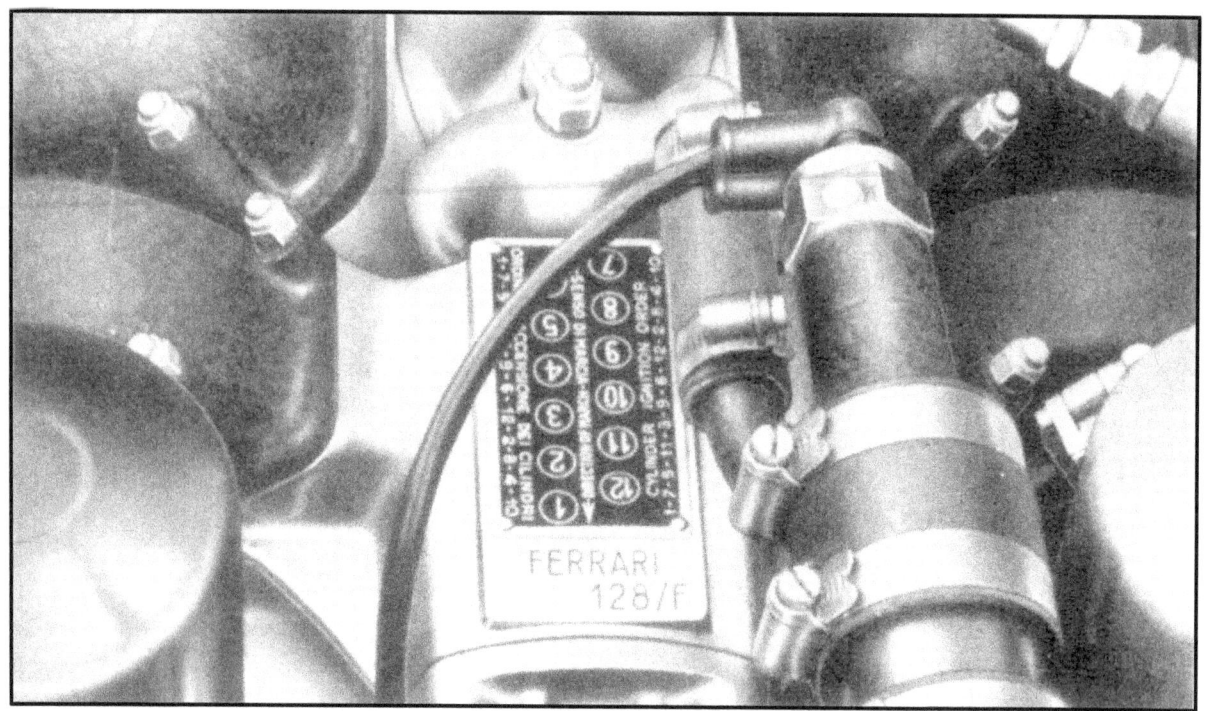

Fig. 33 - Firing order.

	distributor	fixed spark advance	maximum spark advance
Ignition spark advance	Marelli S 85 A V 12°-15°	10°-12°	3600 r.p.m. to 7000 r.p.m. 40°-42°

Engine servicing
page 47

Ignition

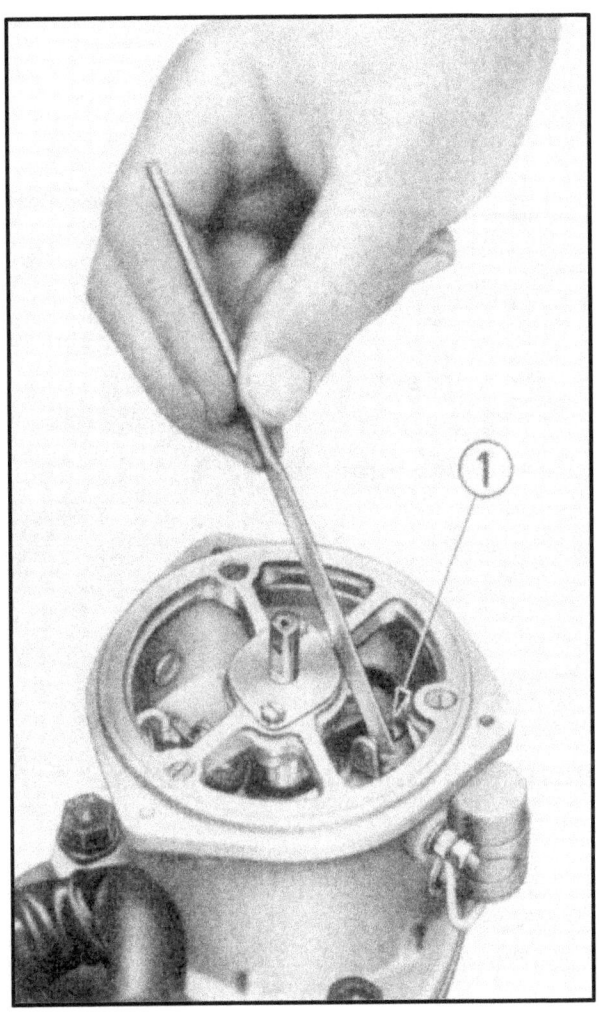

Fig. 34 - Ignition distributor: 1) screw for setting the contacts.

Contact breaker setting

The gap should be .015" - .017"
The adjustment is made on an adjusting screw (screw 1 Fig. 34).
The contacts should be kept clean and if necessary ground with a very fine file.

Every 2,500 miles

Remove the rotor arm - clean the contacts with a cloth soaked in petrol and check the gap setting. Clean the inside of the cap.

Engine servicing

Ignition

Timing check

Offside bank

1) Remove distributor cap and check the contact breaker setting.

2) The static ignition timing is 10° before TDC, marked on the flywheel as AF 10, marked just before 1/6.

It is more accurate to check the automatic advance by stroboscope.

— Remove the flywheel inspection cover and set the engine to 5000-5500 rpm.

— Shine the pistol on the flywheel opposite the datum point, when the mark 42 AM should be coincident. Adjust, if necessary, by turning the distributor.

Nearside bank

The static ignition timing is 10° before TDC, marked on the flywheel as 10 AF, just before 7/12.

Engine servicing

page 49

Ignition

Synchronising the opening of the contacts after stripping, or when replacing the contacts.

The gap between the opening of one set of contacts to the other must be 60° - measured by fitting a dial face on top of the distributor.

Fig. 35 - Reference points engraved on flywheel : 1) reference point 10 AF of spark advance; 2) reference point 42 AM of max. spark advance.

Engine servicing

Ignition

Spark Plugs

Every 2500 miles clean the spark plugs and check the gap between the electrodes; Reset if necessary. The gap between the electrodes should be of 0.55 ÷ 0.60 mm.

Every 5000 miles. Change the plugs.

We recommend Marchal HF 34 spark plugs.

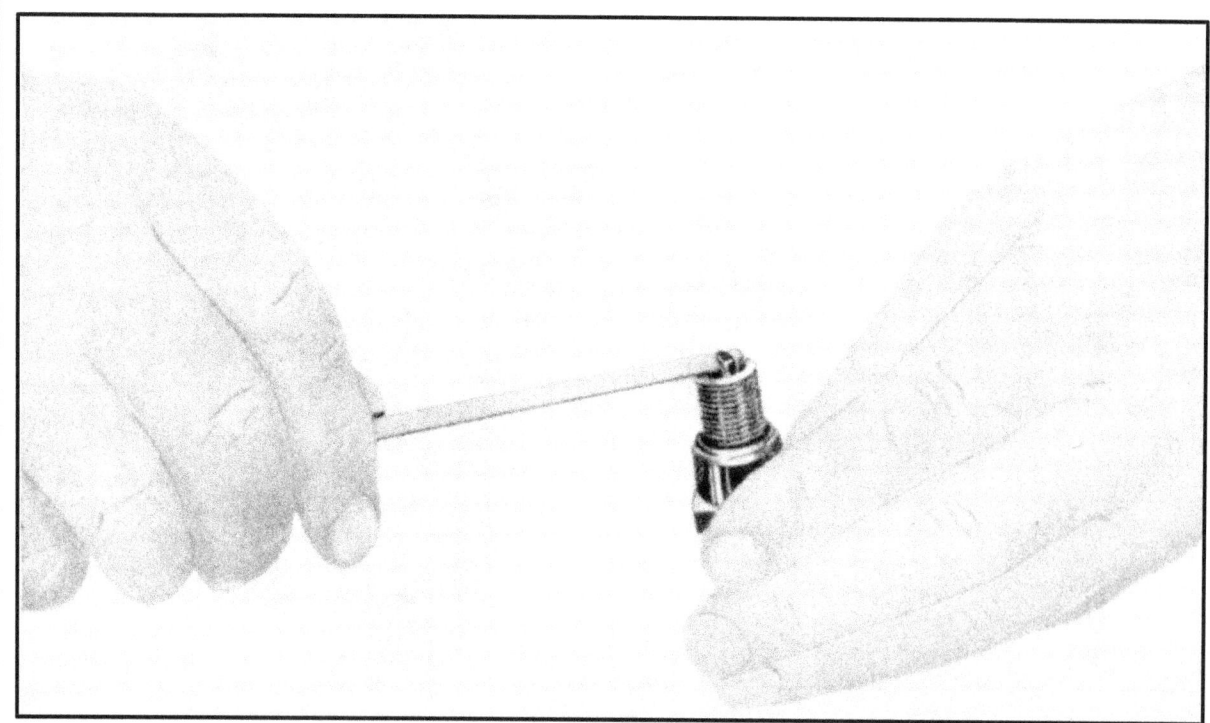

Fig. 36 - Setting the electrodes gap.

Engine servicing

page 51

Cooling system

Water circulation for the cooling of the engine is by means of a centrifugal pump, fixed on the front of the timing housing and driven by its chain.

Every 10,000 miles. Check the sealing of the pump.

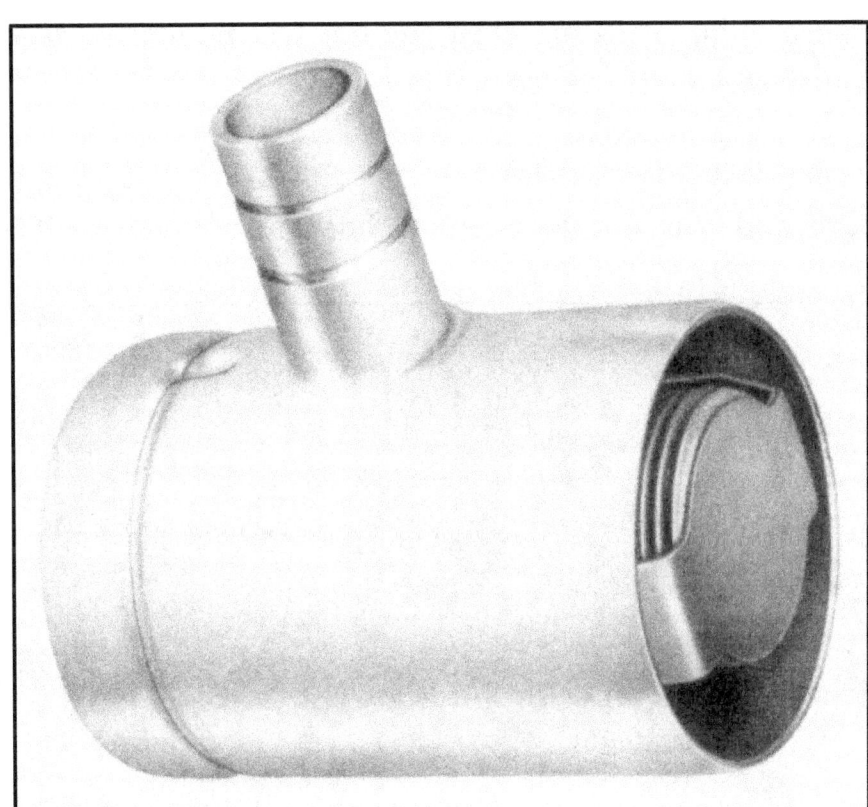

Fig. 37 - Thermostat.

THERMOSTAT

This is situated in the top radiator hose and is set to open at 70° - 77° C/155° - 165° F.

The water temperature should never rise above 90° - 95°C/190° - 195° F.

The system is pressurised at 7 lbs sq.in.

Engine servicing

page 52

Peugeot Fan

There is a thermostatic switch fitted in the top radiator hose, which closes at 84°C/178°F allowing current to pass to an electromagnetic switch engaging the fan. The thermostatic switch disengages the fan when the temperature falls below 75°C/159°F.

There is an adjustment on the electro magnetic switch, to make sure the fan works at the A/M temperatures.

Every 2500 miles Check the lead and brush and the gap between the armature and the electro magnet. The gap should be .004"-014". See Fig. 38.

Fig. 38 - Fan-drive: 1) insulated ring for the contact; 2) gap adjusting screws; 3) gap between the free floating pulley and the driven body of the fan; 4) current brush.

Engine servicing — page 53

Cooling - Radiator

Every 300 miles check the level, if necessary adding soft water - e.g. rain water.

Should the level need constantly topping up, check the radiator cap valve and seating, the hose couplings and the water pump for leaks.

Every so often say 6 monthly or before filling with antifreeze, the system should be flushed through with a solution of $3\,^1/_3$ gallons of water and 14 oz of sodium carbonate.

Allow the engine to idle for 15 mins., drain, allow the engine to cool and then hose clear water through the system, leaving the drain tap open.

Fill with water and allow the engine to tick over for a few minutes.

Drain and refill once more.

Engine servicing

page 54

Cooling

Fig. 39 - Checking the dynamo belt tension.

Every 2,500 miles - check the dynamo belt tension, press down on the belt, which should give ¼" - ½".

If necessary, adjust by loosening the pivot and clamping bolts, and moving the dynamo to the correct tension. Tighten up the bolts. See fig. 39.

Chassis servicing

CLUTCH

The clutch has a single plate and is mechanically operated.

Free travel should measure 1½ - 2".

Every 5000 miles

Adjust the free travel by loosening the lock nuts on linkage (4) fig. 40, tightening the rear nut and then locking up.

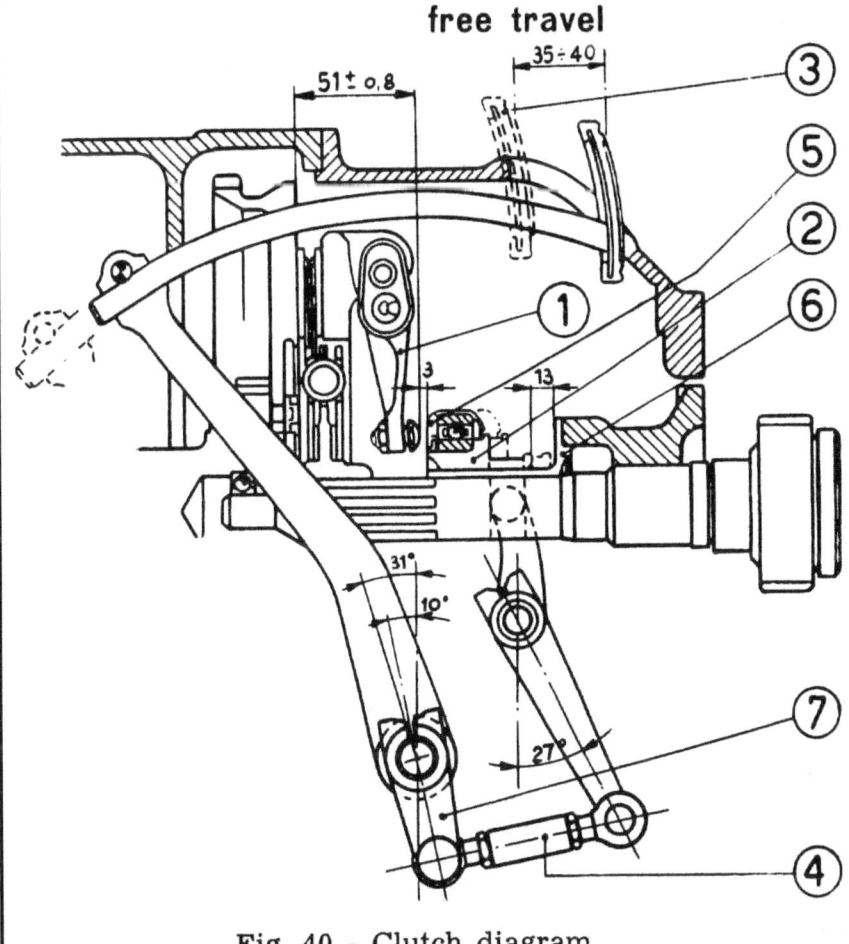

1) Balance lever.
2) Sliding coupling.
3) Clutch pedal.
4) Pedal clearance adjustment idler.
5) Disengagement bearing.
6) Coupling support.
7) Drive lever.

Fig. 40 - Clutch diagram.

Chassis servicing

Gear Box

The gear box is in unit with the engine, and has synchromesh on all four gears, a reverse and an overdrive 5th gear.

Overdrive is higher geared by 22½% allowing the car to maintain high averages with less fuel consumption, and less engine wear.

Engagement is by switch, but:

1. Never use overdrive before the gearbox oil is warm.

2. Slightly release the accelerator on engagement.

3. Accelerate slightly on disengagement.

Chassis servicing

Gearbox and overdrive

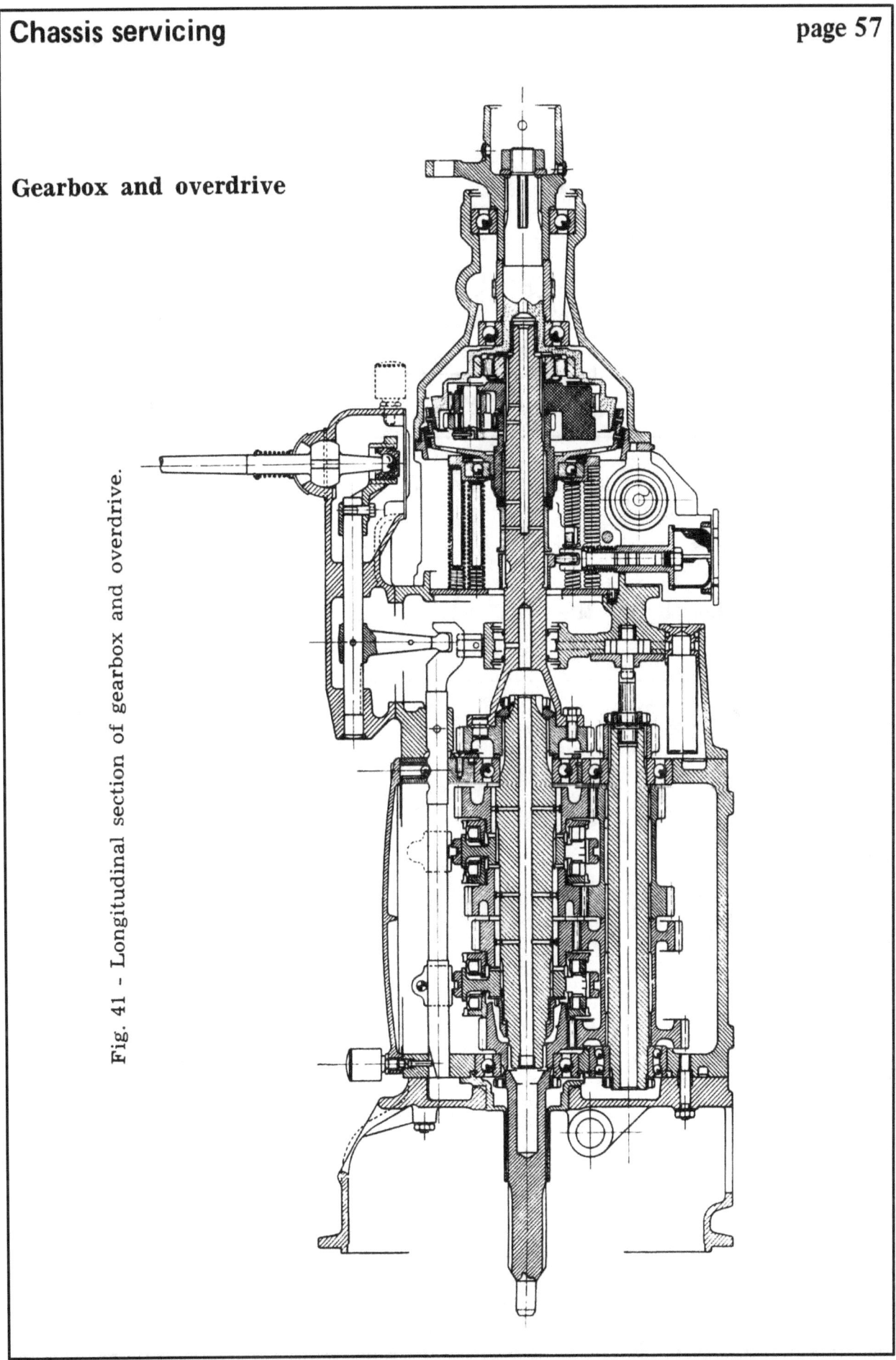

Fig. 41 - Longitudinal section of gearbox and overdrive.

Chassis servicing

Gear ratios

Gear ratio		
	1st. speed	- 1 : 2.536
	2nd. speed	- 1 : 1.777
	3rd. speed	- 1 : 1.256
	4th. speed	- 1 : 1
	5th. speed (overdrive)	- 1 : 0.778
	Reverse	- 1 : 3.218

Every check or adjustment to the gearbox must be performed by a specialised workshop.

Each 2500 miles check that the oil level is still 1 cm. below the filling hole. (See fig. 42).

Each 5000 miles change the oil.

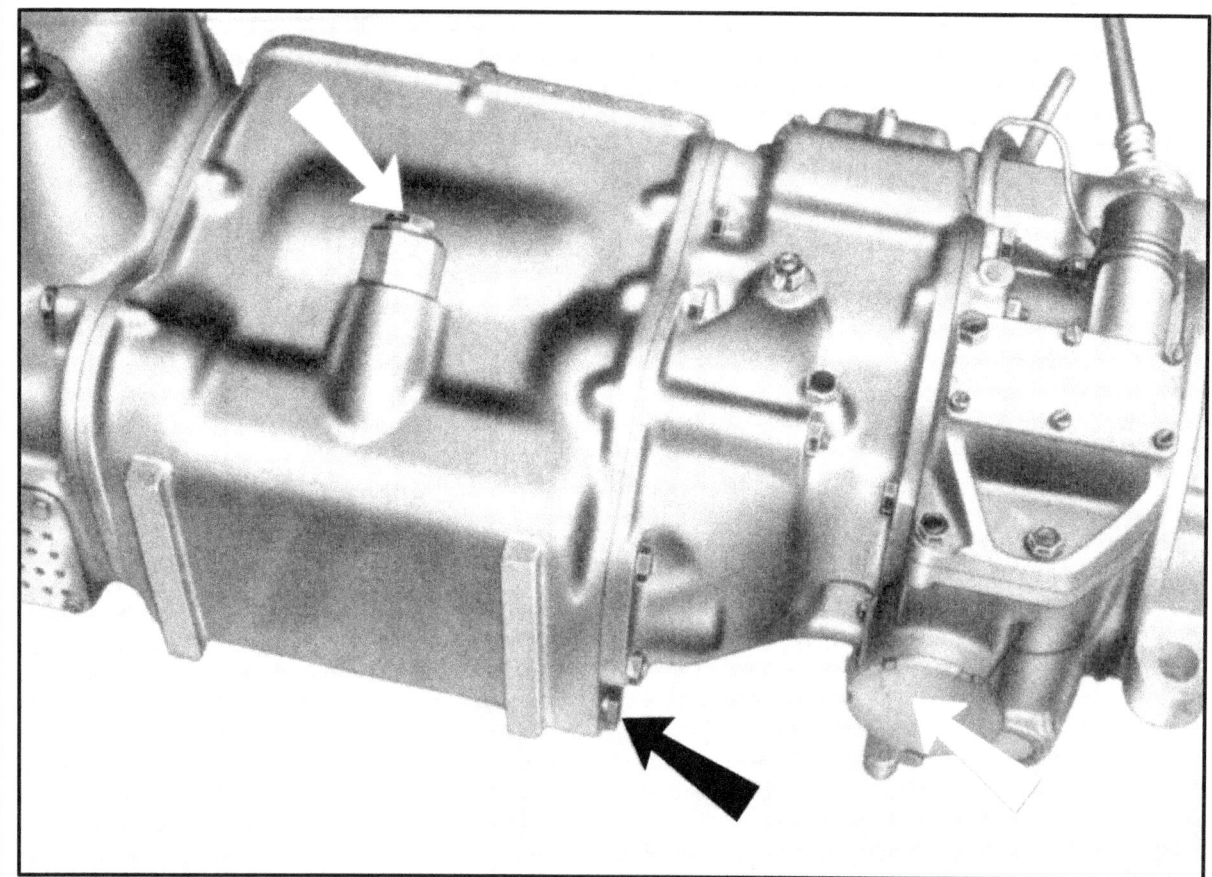

Fig. 42 - Filler and drain plugs.

Chassis servicing

Prop shaft

Every 2500 miles

Pump Retinax A grease into the sliding coupling (2) fig. 43. Remove screw (1) fig. 43, fit a grease nipple in its place, and pump the same type of grease into the universal joint, and also into the ball pin flange centering the prop shaft.
Replace the screw afterwards.

Every 5000 miles

The universal joint must be checked by a Ferrari Concessionaire.

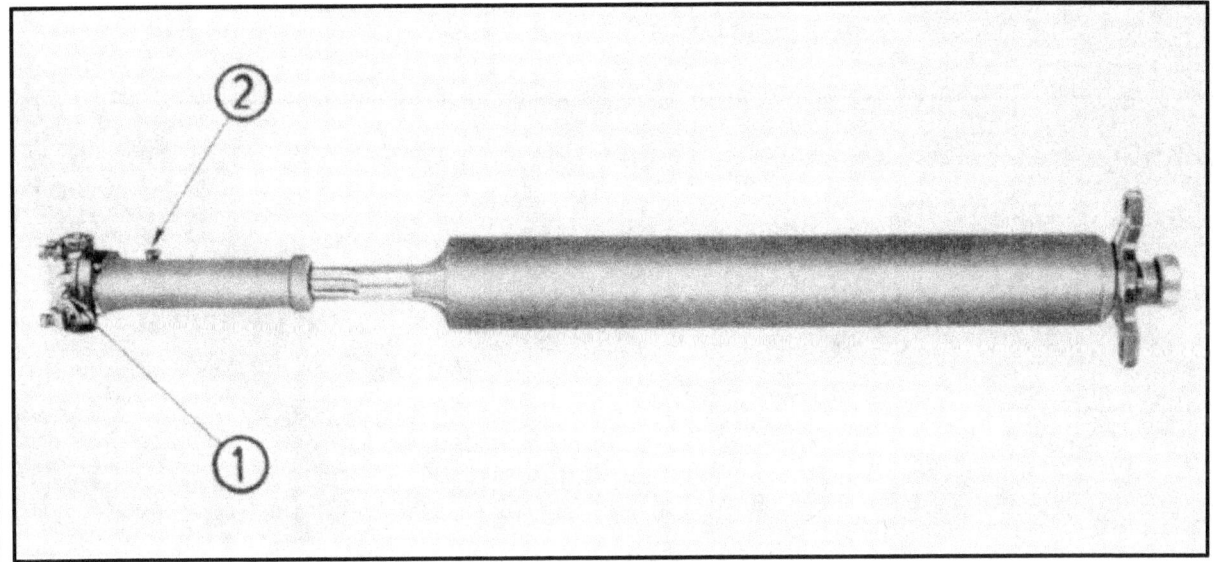

Fig. 43 - Propeller shaft with joints.

Rear axle

The rear axle is located by two pairs of radius arms.
The standard ratio is 7/32 = 4.56 to 1.

Final ratio: gearbox - rear axle with 7/32 crown wheel and pinion	1st. speed	- 1 : 11.59
	2nd. speed	- 1 : 7.76
	3rd. speed	- 1 : 5.72
	4th. speed	- 1 : 4.56
	5th. speed (overdrive)	- 1 : 3.53
	Reverse	- 1 : 14.60

Chassis servicing

Rear axle

Each 2500 miles check the oil level by removing the side plug and, when necessary, filling to the level of the top threads.

Every 10,000 miles adjustments should be carried out by a Ferrari Concessionaire.

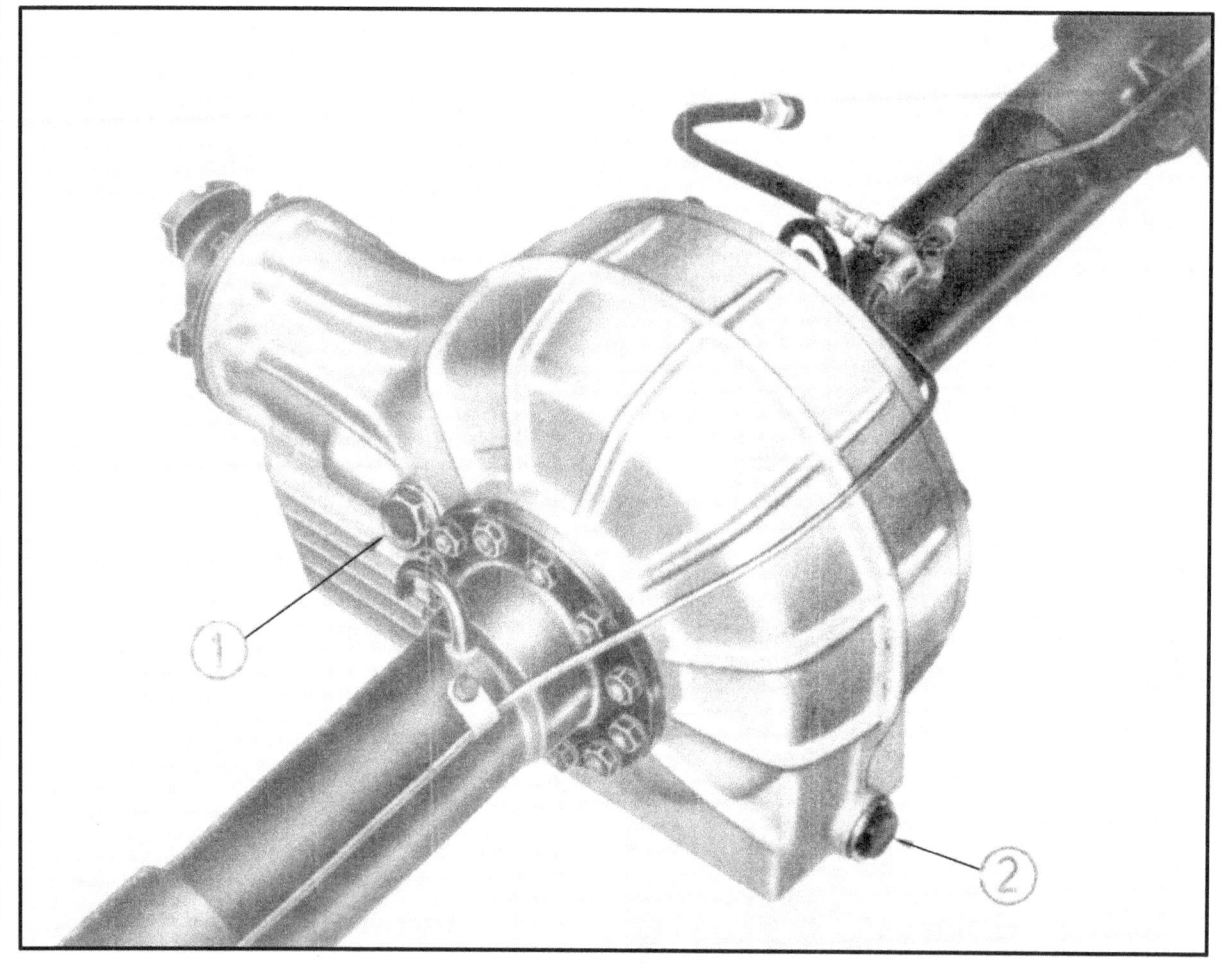

Fig. 44 - Rear axle: 1) Filler plug; 2) oil drain plug.

Chassis servicing

Front wheel suspension

Front suspension is independent by wish bones, helical springs and telescopic shock absorbers. An anti-roll bar is also fitted. (see fig. 45).

Fig. 45 - Front-wheel suspension.

Every 2,500 miles. Grease all the joints and the king pin rollers; also have the shock absorbers checked if damping seems uneven.

Chassis servicing

page 62

Rear suspension

Rear suspension is by semi-elliptic springs with swing shackles fore and aft. Polythene strips are fitted between each leaf, and damping is by telescopic shock absorbers (fig. 46).

Every 5000 miles. Examine shackles, silent blocs radius arms.

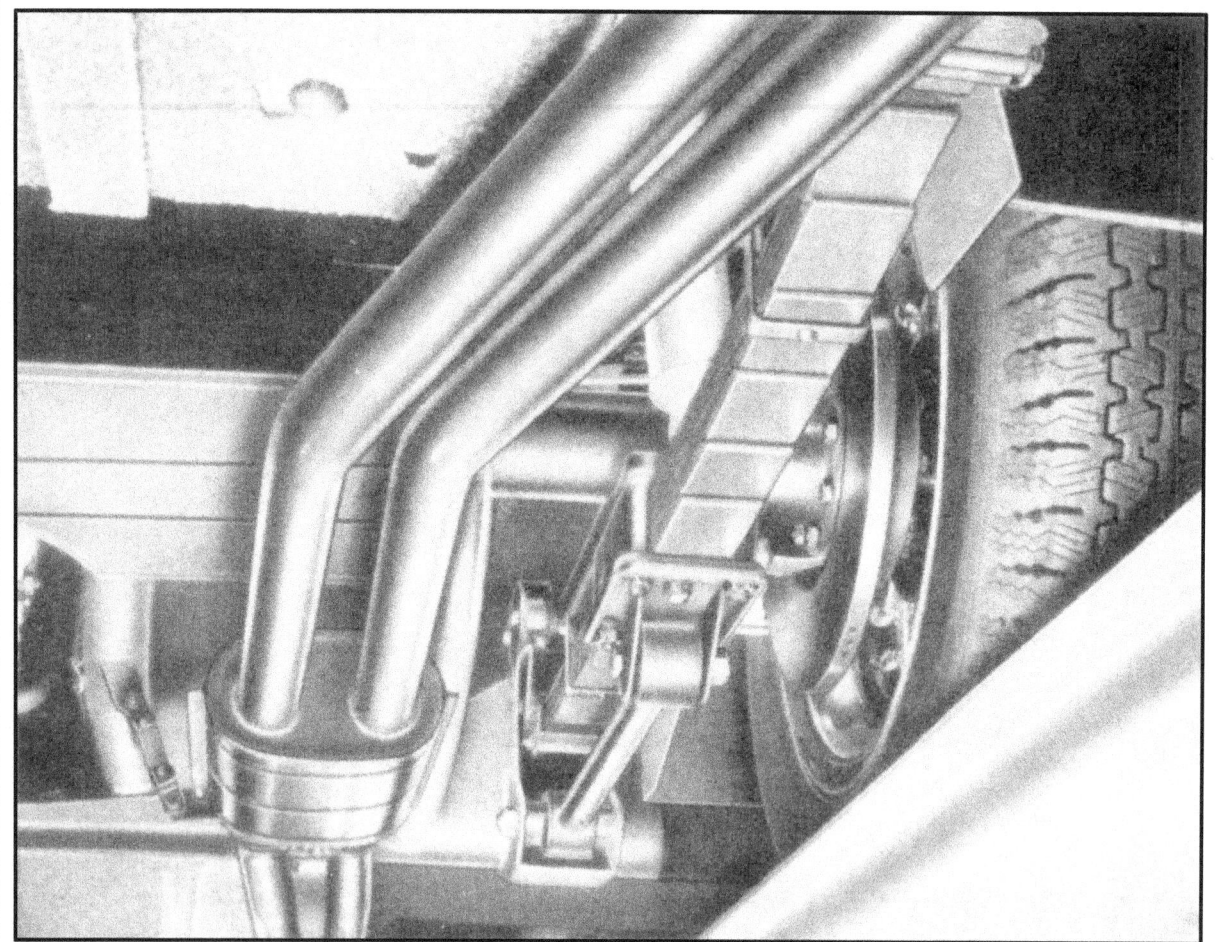

Fig. 46 - Rear suspension.

Chassis servicing

Front Shock absorbers

Calibration : extent : Kgs. 105 - Compression : Kgs. 20.

Calibration diagram

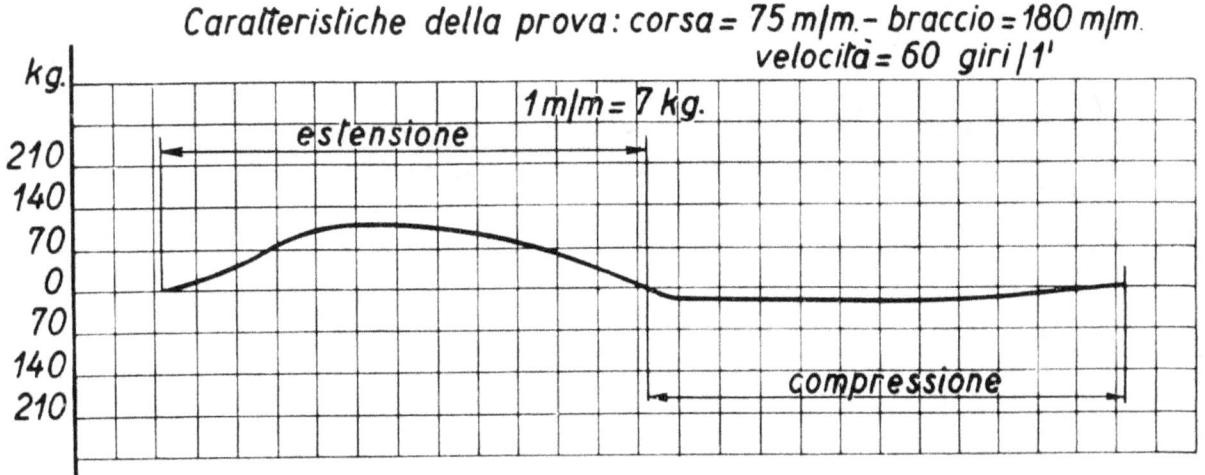

Rear shock absorbers

Calibration : extent : Kgs. 80 - Compression : Kgs. 20.

Calibration diagram

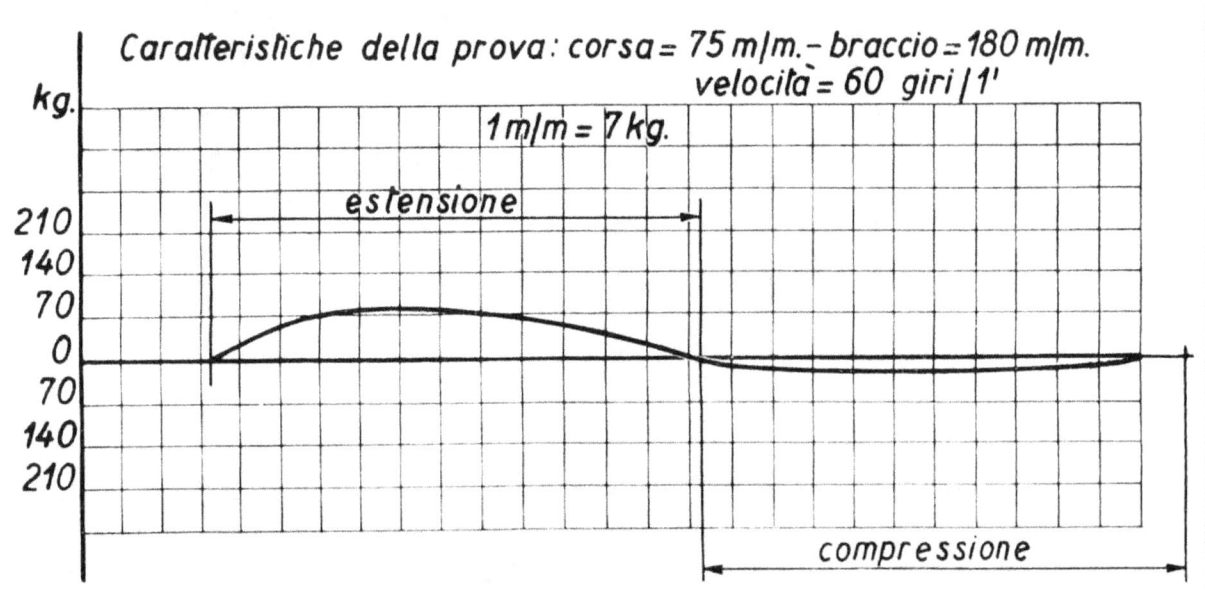

Chassis servicing

Steering

Steering is by worm and peg.

Every 2500 miles check the steering box oil level.
It is important that:
1. There is no wear in the linkage.
2. The wheels are balanced.
3. Toe-out is correctly adjusted.
4. Tyres are at the correct pressures, and evenly worn.
5. The correct amount of play only is allowed in the box.

Every 5000 miles
1. Set the wheels straight.
2. Loosen the lock nut (2).
3. Screw the register pin right in.
4. Lock up.

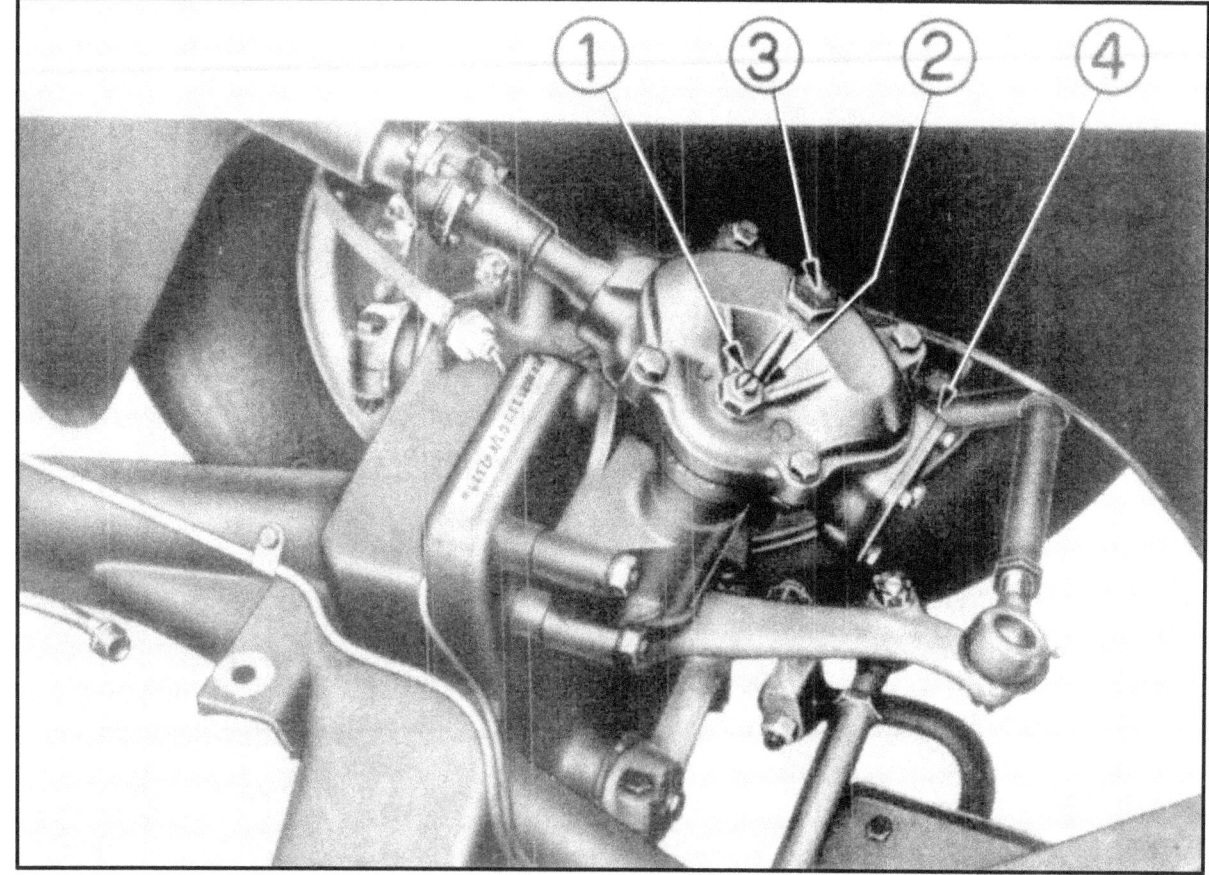

Fig. 47 - Steering box: 1) register screw; 2) lock nut; 3) Oil cap; 4) Bearings adjustment lining.

Chassis servicing

Steering

Track rod ends are fitted with ball joints which should be checked and, if necessary, replaced every 10,000 miles.

Min. turning circle : 40' 1" - this is not adjustable.

Every 2,500 miles lubricate the track rod ends.

Every 5,000 miles check the ball joints for wear.

Fig. 48 - Steering layout diagram.
1) steering box ; 2) steering idler arm and bracket ; 3) track rod ; 4) side tie rods ;
5) turning circle stops.

Chassis servicing

page 66

Front wheels

Every 10,000 miles check the camber and toe-out to avoid abnormal tyre wear and ensure stability.
This must be carried out with the car in full running trim, fuel tank full and 2 people on board, by a Ferrari Concessionaire.

Camber angles with a static load (theoretic 1") fig. 49.

$$B = A + 6 \text{ mm. (minimum value)}$$
$$B = A + 9 \text{ mm. (maximum value)}$$

Camber adjustment

Camber angles cannot be adjusted, but must be checked.

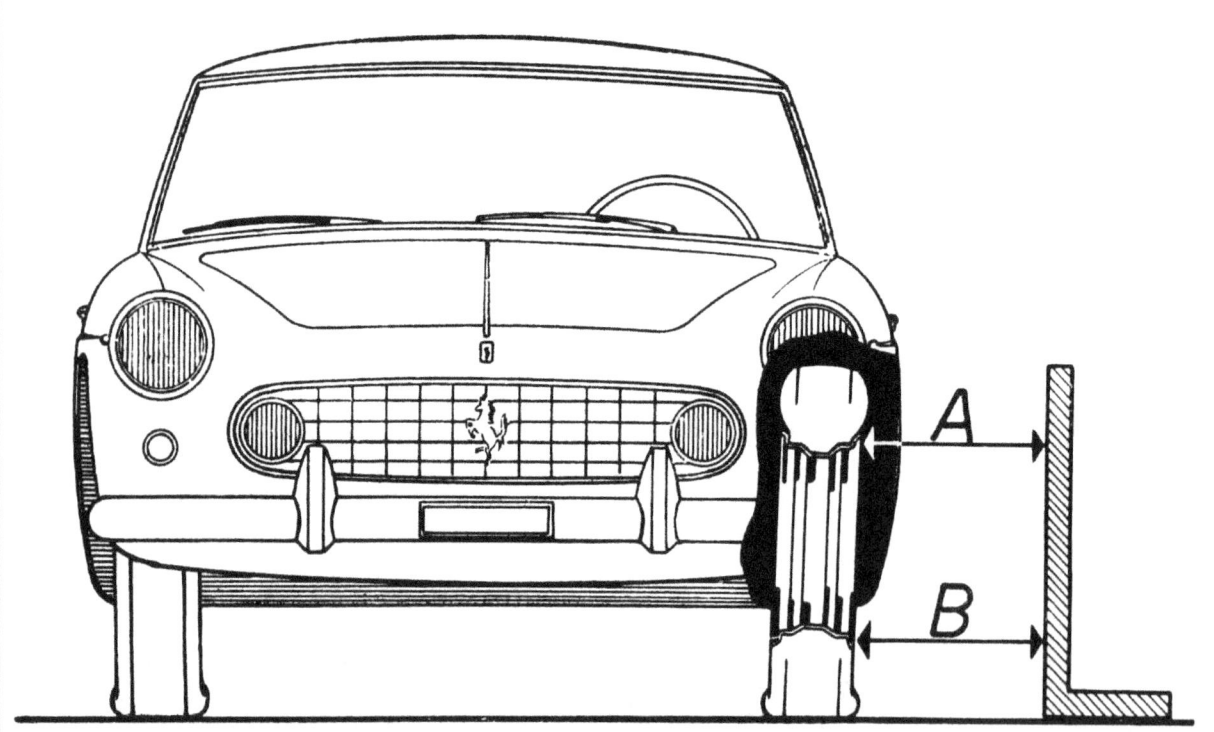

Fig. 49 - Camber check.

Chassis servicing

page 67

Front wheel toe-out adjustment

1. Set the front wheels straight to the front, by aligning the scribe marks on the column and steering-box.
   One of the steering-wheel spokes should be vertical.

2. Adjust the tie-rods to within 1 mm. of 263 mm.

3. Adjust the track rod to give the required toe-out - see fig. 50.

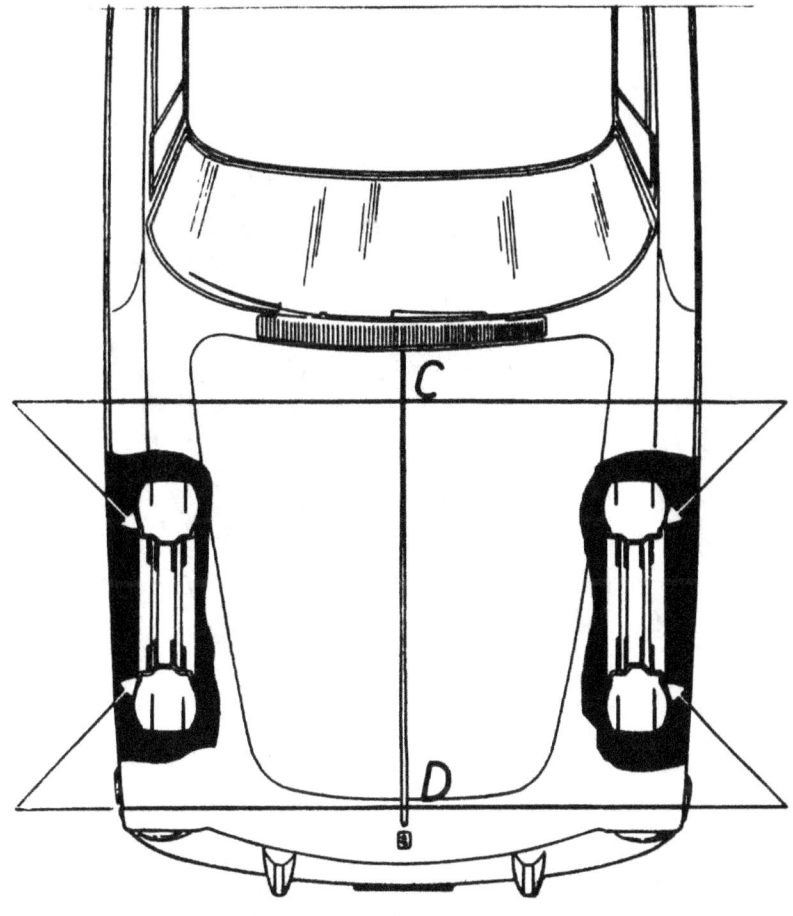

Values of toe-out
(see fig. 50).
Measured between the inside tyre rim:

$$D = C + 1.5 \text{ mm.}$$

Tie rods length
(measured between joint centres):

Lateral 263 mm. ± 2 mm.
Central 630 mm. ± 2 mm.

If these limits do not give the required toe-out the chassis alignment will have to be checked.

Fig. 50 - Adjusting toe-out.

Chassis servicing

Brakes - Layout diagram

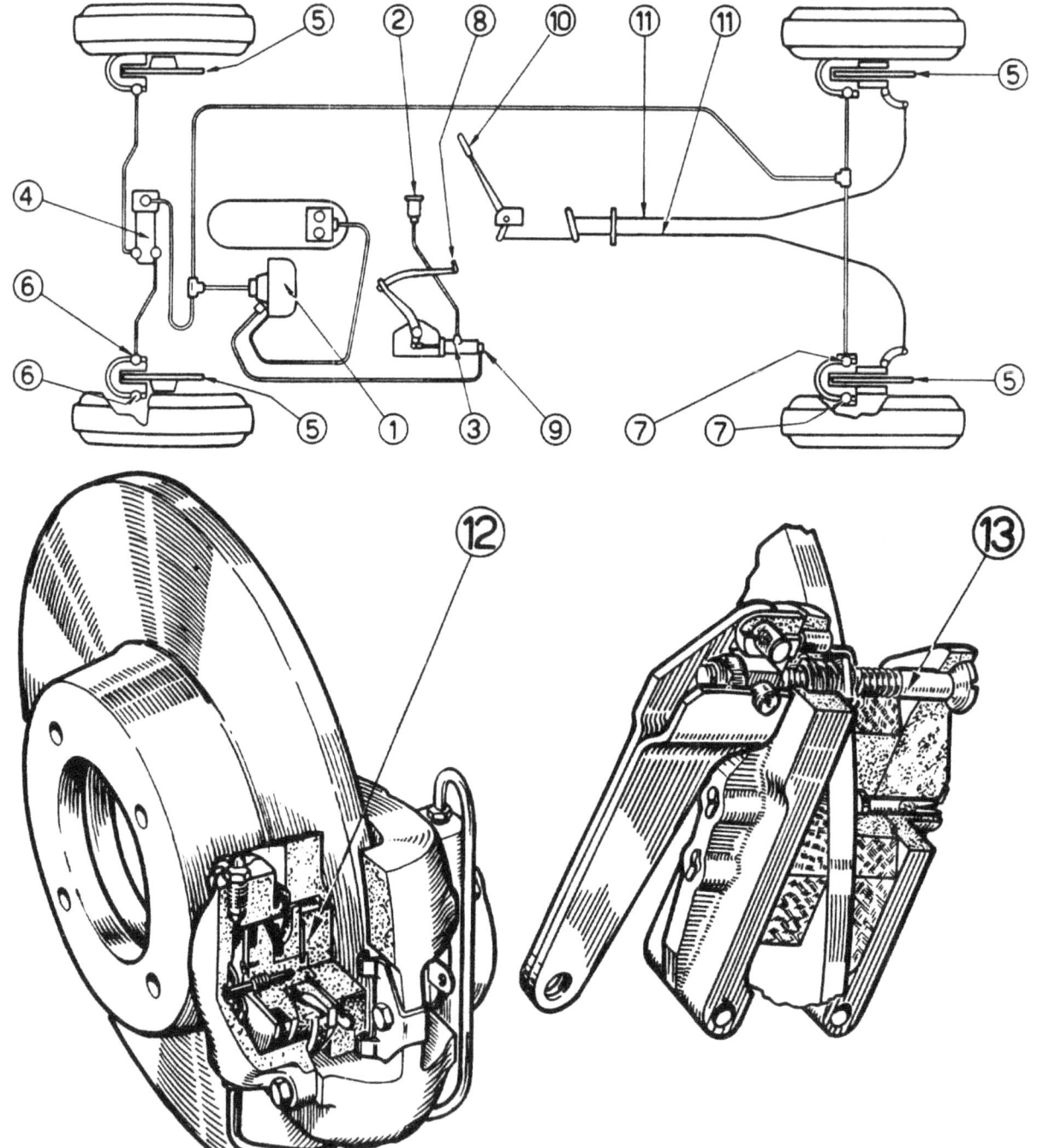

Fig. 51 - Brakes layout diagram:
1) Brake servo; 2) Feed tank; 3) Master cylinder; 4) Booster; 5) Brake discs; 6) Wheel cylinders; 7) Wheel cylinders; 8) Brake pedal; 9) Brake light switch; 10) Hand brake; 11) Hand brake cables; 12) Brake pads; 13) Hand brake adjusting screws.

Chassis servicing

Brakes

The brake system consists of :

— Disc brakes on four wheels, hydraulically operated.
— Servo unit acting on all wheels.
— Booster acting on front wheels only.
— Hand brake acting on rear wheels only.

Hand brake

The hand brake is mechanically operated. The rear wheels should be locked when the brake lever has completed half of its total travel. The correct adjustment is .004" clearance between the pads and the disc.

Hydraulic system

Every 3000 miles check the level in the feed tank - this must never drop below ¼ full. Only use Shell Donax B SAE 70 R3 or Dunlop Racing Brake Fluid (Castrol) oil.

Always replace the fluid throughout when the pads are changed, taking care to use new fluid from sealed tins.

A spongy feel to the brake pedal indicates air in the system.

Chassis servicing

page 70

Brakes

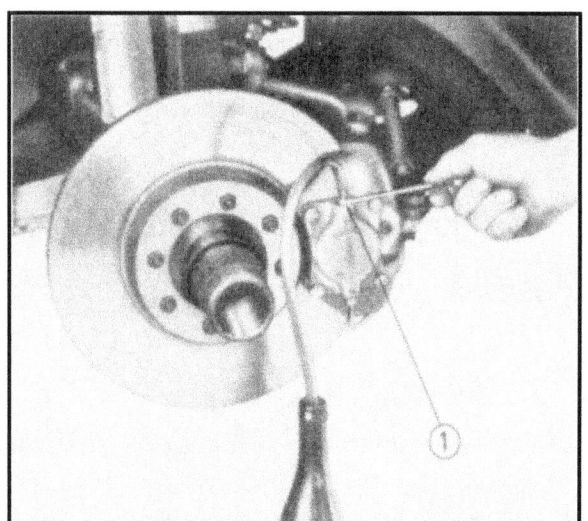

Fig. 52 - Bleeding the brake servo : 1-2) brake servo drainage screws.

Fig. 53 - Bleeding the front and rear wheel cylinders : 1) front cylinder draining screw ; 2) rear cylinder draining screw.

Chassis servicing

Bleeding the brakes

1. During bleeding, the feed tank must be kept over ¾ full with its cap screwed down.

2. Bleeding the servo.

   Fit a rubber pipe onto the bleed valve, the other end hanging into a glass bottle. Press the brake pedal down, closing the bleed valve before allowing the pedal to return. Repeat until no air bubbles come out with the fluid. Then do the same for the other bleed valve on the unit.

3. Follow the same procedure for the front and rear wheels.

4. Finally repeat bleeding on the servo. The pedal should now feel firm, but if it does not, repeat the above.

It is suggested the whole operation be repeated after a road test of about five miles.

There should be a gap of between .040" - .060" between the cap and the driving piston of the master cylinder.

Chassis servicing

page 72

Fig. 54 - Front brake.

Fig. 55 - Rear brake.

Fig. 56 - Hand brake.

Chassis servicing   page 73

Brakes

Every 2500 miles, or when the brakes pull or the pedal free play becomes excessive, it will be necessary to check the pads.

If the pads are not worn more than $^3/_{16}$", and the pistons are free in the wheel cylinders, it should only be necessary to bleed the system.

Every 5000 miles Replace the brake pads, and check the discs.

These may be ground, if scored, providing not more than .040" is removed.

They should also be checked for warping, no more than .002" out of true being permissible.

If the brake pedal does not feel firm after assembly and bleeding, the master and wheel cylinder rubbers should be replaced.

A 30 mile drive will be necessary to bed-in the new pads.

Pads of the following material are recommended.

Front brakes	Mintex VBO 5083
Rear brakes	Mintex VBO 5201

Chassis servicing   page 73

Chassis servicing

page 74

Brakes

Braking room

The stopping distance of a car increases with its speed, and varies according to road conditions, state of the tyres and the load being carried.

A careful driver should always bear his braking distances in mind.

The figures obtained in fig. 57 were taken in perfect conditions.

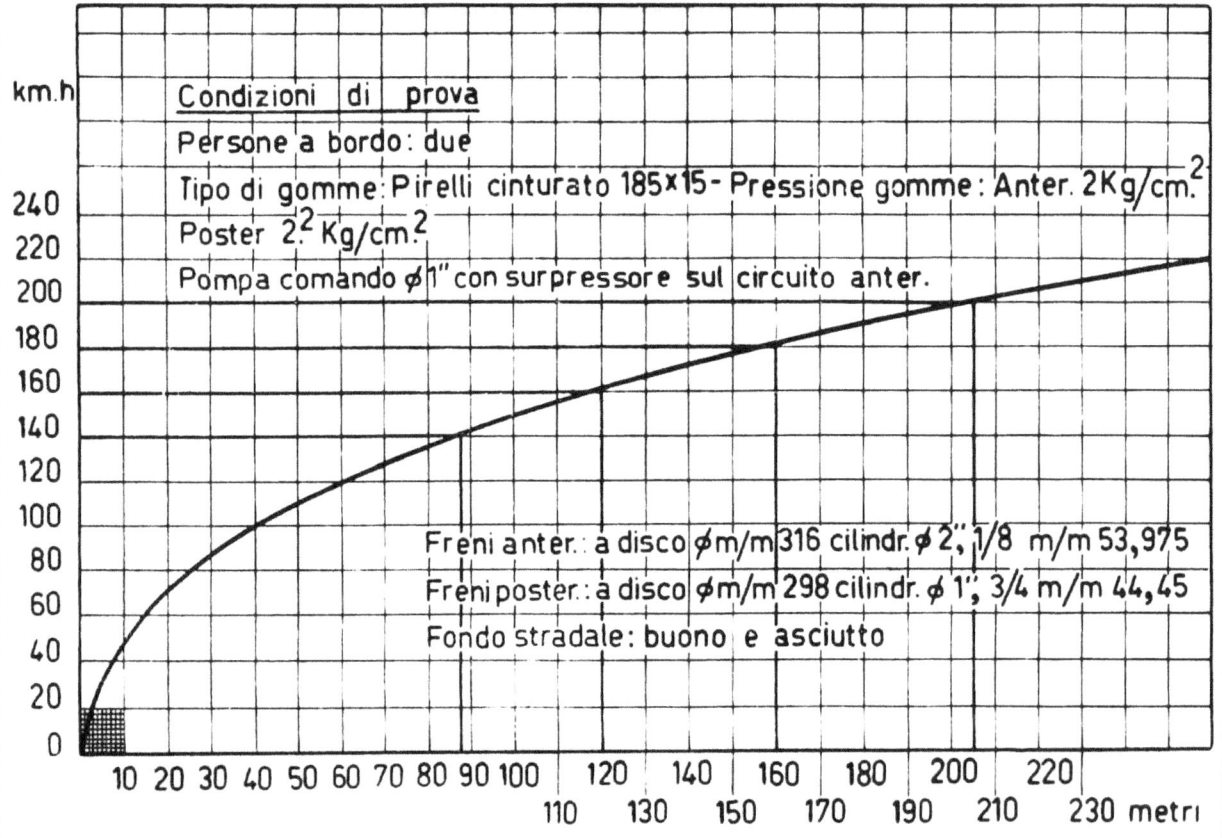

Fig. 57 - Diagram to determine braking distances.

Chassis servicing

Wheels

Wheels are balanced before leaving the factory, and should be re-balanced whenever a tyre is removed.

Unbalanced wheels will cause wear in the steering, uneven tyre wear, and will affect stability.

Every 3000 miles grease the front wheels hub bearings. The rear wheels need no lubrication.

It is necessary to dismantle the hubs to check bearing lubrication and clearances.

It is recommended to have this operation performed on a balancing machine.

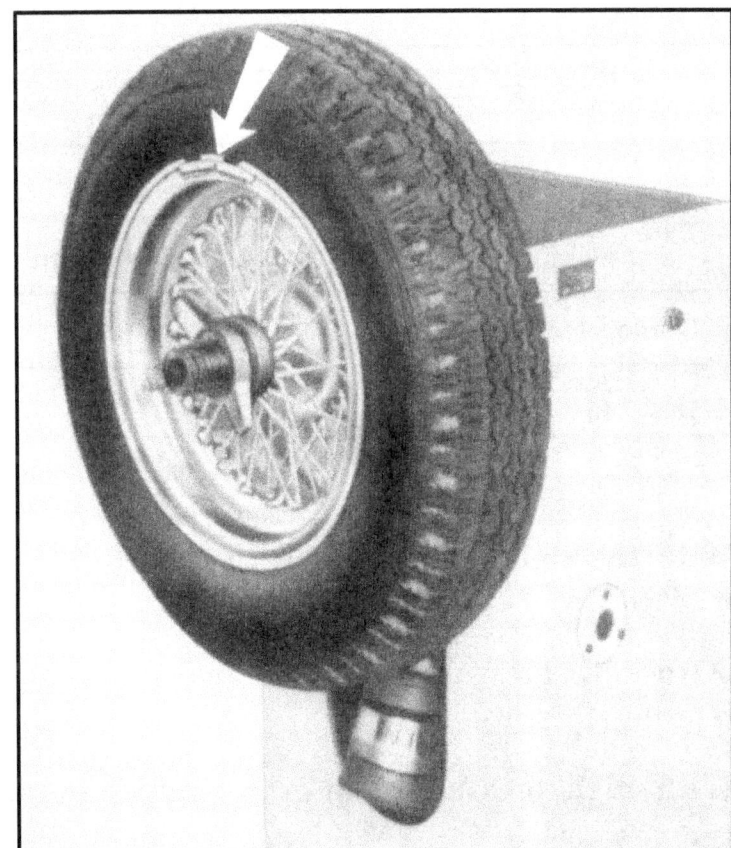

Fig. 58 - Balancing the wheels: balancing weights.

Chassis servicing

Tyres

Inflation pressures - Cold tyres

It is important to keep the tyres at the right pressures to obtain long tyre life.

PRESSIONI PER IMPIEGO NORMALE A MEZZO CARICO NORMAL PRESSURE FOR HALF LOAD				
Pneumatici Tyres	Anteriori Front		Posteriori Rear	
	Kg/cmq.	Lbs/sq. inc.	Kg/cmq.	Lbs/sq. inc.
Dunlop 185/15 SP	1,9	25	2,3	32.7
Cinturato Pirelli 185 × 15	1,9	25	2,3	32.7

PRESSIONI PER IMPIEGO A PIENO CARICO ED AUTOSTRADA PRESSURE FOR FULL LOAD AND ON MOTOR ROAD				
Pneumatici Tyres	Anteriori Front		Posteriori Rear	
	Kg/cmq.	Lbs/sq. inc.	Kg/cmq.	Lbs/sq. inc.
Dunlop 185/15 SP	2,6	37.1	2,9	41.5
Cinturato Pirelli 185 × 15	2,6	37.1	2,9	41.5

With the right pressure, the full width of the tread works, and so wear is uniform.

With low pressure, the tyre overheats and the tread shoulders wear, tending to tear.

With high pressure, comfort is impaired and the tread wears more in the centre.

Chassis servicing

Tyres

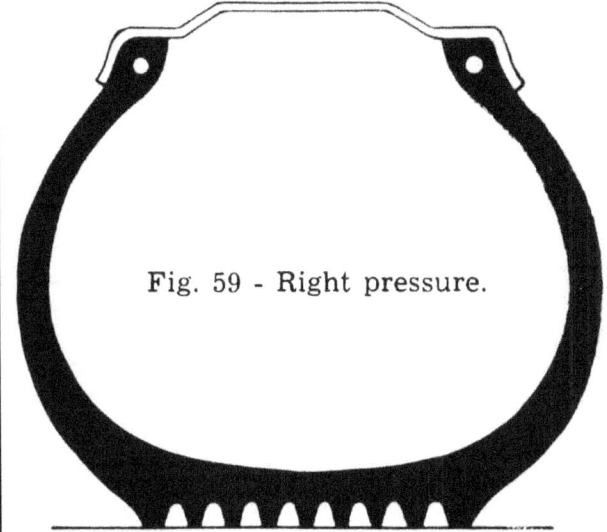

Fig. 59 - Right pressure.

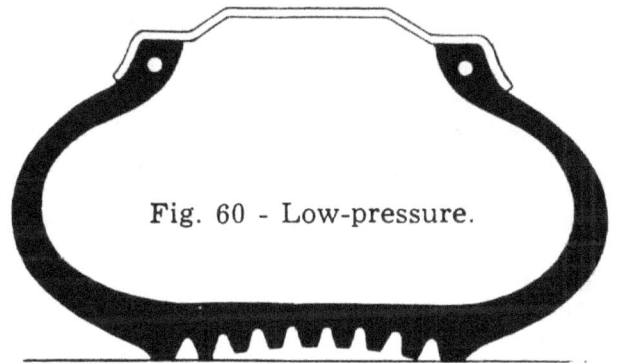

Fig. 60 - Low-pressure.

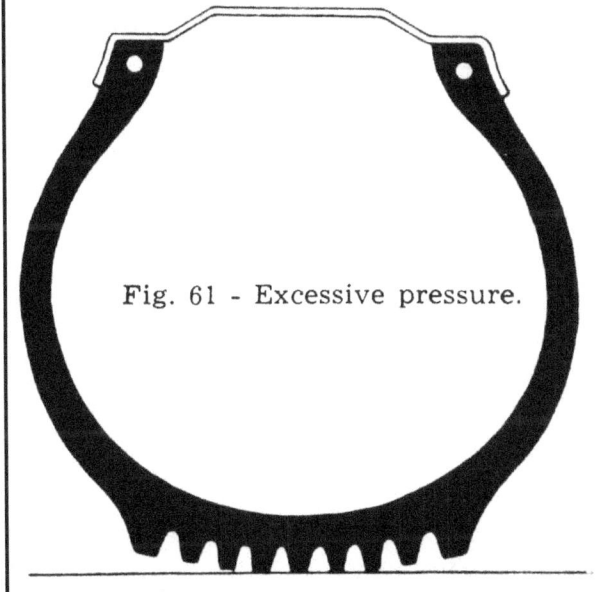

Fig. 61 - Excessive pressure.

Chassis servicing

page 78

Tyres

Exchanging tyres

Change the tyres round as per fig. 62 every 2,500 miles, to ensure even wear.

At the same time, check the wheel balance.

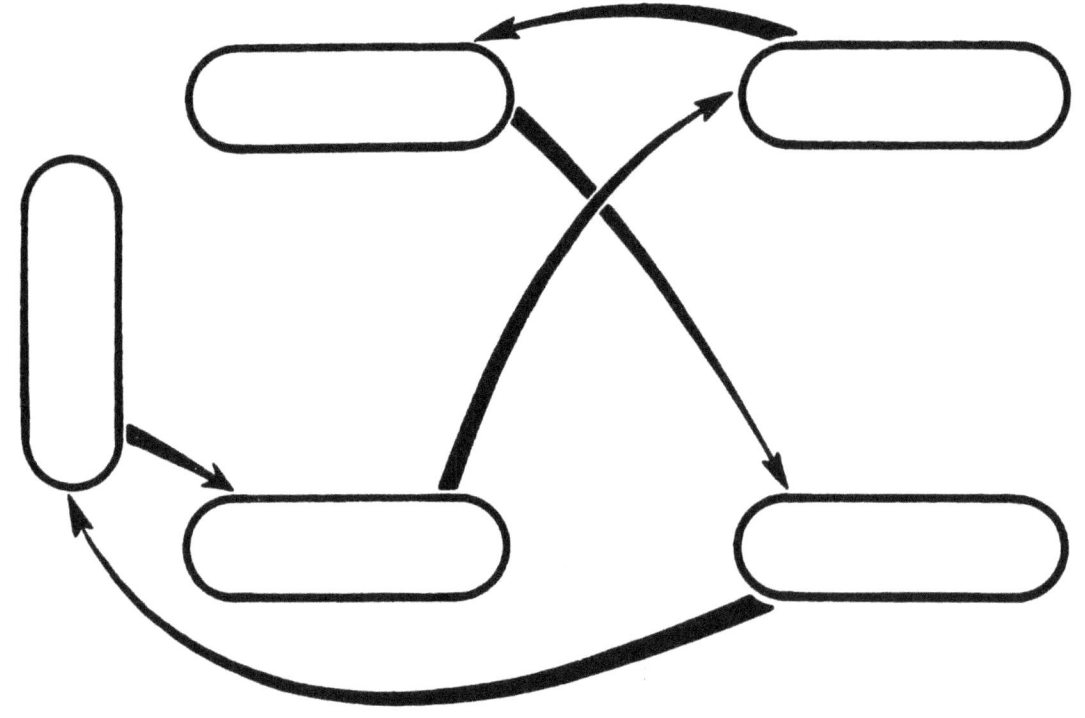

Fig. 62 - Wheel change sequence.

Fifth Part
Electrical installation

General

The 12v electrical installation is insulated throughout and fully fused.

Electric equipment

Battery - capacity	65 A/h.
Dynamo	Marelli DN 51 B = 300/12/2500 S Marelli DN 63 B = 400/12/2300 S
Voltage regulator	Marelli I R 19 E/300/12 - I R 50 A
Starter motor	Marelli MT 21 F = 18/12 D 9
Distributor	Marelli S 85 A - 12 V - 15°
Coil	Marelli 12V - B 202 A - B 2 R 201 A
Windscreen wiper	Lucas = 2 speed

Dynamo and starter motor

Every 2500 miles squirt one or two drops of oil into the oil hole on the dynamo.

Every 5000 miles dynamo, and every **10,000 miles** starter motor.

Check and renew the brushes if worn. Check for ovality or burning on the commutators.

If any is apparent, they will have to be skimmed.

Electrical installation

Battery

— Avoid flattening the battery.
— Use the starter, horn and lights as little as possible.
— Never fit bulbs of a higher wattage.
— Always switch the ignition off when the engine is not running, as damage may occur to the coils.
— Keep the battery clean and dry on the outside, and never rest spanners etc. on the top.

Every 1000 miles check the electrolyte covers the plates by $5/16$" and that the terminals are tight and covered in vasoline. If the car is not being used, arrange for the battery to be charged. Pure distilled water only must be used for topping up.

Fig. 63 - Battery mounting.

Electrical installation

Lighting

Front lights

1. Full and dipped beam headlamps (lamp: 40-45W double filament).
2. Side lights with indicator flashers (lamp: 5-20 W double filament).
3. Fog lights (lamp: 45 W).

Fig. 64 - Front lights.

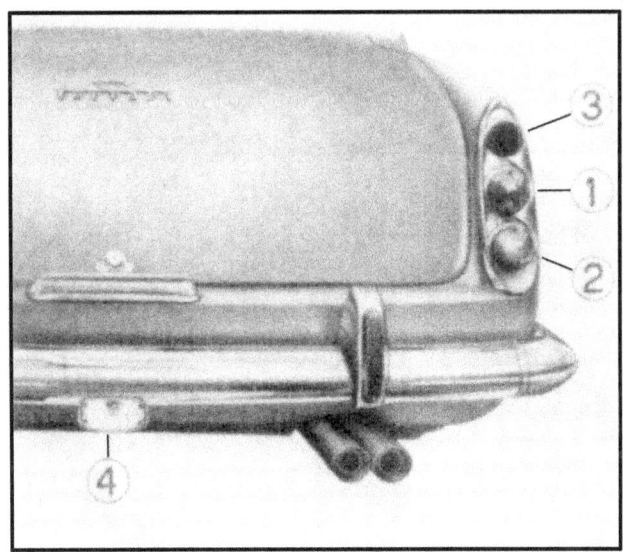

Fig. 65 - Rear lights.

Rear lights

1. Direction indicator (lamp: 20 W).
2. Side lights and stop (lamp: 5-20 W double filament).
3. Reflector.
4. Reverse light. This only operates when the side lights are on and reverse gear is engaged. (Lamp 20 W).

There are also indicator flashers mounted on the side of the wings.

Number plate lights.

Lamps fitted inside the bonnet and boot, and courtesy roof and door lamps.

Electrical installation

page 82

Lighting - Replacing the bulbs

Replacing the headlamp bulbs

It is necessary to remove the lamp and rim from the car, replacing the bulb through the rear of the optique.

Replacing the rear lamp bulbs

Unscrew the plastic lens to remove the bulb.

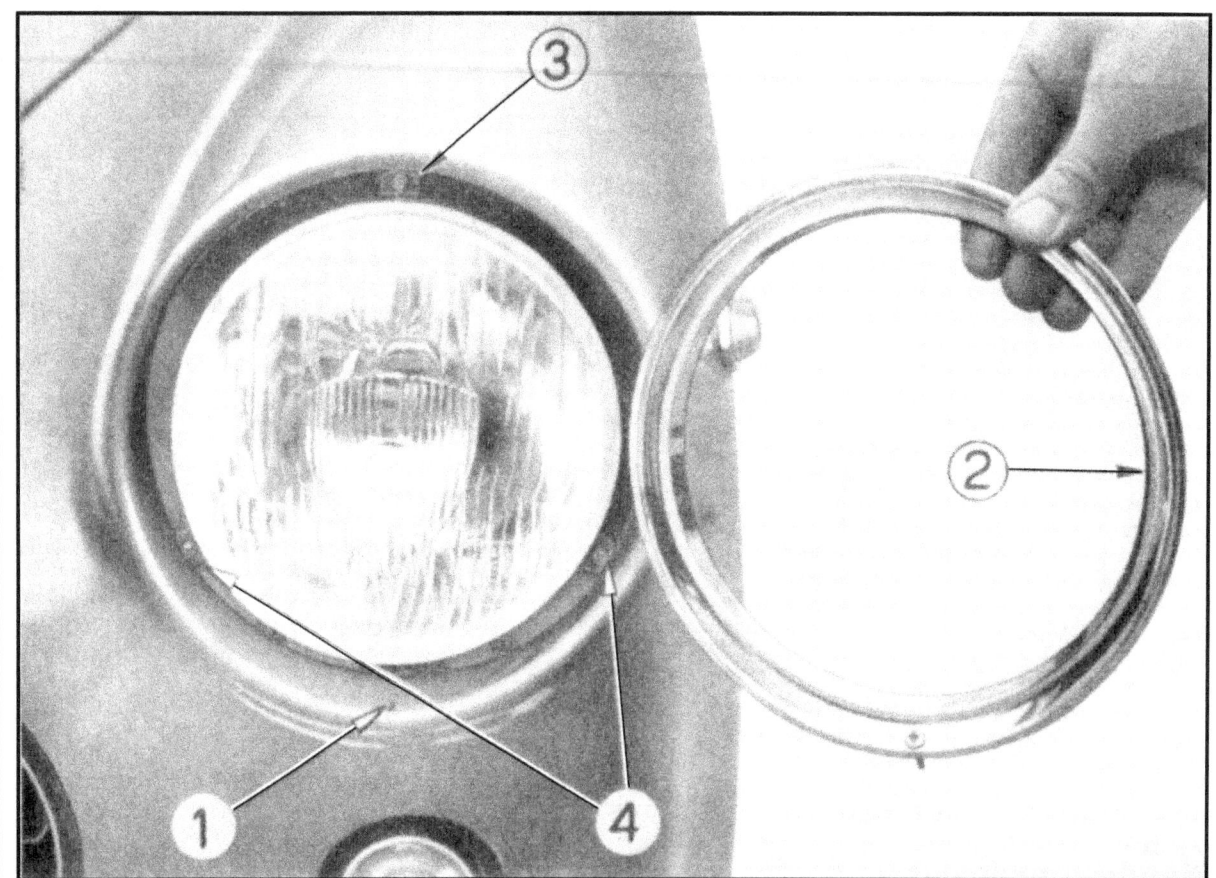

Fig. 66 - Front lamps : 1) rim fixing screws ; 2) Rim ; 3) Adjustment screw for the beam in vertical direction ; 4) adjustment screws for the beam in horizontal direction.

Electrical installation

page 83

Lighting - Focusing the headlamps

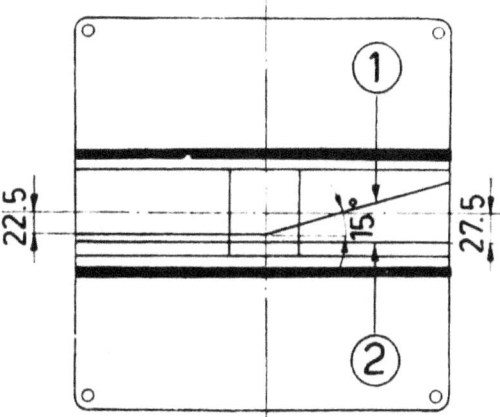

Fig. 67 - Screen with grating for Beamsetter device: 1) reference line for antidazzle; 2) reference line for fog lights.

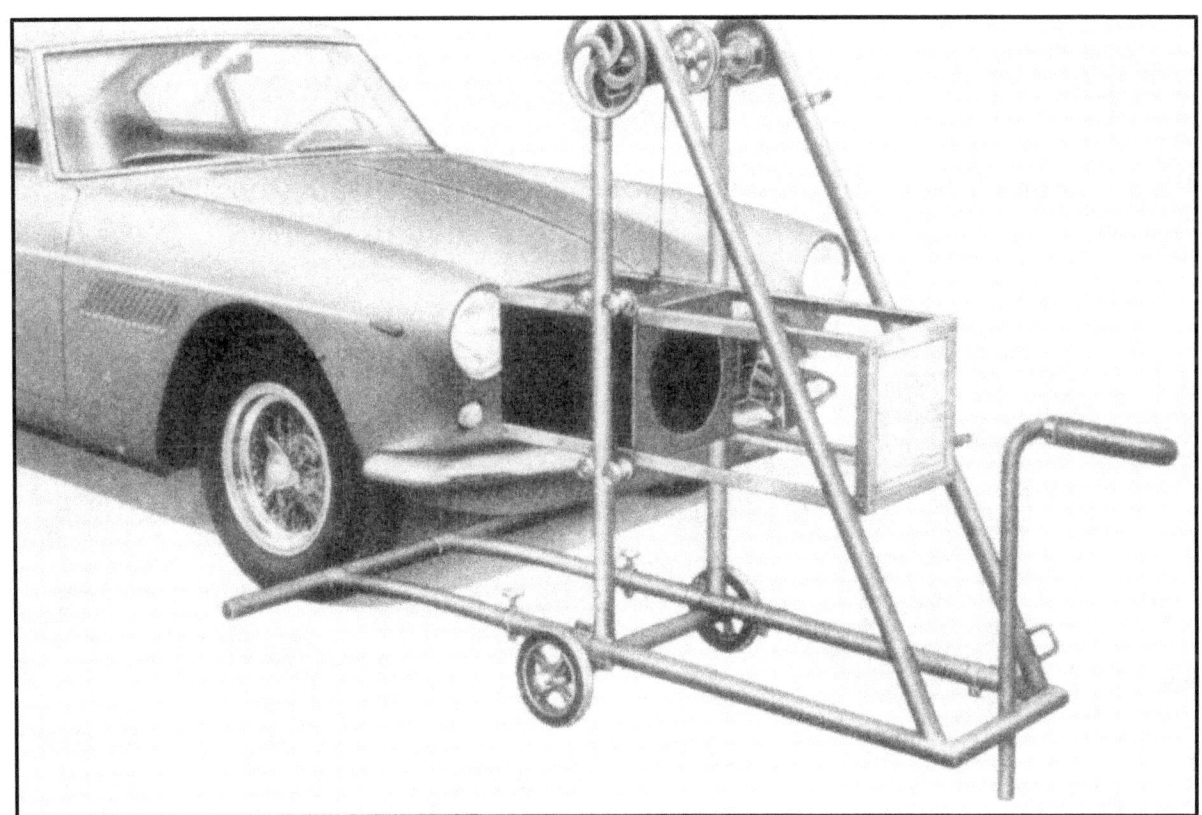

Fig. 68 - Focussing headlamps.

Headlamp alignment

Using a beam setter, place the car on a flat surface, as shown above.

Electrical installation

page 84

Lighting

Headlamps

Data

Projector base	A = 1340 mm. 52.75"
Main beam height	B = 600 mm. 23.62"
Dipper beam height	C = 470 mm. 18.10"
Projector height	D = 780 mm. ± 10 = 30.71" ± 1/3"

Where a beam-setter is not available, adjust the beams on a wall as in Fig. 69.

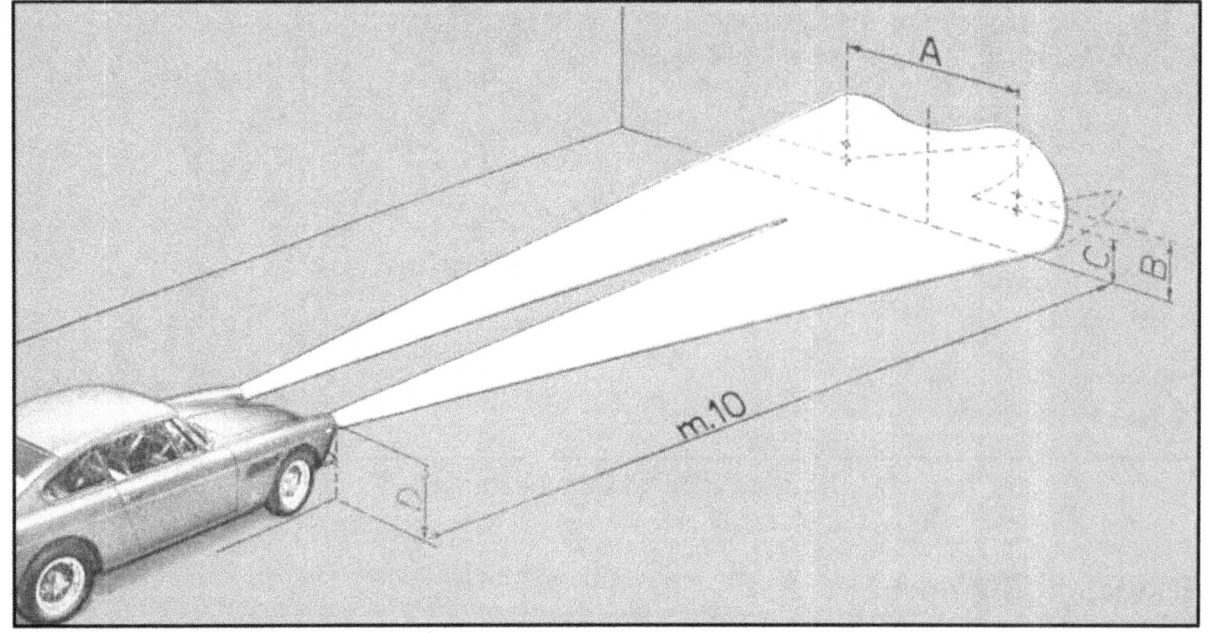

Fig. 69 - Headlamp geometry.

Electrical installation

Lighting

Fog lights

Data

Fog lights base	A = 900 mm.	35.43"
Height of light centre	H = 230 mm.	max. 5.05"

Place the car 33 ft from a wall and adjust the beams as above.

Fig. 70 - Fog light focussing.

Electrical installation

page 86

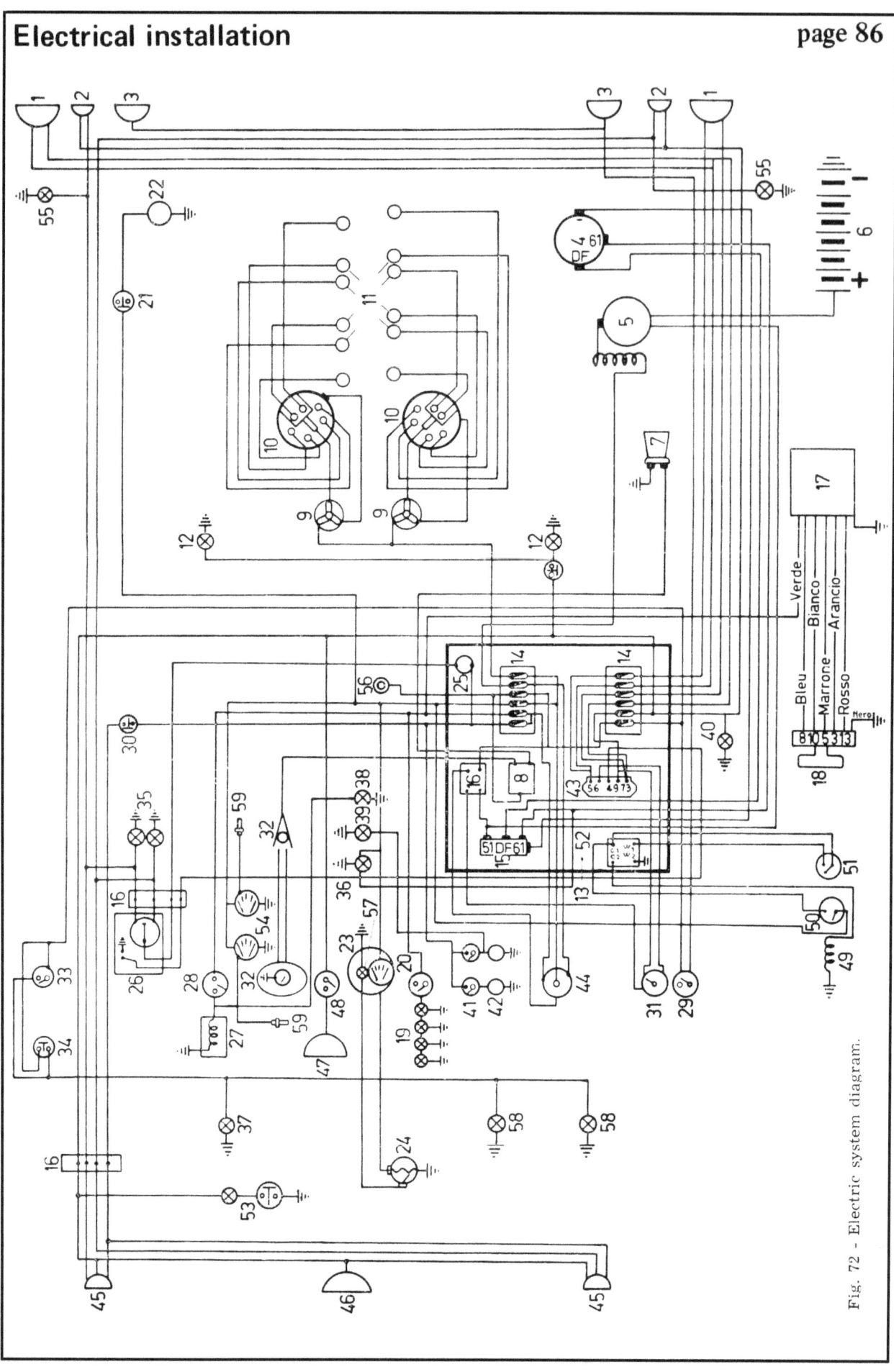

Fig. 72 - Electric system diagram.

Electrical installation

page 87

CAPTION

1) Headlamps and dip
2) Front lights and indicators
3) Fog lights
4) Dynamo
5) Starter
6) Battery
7) Horn
8) Horn relays
9) Ignition coils
10) Distributor
11) Spark plugs
12) Bonnet light
13) Panel
14) Installation fuses
15) Dynamo regulator
16) Terminal board
17) Windscreen wiper motor (2 speeds)
18) Switch for a/m. motor
19) Panel lights
20) Rheostat for panel
21) Thermocontact driving the fan
22) Fan for radiator
23) Petrol gauge
24) Tank level
25) Direction indicator relays
26) Commutator with direction indicator
27) Electric pump
28) Electric pump switch
29) Fog light switch
30) Hydraulic switch for stop lights
31) Outside light commutator
32) Horn push button
33) Inside light switch
34) Automatic switch for inside lights
35) Direction indicator lights
36) Dynamo charge lights
37) Inside lights lamp
38) Indicating lamp for electric pump
39) Heater fan indicating lamp
40) Indicating lamp for headlights
41) Conditioner switches
42) Conditioner electric fans
43) Deviolux (Front light commutator relay)
44) Ignition switch
45) Rear lights
46) Number plate light
47) Reverse lamp
48) Reverse light switch (on the gearbox)
49) Solenoid Overdrive
50) Switch on gearbox driving the Overdrive
51) Switch below the steering for Overdrive
52) Relay driving the Overdrive
53) Boot light
54) Water and oil thermometers
55) Side direction indicators (arrows)
56) Lighter
57) Signaling light for fuel level
58) Side door lamps
59) Thermocontacts for water and oil thermometers

Electrical installation

page 88

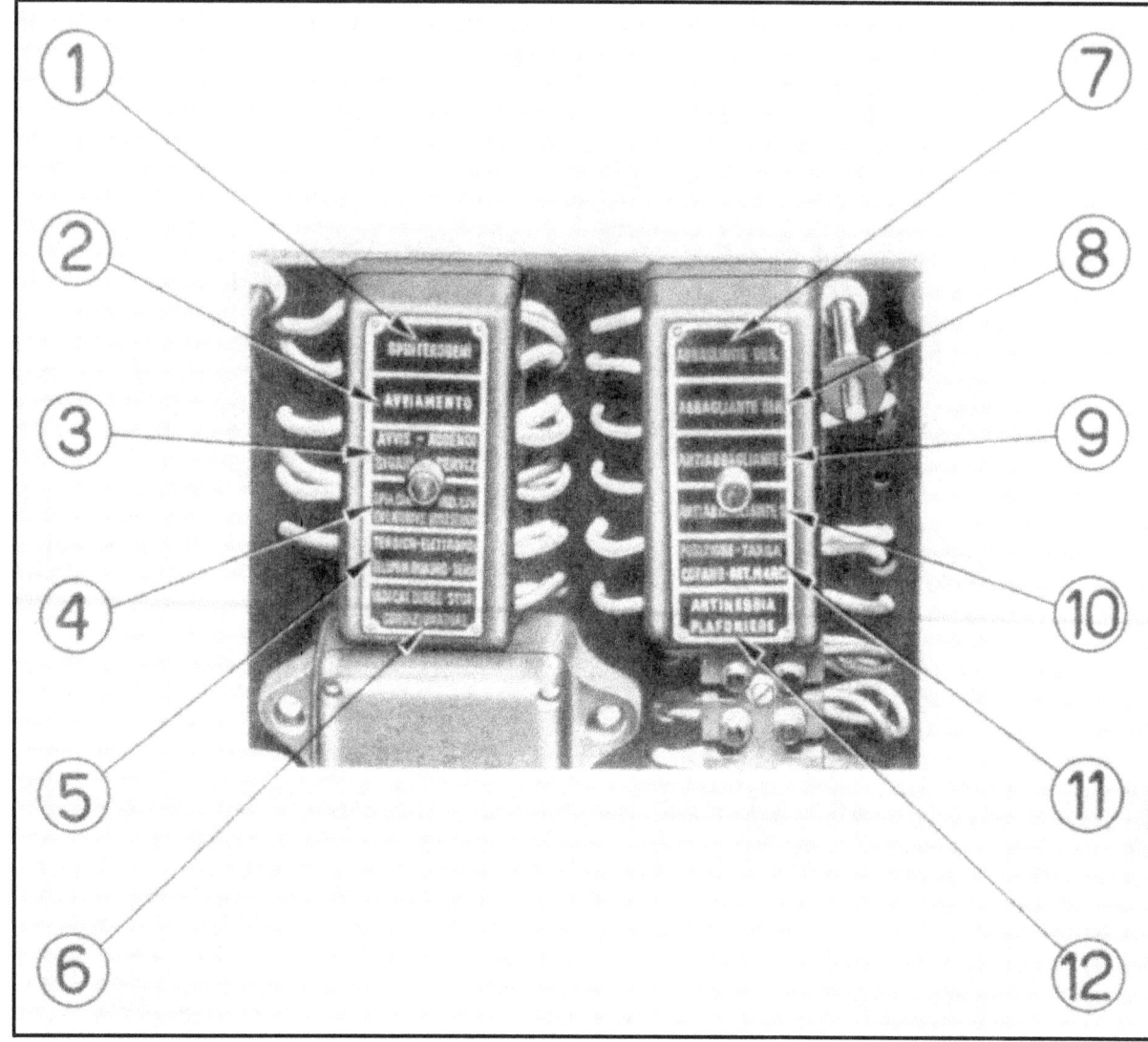

Fig. 71 - Fuse box.

1) Coil ignition.
2) Starter.
3) Horn and cigar lighter.
4) Dynamo warning lamp - fuel level - Overdrive - Fan - Instruments.
5) Windscreen wiper - Electric pump - Panel lights.
6) Stop and indicators - Heater fan.
7) RH. Headlamp main beam.
8) LH. Headlamp main beam.
9) RH. Headlamp dipped beam.
10) LH. Headlamp dipped beam.
11) Number plate - bonnet - Reverse lamp.
12) Fog lights. Roof lamp.

Tool Kit

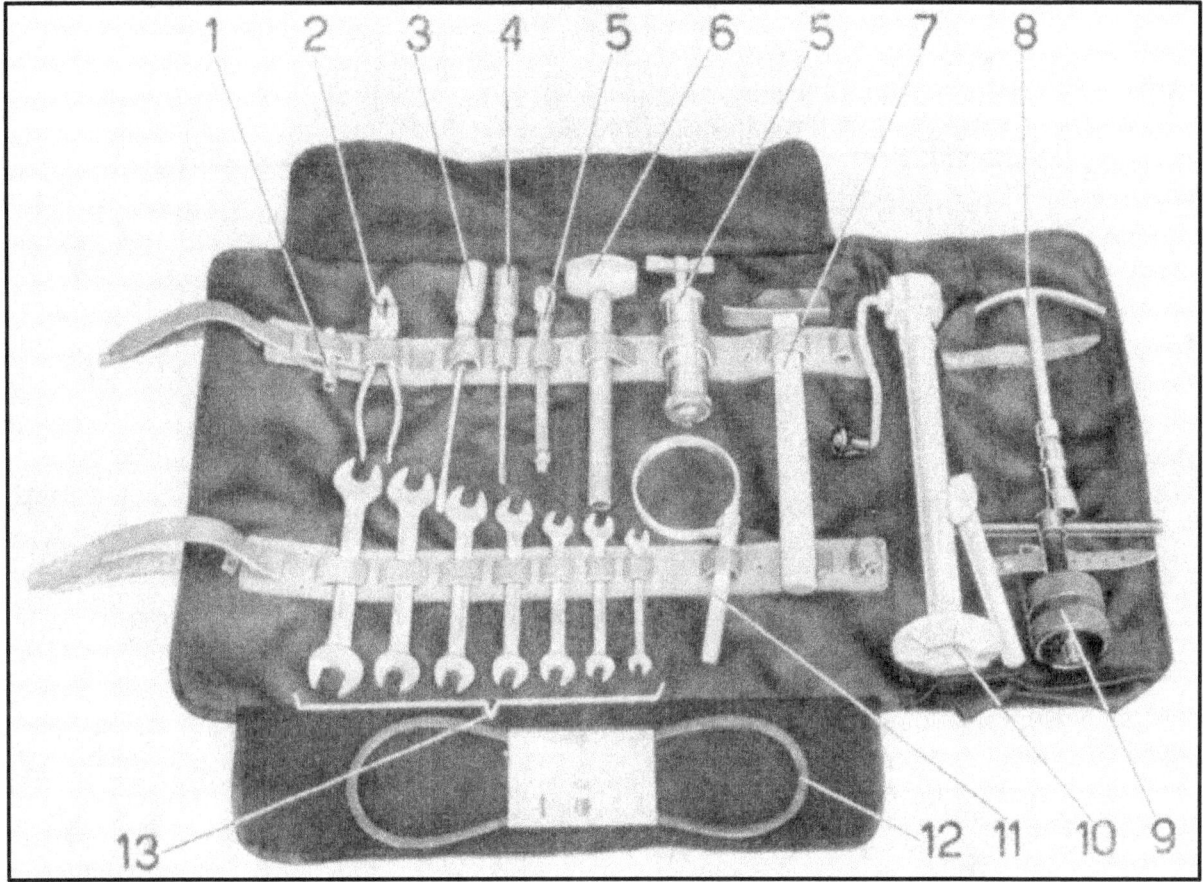

Fig. 73 - Tool kit.

1) Jet Key.
2) Pliers.
3) Screwdriver.
4) Screwdriver.
5) Grease gun and nozzle.
6) Copper hammer.
7) Hammer.
8) Plug spanner.
9) Hub puller.
10) Jack.
11) Filter remover.
12) Dynamo Belt.
13) Set of spanners.

VELOCEPRESS MANUALS – AUTOMOBILE BY MAKE

ALFA ROMEO GIULIA WORKSHOP MANUAL 1300 TO 2000cc 1962-1975
ALFA ROMEO GIULIA TECH MANUAL CARBURETED CARS FROM 1962
ALFA ROMEO GIULIA TECH MANUAL FUEL INJECTED CARS FROM 1969
ALFA ROMEO GIULIETTA & GIULIA 750 & 101 SERIES 1955-1965 WSM
AUSTIN-HEALEY SPRITE & MG MIDGET WORKSHOP MANUAL 1958-1971
BMW 600 LIMOUSINE FACTORY WORKSHOP MANUAL
BMW 600 LIMOUSINE OWNERS HAND BOOK & SERVICE MANUAL
BMW 2000 & 2002 1966-1976 WORKSHOP MANUAL
CORVAIR 1960-1969 WORKSHOP MANUAL
CORVETTE V8 1955-1962 WORKSHOP MANUAL
FERRARI HANDBOOK ROAD & RACE CARS (SERVICE/SPECS) 1948-1958
FERRARI 250GT SERVICE & MAINTENANCE by JIM RIFF 1956-1965
FERRARI 250GT & 250GTE FACTORY PARTS AND REPAIR MANUALS
FIAT 500 FACTORY WORKSHOP MANUAL 1957-1973
FIAT 600, 600D & MULTIPLA FACTORY WORKSHOP MANUAL 1955-1969
JAGUAR E-TYPE 3.8 & 4.2 SERIES 1 & 2 WORKSHOP MANUAL
JAGUAR MK 7, 8, 9 & XK120, 140, 150 WORKSHOP MANUAL 1948-1961
METROPOLITAN FACTORY WORKSHOP MANUAL
MGA & MGB OWNERS HANDBOOK & WORKSHOP MANUAL
MG MIDGET TC, TD, TF & TF1500 WORKSHOP MANUAL
PORSCHE 356 1948-1965 WORKSHOP MANUAL
PORSCHE 911 2.0, 2.2, 2.4 LITRE 1964-1973 WORKSHOP MANUAL
PORSCHE 911 2.7, 3.0, 3.2 LITRE 1973-1989 WORKSHOP MANUAL
PORSCHE 912 WORKSHOP MANUAL
PORSCHE 914/4 & 914/6 1.7, 1.8, 2.0 LITRE 1970-1976 WSM
TRIUMPH TR2, TR3, TR4 1953-1965 WORKSHOP MANUAL
VOLKSWAGEN TRANSPORTER, TRUCKS & WAGONS 1950-1979 WSM
VOLVO 1944-1968 ALL MODELS WORKSHOP MANUAL

VELOCEPRESS TECHNICAL BOOKS - AUTOMOBILE

HOW TO BUILD A FIBERGLASS CAR
HOW TO BUILD A RACING CAR
HOW TO RESTORE THE MODEL 'A' FORD
MASERATI OWNER'S HANDBOOK
PERFORMANCE TUNING THE SUNBEAM TIGER
SOUPING THE VOLKSWAGEN
SOLEX CARBURETORS (EMPHASIS ON UK & EU AUTOMOBILES)
SU CARBURETORS (EMPHASIS ON UK AUTOMOBILES)
WEBER CARBURETORS (EMPHASIS ON ALFA & FIAT)

VELOCEPRESS BOOKS & GUIDES - AUTOMOBILE

COMPLETE CATALOG OF JAPANESE MOTOR VEHICLES
FERRARI 308 SERIES BUYER'S AND OWNER'S GUIDE
FERRARI BROCHURES AND SALES LITERATURE 1968-1989
FERRARI SERIAL NUMBERS PART I - ODD NUMBERS TO 21399
FERRARI SERIAL NUMBERS PART II - EVEN NUMBERS TO 1050
HENRY'S FABULOUS MODEL "A" FORD
MASERATI BROCHURES AND SALES LITERATURE

VELOCEPRESS BOOKS – AUTO RACING

CARRERA PANAMERICANA - MEXICAN ROAD RACE (BOOK OF)
DIALED IN - THE JAN OPPERMAN STORY
VEDA ORR'S NEW REVISED HOT ROD PICTORIAL

www.VelocePress.com

www.ingramcontent.com/pod-product-compliance
Lightning Source LLC
Chambersburg PA
CBHW080740300426
44114CB00019B/2639